MAP OF

TURKEY AND PERSIA.

SCALE OF MILES.

H.W. Longfellow & Co. Lith. Boston.

Pioneers East

HARVARD MIDDLE EASTERN STUDIES 13

Pioneers East

The Early American Experience
in the Middle East

By *DAVID H. FINNIE*

HARVARD UNIVERSITY PRESS
Cambridge, Massachusetts, 1967

In Loving Memory of
ISABELLA HOLT FINNIE
(1892–1962)

Preface

In pursuing over a number of years an academic and professional interest in American relations with the Middle East, I kept coming across occasional vague references to early points of contact which I had not expected. In due course I found the opportunity to look into the subject in detail, and this book is the result. Granting the importance of missionary activity, it turned out that there were many other fields of interest and activity which deserve more attention than they have received. In particular the role of Americans in Ottoman naval affairs in the 1830's (Chapter 3) has been a revelation to me, and I believe it will be to others as well.

Many people have helped and encouraged my research and writing. Debts to Middle Eastern scholars and various amiable volunteers are acknowledged later in the context of the assistance they provided, but it is appropriate to mention here that Elliott Nixon and Janet Finnie have been particularly helpful in many ways. For voluntary secretarial service beyond the call of duty I am grateful to Betty Barratt, Helen Cullen, Betty Hicks, and Jane Kendrigan. Special thanks are due to a young lady who has gladly met my requirements for staples and Scotch tape. Above all I have depended on the advice, encouragement, and patient understanding of my wife, for whom the production of a book on family time over five years has been an undertaking fully and most cheerfully shared.

D. H. F.

New Canaan, Connecticut
July, 1966

Contents

ILLUSTRATIONS (*Following page 18*)

Pioneers East

1. Introduction

HENRY JESSUP, WHO CAME TO SYRIA as a missionary in 1856 and stayed on to become the first president of the Syrian Protestant College at Beirut, was startled and amused in the 1870's by people who asked if he had been the first American missionary there. Of course he hadn't; the first of them were in the Levant in 1820. But along with the early missionaries were an abundant variety of other Americans in the Middle East.* Apart from some anonymous New England traders who plied the Eastern Mediterranean as early as the seventeenth century, the story begins with the headstrong adventurer from Connecticut, John Ledyard, who in 1788 left his lonely bones in Cairo. (See Chapter 6.) It ends, as far as the present effort is concerned, about 1850. By that time positions

* In this book "Middle East" means the territory now occupied by Turkey, Iran, Israel, and the Arab countries east of Libya. In the early nineteenth century this was the area covered by the Ottoman Empire, excluding the Balkans, Greece, and the Barbary States, but including Egypt, Palestine, Syria, Mesopotamia, and Arabia; plus Persia. G. Etzel Pearcy, "The Middle East — An Indefinable Region," *Department of State Bulletin*, March 23, 1959, has a map showing "areas generally conceded to be in the Middle East," which match the definition given above.

were pretty well established: since 1830 the United States had had a treaty with the Ottoman Empire; there was a minister at Constantinople and consulates at such places as Alexandria, Beirut, and Smyrna. (America also had a treaty with Muscat, the first of any Western country with that remote Arab land.) Trade had weathered wars and piracy and had settled down to a routine; many tourists were beginning to treat the Orient as rather less of an adventure to write home — and publish — about (though others sturdily carried on the tradition); the first generation of missionaries had about run its course. The Middle East was becoming better known. The American Oriental Society was formed in Boston in 1842, though its journal, after a reasonably lively start, soon turned into a dreary skirmishing ground for pedants, mainly philological. By mid-century the major writers — Whittier, Melville, Bryant, Irving — had begun to exploit the romantic reaches of the East for a receptive public.

The commonly accepted view, even among specialists, is that aside from the missions there was little interest in the Middle East on the part of Americans until well into the present century.* From the purely political standpoint this is certainly true. Even as late as 1940 President Franklin Roosevelt scribbled this note on a policy paper handed him by Harry Hopkins: "Arabia is too far afield for us. Can't you get the British to do something?" [1] Roosevelt's reserve had venerable roots. George Washington had advised the nation in his Farewell Address to have "as little political connection as possible" with other countries, and this counsel was in effect ratified by the Monroe Doctrine (1823): "In

---

* "The Middle East held few lures for Americans in the nineteenth and early twentieth centuries. . . . Almost the sole exception was the American missionary." William R. Polk, "A Decade of Discovery: America in the Middle East, 1947–1958," *St. Antony's Papers Number 11, Middle Eastern Affairs, Number Two* (London, 1961), p. 50.

the wars of the European powers in matters relating to themselves we have never taken any part, nor does it comport with our policy to do so." This book will amply demonstrate the extension of America's aloof European policy to more remote regions farther east. But this is not the whole story. Neither Washington nor Monroe (nor Roosevelt for that matter) proscribed commercial or other nonpolitical activity. The first half of the nineteenth century saw a constant procession of essentially nonpolitical Americans to the Middle East: missionaries, of course, but also merchants, engineers, inventors, promoters, and artisans; scientists, scholars, and literary figures; philanthropists, adventurers, tourists, and eccentrics; naval officers and sailors; and even a farmer or two. By mid-century many individual Americans in the East had made a contribution, for good or ill: the vivacious Asahel Grant, for instance, without whom a slaughter of several thousand Christians in Kurdistan might not have taken place; Eckford and Rhodes, whose shipbuilding skill rehabilitated the Turkish navy; Dwight and Goodell, who helped engineer a precarious toleration for the tiny Protestant minority among the Turks; Robinson, who laid the groundwork for the study of the archaeology of the Holy Land; Lynch, the first successful navigator of the Jordan River; and the Yankee traders whose hustling efficiency made Turkish opium available in such profusion in the Far East. These, and others like them, who by and large left their mark only on the margin of their own time, are interesting for their characters and their circumstances. What were these early men and women like? How did they live and why did they die? What did they see and how did they react to this vastly alien environment? How different were they really from the Americans of today? What were they coming from in the New World, and what were they seeking in the Old? What polarity split them from the sage of Walden Pond, whose tribute to the West echoed the beat of so many young American hearts: "Eastward I go only by force, but Westward I go free. . . . It is hard to believe that I shall find fair landscapes or sufficient wildness and freedom beyond the eastern horizon. . . . I must walk toward Oregon, and not toward Europe." Hundreds of Americans of Thoreau's time went not only toward Europe but beyond it; for some there was frontier-like adventure that even he would have approved of. And after all the description and analysis, we will often have cause to come back to the haunting observation of Kinglake: "I can hardly tell why it should be, but there is a longing for the East very commonly felt by proud-hearted people when goaded by sorrow." *

INTRODUCING STEPHENS

Camping out on a plain near Ephesus in Asia Minor in the spring of 1835, John Lloyd Stephens was so weary after a long day on horseback that he had no trouble falling asleep on the rocky ground. "I ought to have spent half the night," he confessed, "in musing upon the strange concatenation of circumstances which had broken up a quiet practising attorney, and sent him a straggler from a busy, money-getting land, to meditate among the ruins of ancient cities, and sleep pell-mell with turbaned Turks." Of all the Americans who ventured to the Middle East in the first part of the nineteenth century none would have been a more agreeable companion than Stephens. Born in Shrewsbury, New Jersey, the son of a successful New York merchant, Stephens was a graduate of Columbia College (1822) and had studied his law at Litchfield. A bright young Tammany politician when "Tammany"

* A debt is due to the late Edward H. Brown for drawing attention to this passage in Kinglake's travel classic, *Eothen* (1844). At the time of his tragic death in 1959 Brown himself was at work on a book of Middle Eastern travel, to be called "A Longing for the East."

was not yet a dirty word, he was a bachelor of twenty-eight when he left the United States in 1834. Nowhere does he explain the "concatenation of circumstances" that led him to do so, though a modern biographer suggests that they included doctor's orders: he had an infected throat from too much Democratic orating. Stephens produced two excellent books, with awkward titles, about his Eastern travels: *Incidents of Travel in Egypt, Arabia Petraea, and the Holy Land* (1837) and *Incidents of Travel in the Russian and Turkish Empires* (1839). In an age when the British held undisputed first place in travel literature generally, both of Stephens' books were phenomenally successful in America and Europe. He became a literary lion almost overnight, and his royalties ultimately reached $25,000, an astonishing figure for the time.* Herman Melville, in his autobiographical *Redburn*, recalls that as a small boy he saw this "wonderful Arabian traveler" in church and wanted to follow him home. *Egypt*, which sold 21,000 copies in two years,[2] was widely reviewed on both sides of the Atlantic, most notably perhaps by Edgar Allan Poe in the *New York Review*, October, 1837. Poe found it "highly agreeable, interesting, and instructive," with "claims to public attention possessed by no other book of its kind." In Stephens' style Poe found "a freshness of manner [and] a manliness of feeling, both worthy of high consideration. . . . The volumes are written in general with a freedom, a frankness, and an utter absence of pretension which

---

* After his return from the East Stephens became the first modern explorer of Central America and Yucatán, whence two further books of *Incidents* appeared in 1841 and 1843. He also had a business career as an official of the Ocean Steam Navigation Company and president of the Panama Railway Company. He fell sick in Panama and died on October 13, 1852, leaving his papers to his father. They have never been found. Victor Wolfgang Von Hagen, *Maya Explorer: John Lloyd Stephens and the Lost Cities of Central America and Yucatán* (Norman, Oklahoma, 1947). See also *Dictionary of American Biography*.

will secure them the respect and good-will of all parties. . . .
Mr. Stephens writes like a man of good sense and sound feeling." An eminent modern critic, Van Wyck Brooks, has
singled out Stephens as "the greatest of American travel
writers." [3] He had a keen eye, a kind heart, and a sure sense
of proportion when describing for his American readers a
region so remote that the vast majority of his generation
would never see it for themselves. Beyond this he was especially interested in the other Americans he met on his travels,
and went out of his way to discover and describe how life in
the East affected them. He always enjoyed visiting the foreign households of his countrymen, and one of his comments
is characteristic of his homely attention: "There was scarcely
a house in which I did not find an article unknown except
among Americans, a Boston rocking chair." [4]

Stephens took the Middle East in two bites: the first, in
early 1835, brought him from Greece to Smyrna (now Izmir), Turkey's leading port and commercial center; and
thence through the Dardanelles to Constantinople (Istanbul),
the capital of the Ottoman Empire. His second excursion, the
following year, was by way of Malta to Egypt, Sinai, the
Holy Land, and Syria. Since his books afford us a unique in-
sight into the Middle East as it was known to the Americans
of his day, one could do worse than to follow in his energetic
footsteps — making a number of calculated digressions (for
many Americans penetrated farther than he did).

INTRODUCING THE AREA

At its zenith in the sixteenth century the Ottoman Empire,
rich and powerful, had stretched from the Atlas Mountains
to the Indian Ocean and across Europe as far as the gates of
Vienna. But this empire, which has recently been characterized as "fundamentally never much more than an army in

occupation of territories Christian and Muslim," [5] had fallen upon unhappy times. Effective control of it had broken down. The Sultanate could (and often did) react fretfully or even forcefully to events, but it could not consolidate or govern. By the turn of the nineteenth century North Africa was as good as lost to the Sultan. In 1808 Mohammed Ali seized control of Egypt. Thereafter, while styled "viceroy," this nominal vassal of the Grand Seigneur paid but little regard to his overlord and for long periods was actually at war with him. The most dramatic and conclusive defection of all was that of the Greeks, who rose in rebellion in 1821 and achieved independence after almost a decade of bloody struggle. (One vital skill thereby lost to the Empire was seamanship, a talent in which the Turks themselves were notably deficient.) Palestine and Syria, occupying the land link between Egypt in the south and Turkey proper in the north, tempted the viceroy and his aggressive son, Ibrahim Pasha, and became an intermittent battleground, conquered by slow degrees from the Turks during the 1830's and returned to the Sultan in 1840 only through the active intervention of the European Powers.

Indeed, big as such frogs as Mohammed Ali were in their provincial ponds, they had no independent viability in the Europe-dominated world of the early nineteenth century. And, just as it is today, the area was too important for the Great Powers to neglect. If in the first decades following Waterloo, Europe was too weary and too cautious to bring itself to fight another major war, the Powers were still alert enough to see the importance of denying control to a potential enemy. As the Ottoman Empire crumbled, the temptations to interfere increased, as well as the opportunities to do so. Russia, as she had since Peter the Great, sought warm-water ports and access to the West through the narrow straits that lapped at the very landing stages of the Sultan's various palaces along the Bosphorus. By treaties with Turkey in 1829 and 1833 the Russians acquired an important influence. Britain in turn awoke to the Russian threat to its access to India and judged that it could not tolerate a potential highwayman along its imperial path. France and Austria pursued interests of their own. For the major European Powers, in the period leading up to the Crimean War, the Ottoman Empire and Persia became the principal outlet for their political and military nervous energy and a fertile ground for diplomatic maneuver and intrigue. It is unnecessary here to detail the convolutions of policy, the shifting alliances, the military marching and countermarching — in none of which the United States played any part except occasionally by inadvertence.[6] It is sufficient to note that if ever in modern history there was scope for foreign intrusion, it was in the Sick Man of Europe: Turkey. The ultimate surgery, which cured its sickness while the patient died, was World War I.

At the core of Ottoman decadence was the notorious corruption of its ruling institutions. The palace itself reflected the decay: "Offices and corridors swarmed with officials, secretaries, petitioners, servants, vendors, and professional story tellers. These sat on divans or stood about while state business was transacted before their eyes." [7] The Caliphate, which united Islam and the State in the person of the Sultan, was viable as long as a saber charge could win a major battle. But Holy War as an effective instrument of international policy was dead after 1798, when the flower of the Ottoman army was cut down by Napoleon's guns at the Pyramids. The Terrible Turks looked fierce enough, but they simply were not equal to modern warfare.

And decay pervaded society generally. Education in the Ottoman Empire was largely Koranic. Americans, proud of their own seventy-nine colleges, twenty-three medical schools, and nine law schools (1835), not to mention a system of public education that taught every boy and girl to read and write and cast accounts, found nothing comparable in all the East. America had two thousand daily newspapers, Turkey an ephemeral handful. The Industrial Revolution, then in full swing, left the Turks hopelessly behind. Ancient farming methods drew but little sustenance from a depleted soil. There were no decent roads and, except at the capital itself, almost no wheeled vehicles of any kind. By 1831 two hundred steamboats plied the inland waters of America, while the Ottoman Empire had none. When one finally arrived in the early 1830's, an American wrote from Constantinople: "The Turks have been squatting down here for ages, smoking their pipes with all gravity, and reading the Koran without once being disturbed; when lo! a steamer dashes right in among them, and they have to scramble out of the way." [8] Industry was almost unknown. Government revenues declined through inability to enforce collection of taxes. Governors and lesser officials were venal. It was becoming plain to outsiders, if not to the Turks themselves, that survival of a Turkey dependent upon its own resources was almost hopeless. John Lloyd Stephens took a certain nostalgic pity on the Empire, "which once sent forth large and terrible armies, burning, slaying, and destroying, shaking the hearts of princes and peoples, now lying like a fallen giant, huge, unwieldy, and helpless, ready to fall into the hands of the first invader, and dragging out a precarious and ignoble existence but by the mercy of the great Christian powers." [9]

Sultan Mahmud II, who succeeded to power in 1808 and lived until 1839, was at least aware of the situation. Although the great period of Ottoman "reform" came later, by Stephens' time the Sultan had already begun to make some halting efforts to modernize his administration. The essential first step, removal of the military clique of janissaries, had been accomplished (by simple massacre) in 1826. The Sultan and some of his key officials recognized the need for technical help from outside, though there were immense political, religious, and emotional obstacles to soliciting it from the intriguing European Powers. In this situation, as we shall see, Mahmud turned quietly to the Americans, who played a role in Ottoman naval and educational reforms in the 1830's that was not acknowledged at the time and is not generally recognized even now.[10] (See Chapters 3 and 4.) Moreover, the presence of American missionaries, intermittently supported by their home government, was a significant factor, not always beneficial, in the evolution of the status of the established Christian minorities (*millets*) of the Empire. (See Chapter 5.)

Actually, many Americans in the young, westward-seeking republic on the other side of the globe knew more about the East than might at first be supposed. It was natural that American awareness of the Middle East should lag behind its awareness of Europe, but the gap was of no more than a generation or so. Rome, for instance, had two or three hundred tourists from the United States in 1835, a figure surpassed in Cairo before the Civil War. Strangely enough, the first recorded death of an American in Egypt took place in 1788, while Italy waited until 1803 for equal treatment in this melancholy respect. American merchant ships called regularly at Mediterranean ports (and occasionally in the Red Sea and the Persian Gulf), and John Lloyd Stephens could excuse himself from describing Smyrna in detail on the ground that "every Cape Cod sailor" knew the place better than he did. The first Egyptian mummy to cross the Atlantic arrived in 1823, and some merchants from Smyrna settled in Boston in 1830. The 1850 census enumerated 192 people who owned to having been born in the Ottoman Empire. *Al-Sultanah*, the first Arab vessel to reach the Western Hemisphere, took New York by storm in 1840: her officers were feted by the Common Council and treated to a ride on the Long Island Railroad, while the seamen were being introduced by curious Manhattanites to the city's bars. According to a British official then in New York, the crew "were tormented continually by the mob crowding to see the Arabs, looking on them as a curiosity. . . . They were pulled by the beards and otherwise insulted." Police had to be called in to protect them. Most of New York's ten newspapers gave continuous coverage to the exotic visitors for the two months before the vessel set sail again for Zanzibar and Muscat.[11]

But inevitably much of America's knowledge of the East was secondhand. The first significant American book about the area, Henry A. S. Dearborn's stately *A Memoir on the Commerce and Navigation of the Black Sea, and the Trade and Maritime Geography of Turkey and Egypt*, in two volumes (1819), was by a man who had never been there.* The Reverend William Bentley of Salem mastered the classical Arabic in his own study well enough to correspond with the literati of the Red Sea port of Mocha as early as 1805, and some of the early Boston Brahmins were wont to parade Oriental languages as a stunt after they had wearied of German and Italian.[12] For most of the rest, it was a question of the

---

* Another slim little book, much less interesting (and much rarer), appeared in the same year in New York: the anonymous *Letters from Asia, Written by a Gentleman of Boston to His Friend in That Place*. Similarities between this and Dearborn's book suggest that Dearborn may have been the recipient of the *Letters*, or at least had seen them. In his introduction Dearborn acknowledges the assistance of three "gentlemen of Boston," Charles W. Greene, J. W. Langdon, and George Barrell, any one of whom might have been the author of the *Letters*. Dearborn, I, xiv.

classics, the Bible, and the books of modern European travelers (mainly English), which could be found in the library of many an educated gentleman of Boston, Richmond, or Charleston.

THE FIRST TRAVELERS

While Stephens was by no means the first American traveler in the Middle East, few before him went there purely for pleasure or edification. The East was not yet geared up for tourism: "There is a good chance for an enterprising Connecticut man to set up a hotel in Constantinople," Stephens noted briskly,[13] anticipating Mr. Hilton by more than a century. The distance from home was a formidable barrier, as compared to distances from Europe, and even travelers from Europe were comparatively rare. Some of the Americans, like Stephens, took the packet to Liverpool (three or four weeks), then went overland by stagecoach through Europe to, say, Marseilles or Trieste to catch a vessel to Smyrna or Alexandria. But many traveled directly from New York or Boston all the way to the heart of the Mediterranean. Merchant ships of those days (steam began to take over only in the 1840's) were commonly of no more than two hundred tons burden, carried a crew of perhaps ten or a dozen, and offered few amenities. It was a tedious and often frustrating voyage of several weeks (almost everyone seems to have been seasick for an incredibly long time) before one sighted the Azores, then presently the Moroccan coast, Gibraltar, and finally dropped anchor in, say, Malta. When Josiah Brewer sailed from Boston in 1826, he paid $70 for his passage to Gibraltar. Included in the fare were rations consisting of hard bread, salt meat, a few vegetables early in the journey, occasionally warm wheat or Indian cake at breakfast, and on Sundays a pudding. "Our soda powders," he commented, "have been exceedingly grateful." Dr. Cornelius Van Dyck traveled in 1840 with several other missionaries, all with their wives, on the Boston bark *Emma Isadora,* two hundred tons. The cabin was about ten by thirteen feet. Small pens called staterooms had been knocked up in the afterhold, and five married couples were crowded into them. Van Dyck slept in the deckhouse over the companionway. "On a previous voyage to the West Indies, coffee had been spilled in the hold, and decayed, and produced a bilge the smell of which was simply indescribable. There is nothing vile enough to compare with it. The agent of the Boston mission house had bought as his sleeping outfit a small blanket, too short at both ends, and as thin as a lady's veil, and a thin cotton spread, and this for a winter voyage. But for a buffalo robe he brought with him from home and a thick overcoat, he might have suffered. He was young and in robust health and did not mind matters at all. But the case was different with those five poor ladies, who were shut up below, and compelled to endure the smell of the bilge. A strong current of air drew down from the foresail into the forecastle, whence it drew through the hold to the cabin, taking the whole abominable compound of stinks, and keeping it up, on those poor creatures below, whence it came up through the companionway under the dining table in the deck house." [14]

Eventually the American traveler found his way, generally by a still smaller vessel of Mediterranean provenance, to Alexandria, Smyrna, or Beirut (steam packets were introduced between Liverpool and the Mediterranean in 1833). When he reached his destination he might be kept in quarantine for anything from a week to a month to make sure he was not harboring some disease such as cholera or plague. With impediments like these, it is a wonder that so many Americans made the trip at all — not only the merchants who came to spend years or a lifetime among the colony of "Franks" (as Westerners were called) at Smyrna, or missionaries prepared to live and die in places like Trebizond or Mosul, but also plain tourists, traveling for their health or just out of curiosity.

The earliest American "tourists" — the word was a new one, and "travelers" was more common — left little record. It would seem that two Charleston men, Joseph Allen Smith and Joel Roberts Poinsett, must have been among the first. Smith spent a winter in Constantinople and visited Smyrna in about 1806. Poinsett's link with the Middle East is even more tenuous. He reached northern Persia from Russia in 1806, but he is better remembered as the developer of the flower that bears his name.[15]

An American yacht, of all things, toured the Mediterranean in 1817 and is said to have reached the Dardanelles. She was *Cleopatra's Barge*, owned by George Crowninshield, a Salem merchant and ship owner. His cousin, Benjamin C. Crowninshield, was the skipper, and also aboard was a friend, Samuel Curwen Ward. The yacht was a sensation wherever she called, and it seems a good time was had by all. "The cook . . . was a master of his craft, the stock of wine was choice and abundant."[16]

In 1819 Edward Everett and Theodore Lyman, Jr., a pair of recent Harvard graduates on a *Wanderjahr*, traveled through Constantinople on their way from Greece to Rumania. Stephen Grellet, a French-born, naturalized American Quaker leader, came through in the other direction in the same year. A prominent social reformer, Grellet visited prisons, asylums, and harems, and distributed Greek testaments. He also stopped at Smyrna, where he was welcomed warmly by the merchant David Offley, whom he had known as a boy of a Quaker family in Philadelphia.[17]

For the next few years, owing mainly to disturbed travel conditions resulting from the Greek War of Independence, American travelers were very few. But the war itself brought a number of Philhellenes to Greece, a few of whom found their way as far as Smyrna and Constantinople. Among them were John M. Allen and Richard W. Ruddock, who appeared on Consul David Offley's doorstep in 1825. Sick and out of funds, they were put up at Offley's home, and he advanced them money for medical attention. In the same year came Lieutenant William Townshend Washington of Virginia, whose first call upon Offley's services was for assistance in renouncing his American citizenship. (Offley had doubts whether his jurisdiction extended so far.) Washington, who did not deny the kinship to George attributed to him by the Smyrna press but would have been hard put to document it, had left West Point without graduating, but his commission in the U.S. Army was authentic. He died two years later in Greece at the age of twenty-four.[18]

One is also rather taken by the young American going by the name of "Captain Richards," who showed up at Smyrna in the spring of 1828. He announced that he had two plans to present to the Turks — one for military defense, the other for economic development. At the home of Joseph Langdon, an American merchant, he gave a talk about his schemes. The assembled Franks found Richards quite incomprehensible; his ideas "seemed so absurd that we began to doubt whether he had entirely taken leave of his senses." The Turkish Government invited him to Constantinople, all expenses paid. There he was treated with great courtesy, but his ideas were too baffling even for the hapless Turks.[19]

Other American Philhellenes who got as far as Turkey included Samuel Woodruff and the Reverend Samuel Gridley Howe, the best known among them.[20] Then there was Henry

Albertson Van Zo Post. A Columbia College contemporary
of Stephens, Post was a well-meaning fellow, the agent of the
New York Greek Committee, organized to raise money for
the relief of the suffering people of Greece. He left New
York in 1827 in charge of a charitable cargo of provisions;
and early in 1828, his work in Greece accomplished, he took
a short side trip to Smyrna and Constantinople. The book he
published on his return is full of good stories that he had
picked up — and indeed one can hardly resist the impression
that this good little man may have been a bit gullible. Strongly
pro-Greek, he was willing to believe almost anything that
discredited the Turks. For instance someone, impressing him
with the touchiness of the Muslims about the sanctity of their
mosques, told him about the wife of a European ambassador
who "once spit upon the pavement of one in Constantinople;
the indignation of a bystander was aroused to such a pitch,
that in the vehemence of his wrath he smote the unconscious
offender." Who this innocent lady was he does not say, but
it makes a good story — one that finds no echo outside Post's
own narrative.

Or take the strange American he met in Smyrna: "According to his own story, he came to the place on business a number of years ago, and thoughtlessly entered a mosque with
muddy boots. The Turks seized him, threw him into prison,
and gave him the alternative of renouncing his religion or
forfeiting his head. He chose the former course, and was for
some time in a deranged state of mind, through terror and re-
morse. He has continued ever since to wear the Turkish costume, and to practise an outward observance of the cere-
monies of their religion; being poor, he says, and without
means of getting out of the country."

Upon reflection, even Post came to suspect that this may

have been a leg-pull: "There is reason to believe, that the account which he gives of himself is a fabrication, and that his assumption of the turban was a purely voluntary act." Maybe so; in any case no one else writing from Smyrna in this era mentions the supposed renegade.

One day Post was taken aside by an old-timer and given a real hair-raiser about the slaughter of the Smyrna Greeks by the Turks in 1821: "The Captain of an American vessel which happened to be here at the time informed me, that as he was walking out one morning, during a period of momentary tranquillity, he saw a Turk draw his pistol, and deliberately shoot through the head a poor Greek who was about to pass him; he was so near the spot . . . that his clothes were bespattered with the brains of the unhappy victim."

Henry Post himself was anything but bloodthirsty. In Constantinople he arranged for a guide from the British embassy to show him the sights. In those early days Franks roaming the streets were subject to much jostling and raillery, including such epithets as "infidel, pimp and dog," and Post noted regretfully that the guide, a native Christian, pretended not to know him when things began to get unpleasant. The women, from behind their veils, were especially insulting. Very sensibly, Post took all this in his stride: "I always laid in a good store of patience and forbearance whenever I crossed over to the city; making it a rule to heed no insult however galling, if jostled to pass quietly on, and if buffeted, to bear all without a murmur or a frown. These severe mortifications were the lowest price at which the gratification of my curiosity could be purchased at that period of popular uneasiness." [21]

The only American literary figure to antedate Stephens in the East was Nathaniel Parker Willis. In *Pencillings by the*

Way Willis presents the lighthearted view of a passenger aboard the frigate *United States* on its cruise of the Eastern Mediterranean in 1833. As a Yale undergraduate he had won widespread attention for what Van Wyck Brooks calls his "deft though somewhat watery verses." Now twenty-seven, he was "tall, good-looking, lively and clever, always in good spirits and always a little over-dressed. Light of heart, as of hand and head, he preferred the immediate and the present to the past or future." Henry Beers, Willis' biographer, noted that "his nature reveled in the barbaric riches of the East and cheerfully blinked the discomforts and the dirt." [22]

Pencillings is entertaining enough. One can almost see this young dandy lounging perhaps in a hammock on the deck of the American frigate, writing, "A summer cruise in the Mediterranean is certainly the perfection of sight-seeing" or "The twilights in this part of the world are unparalleled. . . . Each one comes as if there had never been and never were to be another. . . . You must come to Asia and *feel* sunsets. You cannot get them by paying postage." Like many another visitor to the East — but more ably than most — he describes his first experience in a Turkish bath, gives a hair-raising account of the multitude of wild dogs in Constantinople, takes note of the Hero-Leander legend as he contemplates the Dardanelles ("The Hellespont of matrimony may be crossed with the tide. The deuce is to get back"), and visits the slave market ("a tall, arrow-straight lass of about eighteen, with the form of a nymph, and the head of a baboon"). If anything gets a bit tiresome about Willis, it is his rather sophomoric voyeurism as applied to the women he comes across. *Pencillings* is littered with passages like "A pretty female figure, closely enveloped in her veil, and showing, as she ran across the street, a dainty pair of feet in small yellow slippers"

John Lloyd Stephens, Eastern adventurer and "the greatest of American travel writers."

*Henry Eckford, "eminent naval architect of New York,"
who was engaged by the Turks to build a fleet.*

Jonas King: he startled his missionary colleagues by adopting Arab dress.

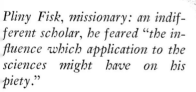

Pliny Fisk, missionary: an indifferent scholar, he feared "the influence which application to the sciences might have on his piety."

Rev. Wm. Thomson's impression of the belly dance:
"preposterous attitudes, languishing, lascivious and
sometimes indecent."

John Lowell, "Junior," in Turkey, as portrayed by an artistic traveling companion.

Harriet Livermore, quick-tempered evangelist; she won a heated argument with "The Mad Nun of Lebanon."

Sarah Smith of Norwich, Connecticut: "I think that America should send forth her best to foreign lands."

William Goodell reasoning with bandits, Beirut, 1826: "They saw from my dress that I was not a native."

Lynch sets out for the Jordan River, 1848: "The experiment of substituting camels for draught horses was tried and proved successful . . . my heart throbbed with gratitude."

and "I tried in vain to get a peep at the camel-driver's daughter, but she seemed jealous of showing even her eye-brow." Nevertheless, *Pencillings by the Way* is still tasty if insubstantial fare, and, unlike Stephens' much better books, it is at least available in a modern edition.[23]

To those who delight in good
cheer, at a reasonable price,
Smyrna is probably the most
inviting place in the world.

— *Samuel Woodruff of
Connecticut, 1828* [1]

2. *Smyrna*

A LITTLE GREEK SAILING VESSEL brought John Lloyd Stephens
across the Aegean to Asia Minor in April, 1835. Characteristically, too impatient to wait for favorable winds, he abandoned the craft at the village of Foggi, near the western end
of the Gulf of Smyrna, and made his way on horseback the
last few miles to Smyrna itself. Early Sunday morning, April
26, "picking my way among caravans, which for ages have
continued to cross this bridge laden with all the riches of the
East, I entered the long-looked-for city of Smyrna." [2]

To the Franks it was the "Pearl of the Levant"; to the
Turks, "infidel Smyrna." Gay, prosperous, and cosmopolitan,
with a population of perhaps 150,000, Smyrna (now called
Izmir) was Turkey's commercial capital. Because of its loca-
tion it was a crossroads for Eastern travelers. It was rather in
the same position, and had much of the same flavor, as Beirut
today. And like modern Beirut, Smyrna in a sense was in the
East but not entirely *of* it.

The Frank community, which dominated the society of
the city, consisted mainly of merchants. The British traders

were members of the Levant Company, which like the com-
plementary East India Company had been chartered in the
time of Elizabeth. (Its charter had been revoked in 1825, but
its spirit lingered on.) British families had lived there for
generations. By the time of Stephens' visit a genial social pattern had developed into which the other Franks willingly
found their way. There was much entertainment and protocol,
and an emphasis on hospitality and good manners. The New
York-bred Stephens noticed that "one of the amiable customs of our own city was in full force here . . . that of the
young gentlemen, with light sticks in their hands, gathering
around the door of the fashionable church to stare at the
ladies as they came out." Life was easy and gracious. Everyone
rode on donkeys, a switch in one hand and a parasol in the
other. In his stiff hat and frock coat Stephens must have been
easily recognized as a stranger, for the customary Frank dress
in good weather was a white linen suit and white straw hat,
worn even on rather formal occasions. Smart shops stocked
European goods for the ladies. There were a number of acceptable places to stay, including the Pension Suisse, where
Stephens put up.[3]

Normally Smyrna was relatively free of the fanaticism of
the more purely Muslim centers of the Ottoman Empire.
The anonymous "Gentleman of Boston" who published a
series of letters in 1819 wrote: "The unhappy prejudices of
the Christian world against the professors of Mahomet's
creed, which had been instilled into my mind, led me to fear
a thousand dangers where none existed. . . . When the seaman approaches that part of Asia inhabited by the Turks, he
may with safety bury all alarm, and rest satisfied, that although he is not near a Christian country, still he will find
among the inhabitants, all the virtues possessed by Christians,
with but few of their vices." [4] Henry Post of New York

(1828) was impressed by the lack of press censorship: "the gazettes and periodicals of Europe, and even Bibles and Christian tracts, circulate unobstructed through the city." [5] By 1840 Smyrna even had its own French and English newspapers.*

The merchants lived along "Frank Street," a rough thoroughfare about fifteen or twenty feet wide, running parallel to the shore through the northern part of the city. Their houses were protected by heavy gates, secured at night by locks and chains. At the rear were terraces forming roofs to their warehouses, upon which they could stroll refreshed and command a superb view of the strikingly beautiful harbor, where their vessels rode peacefully at anchor. "One might lie here," wrote the Gentleman of Boston, "from the beginning to the end of the year, without any molestation or expense from the government." Willis observed that the merchants "are responsible only to their consuls, and having no nobility above, and none but dependents below them, live in a state of cordial republican equality that is not found even in America. . . . This living over warehouses of opium, I am inclined to think, is healthy for the heart." [6]

Stephens found: "Every stranger, upon his arrival in Smyrna, is introduced at the Casino. I went there the first time to a concert. It is a large building, erected by a club of merchants, with a suite of rooms on the lower floor, billiards,

---

* The English-language paper was a weekly called *Manzari Shark*, published by an Englishman, William N. Churchill, a former U.S. consular agent at Constantinople. (Commodore David Porter to Secretary of State, Aug. 24, 1841, DSD.) Porter enclosed two issues, No. 21 (Feb. 5, 1841) and No. 49 (Aug. 21, 1841). According to a modern scholar, a William Churchill started a Turkish-language newspaper in Constantinople in 1840 called *Ceride-i Havadis*. Bernard Lewis, "The Middle East versus the West," *Encounter* (October 1963); also, a personal letter from Professor Lewis to the writer, Sept. 14, 1964. If these Churchills were one and the same, he must have been a very busy man in 1840. The French-language *Courrier de Smyrne* was established several years earlier.

cards, reading and sitting room, and a ball-room above covering the whole. The concert was given in the ball-room, and, from what I had seen in the streets, I expected an extraordinary display of beauty; but I was much disappointed. The company consisted only of the aristocracy or higher mercantile classes, the families of the gentlemen composing the club, and excluded the Greek and Smyrniote women, among whom is found a great portion of the beauty of the place. A patent of nobility in Smyrna, as in our own city, is founded upon the time since the possessor gave up selling goods, or the number of consignments he receives in the course of a year. The Casino, by the way, is a very aristocratic institution, and sometimes knotty questions occur in its management. Captains of merchant vessels are not admitted. A man came out here as owner of a vessel and cargo, and also master: *quere*, could he be admitted? His consignee said yes; but the majority, not being interested in the sale of his cargo, went for a strict construction, and excluded him." [7]

Such republican asides rolled easily off the backs of Smyrna society, and the Casino remained for many years the hub of social activity. Balls or "assemblies" were held every other week throughout the winter. A very sophisticated New Yorker, Mrs. Sarah Haight, was amused to note in 1836 that the waltz and the quadrille were the only dances; and another Gothamite, Dr. James De Kay, observed that the waltz was so popular that it was danced even when the orchestra played the quadrille! According to Mrs. Haight, women as well as men patronized the gaming tables, and the stakes seemed to her mighty high. At the end of such an evening she was quite content to put her feet up: "After the ball of last evening we supped at the house of a very worthy family from our own country, settled here, and I have seen nothing so comfortable in all the East as their snug American fireside." [8]

When an intense young American missionary, Pliny Fisk, was living in Smyrna in 1820 and 1821, the city was something less than its usual genial self. The rebellion in Greece had brought reprisals by the Turks against Greek minorities elsewhere, and one of the key trouble spots was infidel Smyrna. Fisk was a horrified witness to unspeakable massacres in June 1821. On one occasion, on the advice of the British consul, he took refuge for several days on the frigate *United States,* then lying in the harbor. "These events," wrote Fisk, "interrupt, but do not prevent the proceedings of merchants and travelers . . . ships come and go; trade is carried on to a great extent." Franks still attended the Casino's assembly room "as though all were peace and security," a practice which Fisk regarded as "thoughtless ill-timed levity." [9]

YANKEE TRADING

John Lloyd Stephens was attracted above all by the commercial atmosphere of Smyrna in 1835: "Society in Smyrna is purely mercantile," he wrote; "and having been so long out of the way of it, [it] was actually grateful to me once more to hear men talking with all their souls about cotton, stocks, exchanges, and other topics of *interest.* . . . Sometimes lounging in a merchant's counting room, I took up an American paper, and heard Boston, and New York, and Baltimore, and cotton, and opium, and freight, and quarter percent less bandied about, until I almost fancied myself at home." [10]

The beginnings of American trade with the Eastern Mediterranean go back to early colonial times. Though forbidden by British law to trade directly with Asia, merchants from the American colonies worked the Mediterranean under the British flag. Yankee traders are said to have called at Alexandretta (Iskenderun) as early as 1676. A Perkins of Boston, a loyalist, sat out the Revolution in Smyrna. Along about 1786 an American flag vessel reached Constantinople, if one can trust the memory of a British consul writing ten years later. (The Stars and Stripes was flown in Constantinople from a French vessel on Bastille Day, 1793, sent by the French government to demonstrate revolutionary principles.)[11]

In April, 1802, President Jefferson appointed William Stewart, a Philadelphia merchant, as the first American consul at Smyrna. Stewart, who spent most of 1803 there, went home again without having seen a single compatriot, although three American vessels had called in the two years before his arrival. Thus unembarrassed by commercial duties, Stewart had plenty of time to reflect on his rather ineffectual role as consul.

The problem was that, in the absence of a treaty between Turkey and the United States, the Turks were inclined to disregard him. By custom American ships calling at Smyrna would be "protected" by the British consul; Stewart had no power or jurisdiction to deal with them. He left somewhat disillusioned, with the strong recommendation that a treaty should be negotiated.

On leaving Stewart appointed a "proconsul," one R. Wilkinson, an Anglo-Levantine with thirty-five years of residence in Smyrna. Wilkinson's duties were also very light, since the few American traders at Smyrna continued to clear their cargoes through the British consul. He took pains to make a record of every American ship that called. His report for the year 1805, for instance, showed six vessels: four from Philadelphia and two from Baltimore; on leaving three said they were headed for the United States and the other three for Canton. They brought with them mainly coffee, pepper, tea, sugar, rum, and Havana sugars. In Smyrna they loaded a great deal of opium (for China), as well as raisins, figs, and salt.[12]

David Offley arrived in 1811. A partner in the Philadelphia trading firm of Woodmas and Offley, which had been trading at Smyrna at least since 1805, he was the son of a leading Quaker (Daniel Offley) and was born and brought up in Philadelphia.[13] He married an Armenian woman (some said she was Greek) and lived in Smyrna for twenty-seven years until his death.

In Smyrna in 1811, Offley saw at once that American traders were at a disadvantage. Since the United States had no treaty with the Turks, there was no official recourse from high and capricious tariffs and the whims of venal, petty officials. Even after American Independence some American merchantmen found that flying British colors sufficed to bring them under the much more favorable customs terms afforded to the British. But early in 1811 the British put an end to this; from now on Americans could still depend on the British for consular protection (for which they paid fees), but they were at the mercy of the Turks as far as customs duties were concerned. The fact that his countrymen, including his own firm, were paying consular dues to the British was irksome to Offley for commercial as well as patriotic reasons. The amounts paid in a year came to some four or five thousand dollars.

Offley's arrival was regarded with deep suspicion by the British, who had been profiting by handling American goods at Smyrna; it was not long before a mutual antipathy grew up which lasted throughout Offley's career. Offley soon became convinced that the Levant Company, the British-chartered merchants' monopoly, was taking advantage of contacts in the Ottoman administration to make things harder for the

Americans. The Turks refused the American merchants customs duties as low as other nations enjoyed (they paid six percent as against two percent). In this Offley was quick to see the hand of the Levant Company and the British ambassador.[14]

As soon as he could he went up to Constantinople to see what might be done about it, and he shortly found himself enmeshed in a typically Ottoman runaround. Officials served him many a cup of coffee and offered him many a hookah, but he found he was getting nowhere. Then he did something which had probably never before occurred to a foreigner: he threatened to intercept Sultan Mahmud himself on his way to Friday Mosque, taking advantage of the traditional Ottoman right of redress in public. This bluff worked. Resistance wilted, and Offley elatedly left Constantinople with an assurance that henceforth American imports would be subject only to the going tariffs. All that now remained was to renounce British "protection" so as to stop the obnoxious practice of paying consular dues to the Levant Company. In this, however, he was frustrated by his fellow American merchants (among them John W. Langdon and Francis Coffin of Boston), who would not cooperate, believing it preferable to continue to enjoy British protection. While this domestic argument was going on, the War of 1812 broke out between the United States and Great Britain, and the matter became academic, for American merchant vessels were unable to penetrate the Royal Navy's very effective blockade of United States shipping. Offley remained alone in Smyrna throughout the war ("nursing his Anglophobia," as Professor Wright put it) and never saw another American vessel until the war ended in 1815. Then he restated his case and quickly won acquiescence from his colleagues.[15] From now on the Americans were on their own.

Or were they? The situation was still clouded by the lack of a Turkish-American treaty. In Smyrna Offley worked out an arrangement with the local governor (or pasha) whereby American traders were recognized as "guests of the Sultan." For a long time this ingenious and precarious fiction worked, a kind of private treaty between Offley and the Porte whereby the American traders got fair commercial treatment from the Turks without outside help. The resourceful Offley even managed to have the arrangement survive the execution in 1816 of his friend the governor (for treason): he approached the capudan pasha, the commander of the Turkish fleet, and won assurance that the "guest" status would continue as before. It cost him $2000 in presents.

By now David Offley was an important and respected figure in Smyrna. Justly so, for he had single-handedly achieved for American citizens what other nationals had obtained only through official negotiations. He wrote of himself in 1825: "Our commerce to this country stands already on a tolerably fair footing, and I may be allowed to add thro' my unauthorized and unassisted means." [16] By the Turks he was treated like any other foreign consul, and he had established a private channel of communication with the capudan pasha, a very influential figure in Ottoman politics. But Offley was still uneasy. Though recognized personally by the Turks as representing American interests, he had no official status as far as his own government was concerned. His position was improved in June, 1823, when he was formally appointed "Consular Commercial Agent." This was better. With his new authority, for instance, he rented a prison (at $60 per year) for locking up disorderly American seamen; until then they had been lodged in the prison at the British consulate and were sometimes induced to buy their freedom by signing onto British warships — or so Offley said, defending the new arrangement. But he still could not issue passports or attend to other official duties for American nationals, who continued to look to the British for "protection." Offley found this an irritant on nationalistic as well as personal grounds; what he needed was a treaty.[17] How he got one, in 1830, is related in the next chapter.

In all this one cannot entirely separate Offley the unpaid patriot-diplomat from Offley the businessman. The firm of Woodmas and Offley prospered. All but twenty-four of the seventy-eight American vessels that called at Smyrna during the years 1811–1820 carried cargoes consigned to the Woodmas and Offley firm. And during this period Offley actually spent $6000 of the firm's money on his negotiations, mainly for presents to helpful and influential Turkish officials.

Maybe David Offley took his own prominence rather too seriously. After all he was quoted on the floor of the United States Senate in 1831 by no less a figure than Daniel Webster; and indeed the burden of his views was that the American Government had no need for a minister at the Turkish capital — a chargé d'affaires would do very nicely. Perhaps he would have agreed with John Lloyd Stephens, who reported that the position of a consul at Smyrna was far more important than that of an ordinary ambassador! "With their janisaries," wrote Stephens, "and their appearance on all public occasions in uniform, [they] are looked up to by the Levantines somewhat like the consuls sent abroad under the Roman Empire, and by the Turks as almost sultans."[18] Offley finally got a Presidential appointment as consul in 1832. David Porter, in charge of the legation at the capital, reported without rancor in 1834 that Offley "considers his obligations and his duties entirely independent of my authority, which I have never attempted to exercise."[19] Regardless of his official status, however, Offley always enjoyed great prestige with the

Turks. During the consternation that followed the news of the defeat of the Turkish fleet at Navarino in 1827, most of the European officials and merchants quietly vanished. Offley was assured by the pasha that American interests would be protected. The U.S.S. *Constitution,* in the harbor at the time, kept in constant signal communication with him, ready to evacuate the Offley family if necessary, but it never was.[20]

Offley's firm was joined in 1816 by Perkins Brothers of Boston and in 1821 by Langdon and Co. (Joseph W. Langdon), also of Boston. Soon afterwards a firm called Issaverdens, Styth & Co. of Baltimore opened an office, with Mr. Griffin Styth in charge. By 1827, then, there were four American "houses" at Smyrna, and indeed for many years there were no American merchants anywhere else in the Levant (except Frederick Bunker at Constantinople briefly in 1832).[21]

The main object of American trade with Smyrna in those days was opium for China. Americans, neutral during most of the period of the Napoleonic wars, opened the opium trade with Smyrna in 1804 and more or less cornered the market. Wartime conditions meant high shipping rates and high profits. There were also high risks. The opium was mainly transshipped at Malta or Gibraltar into larger vessels, especially fitted out for this trade, for the run to the Far East. As popular opinion against the opium trade began to mount, a certain furtiveness developed. The Turks themselves supposed the opium was destined for the United States. As a contemporary Englishman wrote, "the Turks, who are not aware how the purchasers after dispose of it, give the Yankees the credit of having assumed the propensities they themselves have abandoned."[22]

Opium was largely in the hands of a small group of the great family firms of Salem and Boston — notably Perkins and Peabody — which had opened the China trade late in the eighteenth century. Most of it came from a small district near Smyrna; it was brought to the port by local merchants, said to have been Jews and Armenians, and passed along to American shippers through agents like David Offley.[23]

Other Turkish exports included fruit, nuts, silver, raw wool, and hides. Imports from the United States were equally varied: cotton goods, tobacco, gunpowder, and breadstuffs, but the main item was "Boston Particular," good old New England rum. In the first half of 1830, for example, twelve million gallons of it were shipped to Turkey, mainly for transshipment to Russia and Persia via the Black Sea. The legation staff at Constantinople helpfully pointed out to American merchants that the cheapest grade was preferred. "Scarcely an American vessel," the legation reported, "arrives at Smyrna from the United States that does not bring from 50 to 100 casks, much of which finds its way into Persia and the neighboring countries." In fact, rum was the only American manufacture to be seen in the well-stocked bazaars of Tiflis, the capital of Armenia, when the abstemious American missionaries Eli Smith and Harrison Dwight arrived there in 1830. (See Chapter 8.) Smith wrote: "You may suppose that we were gratified to meet the productions of our own country in this commercial market. . . . In the first caravanserai we entered, the day after reaching Tiflis, we stumbled upon a hogshead of New England rum! What a reproof to the Christians of America that, in finding fields of labor for their missionaries, they should allow themselves to be anticipated by her merchants, in finding a market for their poisons! When shall the love of souls cease to be a less powerful motive of enterprise than the love of gain?"[24]

When Commodore David Porter arrived to head up the American legation at Constantinople in 1831, he found that "although the pedlars and hawkers are hourly crying American cottons for sale through the streets, there is not one of them that I have found, who knows of the existence of such a country." Nevertheless, American ships became better known in the Eastern Mediterranean as trade increased. During the decade of the 1810's (excluding the war years) an average of thirteen American vessels called each year at Smyrna. Some found it profitable to run down to Alexandria afterwards, carrying Muslim pilgrims bound for Mecca. By 1832 the number of American ships at Smyrna during the year had climbed to forty-six.

Other Ottoman ports saw American shipping more rarely. William Hodgson saw American cottons on sale at Beirut in 1834, but they had been imported by British merchants through Liverpool. Constantinople, guarded by jealous Turkish guns commanding the Dardanelles, was the most difficult of all. The *Telemachus* of Salem made it in 1809, followed the next year by the *Calumet* of Boston and the *America*, the latter commanded by Captain Joseph Ropes of Salem. Unfortunately the *Calumet* neglected to observe the usual formalities and ran afoul of Turkish officials; she was saved from confiscation only by the timely intervention of the British ambassador. Following this incident, no American ship seems to have run the Dardanelles until 1828, when the Turks gave the brig *Delos* of Boston permission to come up to Constantinople. After a commercial treaty with Turkey was signed in 1830, such events became more common: there were fourteen U.S. ships at the capital in 1832 and again in 1833.[25] Commodore Porter provided a colorful picture of the master of one of them: "The Yankee captain, just promoted; his hands as hard as a jackass' hoof, his new cloth coat with gilt buttons, his hat brushed to look like silk instead of felt; the upper part of his face as brown as a nut, the lower as white as chalk, from the protection afforded it by a beard just shaven, the growth of a ninety days passage." [26]

Trade was the first and most tangible link between America and the East. Separated by an ocean from the civilized world, America was quick to develop its merchant marine. By the 1830's the American merchant fleet was second in size only to Britain's, and it was said that the United States had the highest ratio of mariners to its population of any country in the world. American ships were highly regarded. European merchants sought them out for their speed and efficiency; their masters, half of them New Englanders, were known for their daring and their ability to deliver the goods. Here is the pretty compliment paid by an Englishman in Turkey in 1828: "I may here appropriately introduce a piece of 'advice to travellers' in the Mediterranean: if their object be speed, let them under no consideration embark in any vessel but an English or American." [27]

Although David Offley was the doyen of Americans in Smyrna, his prominence came in time to be shared with his chief commercial rival, Joseph W. Langdon, a leader in the opium trade. Langdon acted incidentally as a banker for visiting Americans. Well known for his hospitable graces, he did a great deal of entertaining of merchants, supercargoes, travelers, and ships' captains. He also acquired a reputation as a humanitarian. When a terrible fire devastated Smyrna on July 29, 1841, it was Langdon who headed the relief donations committee. Only a few Franks bothered to assist the unfortunate Smyrniote Greeks in the 1820's, but Charles MacFarlane, an Englishman, wrote: "Among many other generous and noble actions in favour of the unhappy Greeks, [Langdon] ransomed a fine child (a Sciote), and sent her to his home, to be educated among his relations and friends. . . . Mr. L. does not look for public praise like this, but I have a debt of affection and gratitude to him, for the friendship I experienced while at Smyrna. This instance is not a solitary one."

For those days, a rare tribute from an Englishman! The girl's name was Sappho; she was adopted by the family of Thomas L. Winthrop, Governor of Massachusetts, in 1827. Five years later Elizabeth Cabot Kirkland of Boston, who visited Langdon, reported that he had a Greek wife about sixteen years old and a "very fine boy of six months." Sappho? Mrs. Kirkland unfortunately does not say. According to Samuel Woodruff, who dined at the Langdons' in 1828, "His house is a sort of rendezvous for all foreigners visiting Smyrna in the course of trade or traveling. . . . Without ostentation or parade, he is kind and hospitable, plain and unceremonious, but easy and unaffected in his manner; the stranger, at once, finds himself at home, under the roof and in the society of this friendly man." [28]

But in the end Langdon became the center of a controversy that bitterly divided the American colony at Smyrna. David Offley died suddenly on October 3, 1838, of "water on the heart." He was succeeded as consul by his son, David W. Offley. When the latter died in November, 1846, Langdon made a determined effort to get the consular job. Instead, the new minister resident, Dabney Carr, appointed Edward S. Offley (another son) *ad interim* and recommended to the State Department that this appointment be confirmed. When Langdon got wind of this, he wrote Carr protesting that he was entitled to the job, since he was the only American-born merchant in the Levant. This letter was followed by a petition, signed by a large number of Langdon's friends, demanding his appointment. Carr stood firm, mainly on the fairly reasonable ground that Langdon had gone into bankruptcy and had made no great effort to repay his creditors. Washington agreed with Carr. When Edward Offley's commission finally arrived from Washington in September, 1848, the Langdon faction staged a furious and graceless demonstration. American flags were hung at half mast; the harbor resounded to cannon fire in token of mourning. The editor of the *Courrier de Constantinople* was chided in a letter from eight Langdonites* for having served up an innocent story to the effect that Edward Offley's appointment had been greeted with satisfaction by all who knew him. Offley's friends rallied to his support: missionaries, merchants of other nationalities, and even the Turkish pasha stopped by to wish him well. To what extent Langdon was personally involved in this senseless demonstration is not clear; the noisy partisanship of his supporters at least treated Franks and Smyrniotes to a first-hand glimpse of robust American civic emotionalism.[29]

MEN OF THE CLOTH

Professor Parrington once suggested that the key social figures in our early history were the merchant and the minister.[30] In the microcosm of American life at Smyrna in Stephens' time, this was surely true. Aside from David Offley and Joseph Langdon, Stephens had a letter of introduction to the Reverend Josiah Brewer, a New England Congregational missionary. Stephens, a fairly relaxed Episcopalian, was not well predisposed toward missionaries: the only one he had ever met at home had been a "canting hypocrite." But seeing the missionaries in Smyrna made him change his mind; he found them "gentlemanly and well-educated men, well acquainted with the countries and the places worth visiting, with just the books I wanted, and, I had almost said, the wives;

---

* The signatories, all described as American residents of Smyrna, were F. C. Blackler, Alfred Kenrick, George C. Prior, Joseph Gardner, Charles F. King, Charles Watson, Henry Devine, and H. B. Skinner.

I mean with wives always glad to see a countryman, and to talk about home. There is something exceedingly interesting in a missionary's wife." [31]

Stephens was not the only visitor thus bemused by the gorgeous Emilia Field Brewer, one of the outstanding social beauties of her day before she left Connecticut to share her husband's work in the East. The Reverend E. C. Wines, who met her in 1831, found her "uncommonly beautiful, and a woman of the finest intelligence and most fascinating manners." Wines was irresistibly drawn to the Brewer house (located between Frank Street and the harbor), and during his stay in Smyrna he went there almost every evening. [32]

The Brewers lived in Smyrna from 1830 to 1838. With them had come Emilia's thirteen-year-old brother, Stephen, who later (like the Brewers' own son David, born in 1837) became a distinguished Supreme Court Justice. Brewer, a Yale man, was employed by the Ladies Missionary Society of New Haven, with the object of educating Greek girls. Most visitors found the Brewer operation very impressive. He was much admired for his character ("marked with mildness, modesty, good sense and unaffected piety," according to Wines) and for the fearless way he went out during the plague, attending to the needy. Brewer renounced the salary provided by the New Haven ladies and made a living by keeping school for American and European children, for which the grateful merchants of Smyrna gave him £200 per year. In all his schools Brewer had more than two hundred pupils. [33]

This was Brewer's second missionary assignment in the East. In 1826, as a bachelor of thirty, he had been sent out by the Female Society of Boston and Vicinity for Promoting Christianity among the Jews. (The ladies of the Society could have had little first-hand knowledge of their target, for there were few Jews in New England in those days.) Their parting instructions to him were full of good will of a peculiarly Boston kind: "Mr. Brewer will transmit frequent communications to the Society, and it is hoped that the Ladies will feel for him that tender solicitude and deep interest, which they would feel for a dear brother, or a beloved child, who had left the bosom of his friends to dwell with a rebellious and stiff-necked people. In our nearest approaches to the throne of grace, may we never forget our far distant missionary." Such a demonstration of corporate affection could hardly be left unanswered. Moved by the scene as his ship left Boston harbor on September 16, 1826, Brewer sent his reply ashore with the pilot: "How could our *Pilgrim mothers* have exulted amidst the trials which they were called to endure around this bay, had they foreseen that scarcely two centuries would elapse, before their daughters should be sending back the gospel to Jerusalem!" [34]

Brewer never got to Jerusalem, much to the disappointment of the good females of Boston. Soon after reaching Smyrna he wrote back: "Jerusalem and its vicinity are in a state of anarchy, the governor having revolted against the Pasha of Acre." The distribution of Bibles and tracts in Syria, he pointed out, was almost entirely suspended, whereas it was continuing in Smyrna and Constantinople. Under the circumstances he thought it best to make for Constantinople right away, and he arrived there on February 2, 1827.* In the capital Brewer found lodging in a boarding house run by a Greek Catholic widow, at a dollar a day, which he thought exorbitant. The other boarders, with whom he dined each

---

* His description of his *firman*, or travel document, is interesting: "A sheet of firm paper, a yard in length, and half that in breadth, beginning with the name of the Sultan in large and complex characters. This it behooves every good Mussulman to apply to his lips and his forehead, as a token of loyalty. Like inscriptions on Turkish tombstones, its lines gradually rise towards the left." A scribe charged him one dollar for it.

day at five o'clock, were an English traveler and a Wallachian merchant. His first task each morning was to destroy fifty or sixty vermin in his bed and clothing, but he waxed philosophical about this chore, identifying himself with some illustrious forebears: "From the great uniformity between the style of living in the Apostolic times and the present, there is reason to believe, that the slumbers of Paul and other primitive missionaries were often disturbed by this cause." After several months in Constantinople he visited the Greek islands and embarked for Boston in April, 1828. Brewer had accomplished but little for the good ladies of Boston, and his connection with them was severed soon after his return.[35]

With Josiah Brewer in 1826 was Elnathan Gridley, also a bachelor of thirty, sent out by the American Board of Commissioners for Foreign Missions to work among the Greeks in Turkey. Another Yale graduate, born in nearby Farmington, Gridley was an enthusiastic mountaineer. In September, 1827, he ventured to tackle Mount Argeus, near Caesarea (now Kayseri), about four hundred miles east of Smyrna; he was undoubtedly the first American to have ventured so far into the interior of Asia Minor. Near the top he was overtaken by a hailstorm, caught cold, and died a fortnight later. "He was laid by strangers in his narrow bed," Brewer reported, in the idiom of the time. A legend about Gridley's death grew up among the Turks of Central Anatolia. It seems that Gridley was seeking a rare flower that grew only at the summit. "The plant was guarded by a watchful serpent. . . . The traveler in vain tried to persuade some of the natives to accompany him, and point out the way; none of them would venture, and at length he made the ascent alone. Failing, however, in his attempt to surprise the dragon, he was himself destroyed. He was afterwards discovered, transformed into a book, which was taken to Caesarea, and thence found its way back to Frangistan." [36]

The American Board sent out others to replace the unfortunate and legendary Gridley. By the time of Stephens' visit in 1835 Smyrna had become the center for communication with other missionary stations in Western Asia. In charge of these operations for many years was the Reverend Daniel Temple, a gloomy, austere, sanctimonious New Englander. Yet he seems an oddly sympathetic character. He was born in Reading, Massachusetts, in 1789, the eldest of thirteen children of a pious farmer. "Trained faithfully in the nurture and admonition of the Lord," he worked his way through Dartmouth by teaching grammar and singing and was graduated from Andover Theological Seminary in 1820. His intimate friend for nine years at Phillips Academy, Dartmouth, and Andover, the much more convivial William Goodell, recalled later: "Seven of those years we occupied the same room, ate at the same table, prayed in the same closet, . . . and at night threw ourselves down upon the same couch." Yet throughout a lifetime of correspondence Temple always began his letters "Dear Brother Goodell." (E. C. Wines, comparing Temple to Goodell, found him "a gentleman of milder virtues, of less determined energy of character, and not so deeply versed in Eastern lore." [37])

Temple did not enjoy traveling. Early in his career he wrote unhappily: "I painfully feel the want of that sacred retirement which I would enjoy and did enjoy when I was not obliged to fall almost every day and hour into the society of strangers. . . . If I did not feel that it would be hiding my talent in the earth, I would sink at once into retirement, and the great world should never see me again." Just before leaving for the Mediterranean in January 1822 he wrote gloomily:

"I am praying that our departure may not be on the Sabbath Day." In fact, Temple and his bride (Rachel Dix of Little-ton, Massachusetts) set sail for Malta on a Wednesday, January 2. In the hold of the brig *Cyprus*, Captain Dixon, was a printing press which Temple was to operate for many years, first at Malta, later at Smyrna. On his arrival at Malta in late February, Temple wrote his parents: "To me, the most un-pleasant circumstance on our voyage has been that I could never enjoy a moment's retirement. . . ." Malta was depress-ing to him: "The weather is rather cold here now. We have no fire, except a little in the kitchen for cooking. . . . I re-joice in the thought that you will spend your days in New England, that Eden of this world."

When Rachel died of consumption in 1827, Temple was left with four young children, two of whom soon followed their mother to the grave. He was worried about the other two, Daniel and Charles: "The thought of their being educated in this deeply depraved and ungodly part of the world is truly distressing. All the people in the Mediterranean, I have reason to fear, are by principle and practice liars." (Despite these apprehensions, both boys grew up to become preachers.) In America in 1830, he found them a new mother, Martha Ely of Longmeadow, Massachusetts. The family returned to live three more years at Malta. Then in December, 1833, the Temples and the press moved to Smyrna. Within a month of their arrival, Consul Offley sent for Temple and told him that the pasha had given him ten days to pack up and leave. The printing press, already at work turning out Protestant tracts in Greek, was giving offence to rival religious groups. An Armenian bishop named Carabet, living with the Temple family, must be delivered up to the pasha within three days. But with Offley's cooperation, Carabet was smuggled out of the country, and Temple was allowed to stay.

His work settled into a dull routine. Dutifully he managed
the mail for the brethren in Constantinople, Beirut, Bursa,
Trebizond, Erzurum, and Northern Persia. Once he wrote
Goodell: "With more than forty boxes to be shipped to the
United States, and nearly as many more to go to you [in
Constantinople] and the Syrian mission, I have found myself
more than a little confused. . . . The press, the schools, the
correspondence, receiving and despatching letters and parcels
and boxes, almost without number, and in all directions; all
these things, with many more that are nameless, and must
be nameless, consume my time and distract my mind. . . .
But it is work which someone must do, and why not I, as
well as anybody else?"

Temple confessed in 1839: "Looking back over the years
I have spent in the Mediterranean, I seem to have accomplished very little." For five more years he soldiered on. He
mellowed somewhat, according to Goodell: "As he becomes
more cheerful in his old age and I more sober, we are of course
getting to be somewhat more alike!" Then suddenly, at
fifty-four, he was out of a job. The American Board decided
in 1844 to close down all operations among the Greeks
(though work in Smyrna among the Armenians continued).
Temple bitterly auctioned off his household goods, including
his one luxury, a mahogany table (all his other furniture was
of pine) acquired at the beginning of his career lest any "air
of meanness should lurk around the house of one called to
mingle . . . with the wealthy and refined circles of the
English residents at Malta." Gloom and apprehension possessed him: "The thought of a removal, of a return to our
native land, seems to me like the wandering of a satellite out
of its orbit. . . . I have not the remotest idea of the things
that are to befall us there." On his return to Massachusetts
he found that much had changed: "A railroad is now being

cut through the middle of my father's farm, within forty rods of the house. Modes of living, dress, food, and furniture . . . all is unlike what it was fifteen years ago. . . . The West is a world of wonders and magic." And he expressed a thoroughly modern sentiment shortly after rejoining his two sons who had been in the United States for schooling: "I meet most painful proofs that children are not thoroughly taught to obey their parents."

Temple was still, after all, a preacher, and he had no choice but to ply his trade; he drifted as far west as Ohio and Iowa. Enfeebled by consumption, he took to the sea and saw Panama and England. His sadly unfulfilled life ended on August 9, 1851, in the old farmhouse where he and his father before him were born. He died fretting over the great iron horse chugging past only two hundred yards from his bed. At the end, "longing for the East," he was comforted by William Goodell, temporarily away from his post at Constantinople. Goodell tarried to preach the sermon at his old friend's funeral.[38]

A number of other American Board missionaries came to live at Smyrna in the 1830's. One was John B. Adger. Born into a well-to-do, slave-owning Charleston family in 1810, Adger was a graduate of Union College and Princeton Theological Seminary. He arrived in Smyrna with his bride, a wealthy young Charleston girl named Elizabeth Keith Shrewsbury, in October, 1834. He was a member of the mission there until 1846, but in some ways he was never really a part of it. (Significantly, almost no mention of Adger appears in the copious journal of Daniel Temple.) Perhaps his independent means subtly kept him apart. At least it allowed him to get away from his work for long periods; during his eleven years at Smyrna he and his family traveled twice to

Western Europe for pleasure. (How Daniel Temple must have fumed!) In less than ten years the Adgers had seven children, each baptized by a different American missionary.

The Adgers went home to Charleston in 1846 fully intending to return to their post, but they never did. Adger sensed that the Congregationalist, Yankee-dominated American Board, heavily dependent upon New England Abolitionist money, did not like having Southerners on its staff.* John Adger followed his calling for a solid fifty years after his return to the United States, but he never quite forgave the Board for easing him out.[39]

Finally, there was Henry John Van Lennep, born in Smyrna in 1815 into an old trading family of Dutch extraction. He was a small boy in 1820 when his parents befriended the pioneer missionary Pliny Fisk and invited him in as a boarder. (Fisk mentioned that the Van Lenneps were "respectable and rich.") Henry's parents were apparently so impressed with what they saw of the Americans that they took the extraordinary step — for those days — of packing him off to the United States for schooling. After Amherst ('37) and Andover ('40) he returned to his home town as a missionary of the American Board. With him was his New England bride, Emma, who survived only a few months in the East. Back in the United States in 1843, he married Mary Elizabeth Hawes of Hartford, daughter of a prominent clergyman. She in turn died of dysentery in 1844, at the age of twenty-three. Undaunted, Van Lennep married for a

---

* Two other Board missionaries from the South, Albert L. Holladay of Virginia and John Francis Lanneau of Charleston, also returned from the Middle East in 1846 and were dropped by the Board. Rufus Anderson, in his official history of the American Board, blandly recorded that all three had retired because of bad health. *History of the Missions . . . to the Oriental Churches* (Boston, 1872), I, 278, 333; II, 11.

third time in 1850. He left the Middle East in 1869 and retired in Massachusetts.

Because of the relative openness of its society and the forbearance of the Ottomans, Smyrna in the early nineteenth
century was a natural place for Americans to establish their
first Eastern beachhead. With their curious mixture of commerce and piety, contentiousness and charity, and their somewhat defensive admiration for their British cousins, they
epitomized the America from which they had come. It is a
measure of John Lloyd Stephens' skill that his book caught
this mood so well. Smyrna provided him with a bench mark
by which to gauge the rest of the Eastern journey on which
he now proceeded.

3. Constantinople: The Treaty of 1830 and the Turkish Navy

FROM SMYRNA STEPHENS DECIDED to take the steamer, introduced only the year before, up to Constantinople. It troubled him to do so, he said. "A new and unaccountable respect for the classics almost made me scorn the new-fangled conveyance. . . . Smothering, as well as I could, my sense of shame, I sneaked on board the Maria Dorothea for a race to Constantinople. Join me, now, in this race; and if your heart does not break at going by at the rate of eight or ten miles an hour, I will whip you over a piece of the most classic ground consecrated in history, mythology, or poetry, and in less time than even the swift-footed Achilles could have traveled it." And so he does: Lesbos, Lemnos, Tenedos, Troy ("but hold, stop the engine!"), Mount Ida, the Dardanelles ("in the hands of Europeans, particularly English, improved as country seats, would make one of the loveliest countries in the world"), Gallipoli, the Sea of Marmora ("I went to sleep lulled by the music of a high-pressure engine"), and finally — Constantinople.[1]

Stephens knew, of course, that for almost four years the United States had had a resident chargé d'affaires at the Turkish capital, Commodore David Porter. But the first official American visit to Constantinople took place many years before. It was a singular train of events that led to the establishment, in 1830, of diplomatic relations between the young giant of the West and the lumbering old Ottoman Empire.

1800: THE BAINBRIDGE MISSION

The American ships that sailed the Mediterranean in the early days of the Republic were considered such fair game by the Barbary Pirates that in 1795 the United States negotiated a treaty with the dey of Algiers whereby this uncongenial potentate promised to keep his pirates in check in return for an annual tribute of naval stores to the value of $21,600. However, the fact that the dey of Algiers and his fellow rulers of the Barbary Coast were nominally under the control of the Sultan posed the delicate question as to whether treaties with them were effective unless there were also a treaty with the Ottoman Porte. John Adams and Thomas Jefferson, frankly puzzled, sought expert European diplomatic opinion on this subtle point, the tribute arrangement being well known and accepted by the European Powers generally. Counsels were divided. In the end Adams and Jefferson did nothing, mainly because their attention was diverted to more pressing matters in the life of the young nation. But pressures began to build up for diplomatic relations with the Sultan. Joel Barlow, the roughhewn Connecticut poet, while serving as consul at Algiers in 1796, wrote the Secretary of State advising the establishment of consulates at Smyrna, Alexandria, and Salonika. In 1798 President John Adams actually got as far as appointing a minister to the Porte, one William Loughton Smith of South Carolina, then serving as minister to Portugal. But proper instructions never reached him, and with the outbreak of war that year between France and England the plan was abandoned; it was deemed too risky for the new republic to antagonize either Power by taking a diplomatic initiative which might be regarded as precocious.[2]

Thus it was that the first official American visit to the Ottoman capital was made in 1800 by a naval officer, Captain William Bainbridge, in command at twenty-six of the U.S.S. *George Washington*. It fell to Bainbridge to deliver to the dey of Algiers the naval stores called for under the 1795 treaty. When the *George Washington*, a converted merchant ship and a poor sailer, arrived in Algiers harbor, the dey accepted his booty with pleasure and then asked Bainbridge to do him a favor. He had, he said, some presents for the Sultan: would Bainbridge kindly deliver them to Constantinople? The young captain said he was sorry, that this was not part of his orders, and he made to depart. The dey adopted a firmer tone — did Bainbridge recognize that the *George Washington* was in range of the Algerian shore batteries? Besides, other nations were accustomed to perform such courtesies for the dey; surely the Americans could oblige as well. For better or worse — and it stirred up a storm later — Bainbridge decided to yield rather than lose his ship and doom his crew of one hundred and fifty Yankee seamen to slavery, as had happened on occasion to British and Dutch mariners who had ventured to challenge the dey's authority. But he didn't like it, and he reported to Secretary of the

Navy Benjamin Stoddert: "I hope I may never again be sent to Algiers with *tribute,* unless I am authorized to deliver it from the mouth of our cannon!" [3]

The *George Washington* weighed anchor in Algiers harbor on October 19, 1800. Besides the seething young Bainbridge and his crew, the ship carried the Algerian ambassador and his suite of a hundred persons, a hundred Negro women and children, four horses, one hundred and fifty sheep, twenty-five horned cattle, four lions, four tigers, four antelopes, twelve parrots, and several ostriches, together with funds and regalia amounting to nearly a million dollars in value. Over this floating zoo flew the Algerian flag, but once out of the harbor Bainbridge had it hauled down and ran up the Stars and Stripes instead. Life aboard the crowded vessel was complicated by the five daily prayers of the Muslim passengers, whose efforts to orient themselves to Mecca when the vessel tacked created some mirth among the American sailors.

Bainbridge approached the forbidding Turkish forts at the Dardanelles with caution. Ordinarily, a *firman* from the capital was required for an armed foreign vessel to pass through the Straits, and Bainbridge had none. Improvising, he ordered his crew to pretend they were taking in sail with a view to heaving to for inspection. At the same time he fired a formidably smoky eight-gun salute. When the fort returned the salute, Bainbridge simply sailed on past, taking a chance that the Turkish gunners could not see to hit him. The ruse succeeded. No Western vessel had ever done this sort of thing before, and Bainbridge reported from Constantinople that his success had "astonished every Christian ambassador here." [4]

In Constantinople this strange foreign vessel with its exotic cargo was greeted warmly. An English traveler has left a colorful account of the visit: "When the frigate came to anchor, and a message went to the Porte that an American ship was in the harbour, the Turks were altogether unable to comprehend where the country was situate whose flag they were to salute. A great deal of time was therefore lost in settling this important point, and in considering how to receive the stranger. In the meantime we went on board to visit the captain. We were sitting with him in his cabin, when a messenger came from the Turkish Government to ask whether America were not otherwise called the New World; and, being answered in the affirmative, assured the captain that he was welcome, and that he would be treated with the utmost cordiality and respect. The messengers from the dey were then ordered on board the capudan pasha's ship; who, receiving the letter from their sovereign with great rage, first spat, and then stamped upon it; telling them to go back to their master and inform him that he would be served after the same manner, whenever the Turkish admiral met him. Captain Bainbridge was, however, received with every mark of respect and attention, and he was rewarded with magnificent presents. The fine order of his ship, and the healthy state of her crew, became topics of general conversation in Pera; and the different ministers strove who should first receive him in their palaces. We accompanied him in his longboat to the Black Sea, as he was desirous of hoisting there, for the first time, the American flag; and, upon his return, were amused by a very singular entertainment at his table during dinner. Upon the four corners were as many decanters, containing fresh water from the four quarters of the globe. The natives of Europe, Asia, Africa, and America, sat down together at the same table, and were regaled with flesh, fruit, bread and other viands; while, of every article, a sample from each quarter of the globe was presented at the same time.

The means of accomplishing this are easily explained, by the frigate's having touched at Algiers, in her passage from America, and being at anchor so near to the shores of both Europe and Asia." [5]

Bainbridge acquitted himself with dignity (among other things, he pleaded for clemency for the commander at the Dardanelles who had failed to stop him); the *George Washington* left Constantinople in December and returned peacefully to its normal duties in the western Mediterranean.

TREATY NEGOTIATIONS

During his stay in Constantinople Bainbridge was summoned by the capudan pasha to discuss the possibility of a treaty between the United States and the Ottoman Empire. Nothing came of the idea at the time. But as we have seen (Chapter 2), the Smyrna merchant David Offley, who arrived eleven years later, felt strongly that American commerce with Turkey could never be placed on a sound footing until there was a treaty between the two countries. He constantly buttonholed visiting Americans to make this argument and often stressed it in his reports to Washington. In 1820 he struck a sympathetic chord with John Quincy Adams, then Secretary of State in the Monroe administration. There followed a ten-year period of frustrating negotiations with the corrupt, supine bureaucracy in Constantinople, whose venality and infinite gifts for vacillation baffled Americans unschooled in the labyrinth of Ottoman intrigue. As it turned out American treaty commissioners succeeded in pinning the Turks down only after a combined force of British, French, and Russian ships gunned almost the entire Ottoman navy to the bottom of the sea at Navarino, in Greece, on October 20, 1827. On that date, between 2:30 and 6:00 in the afternoon, the combined Turkish and Egyptian fleets lost sixty vessels. According to a French officer on the scene, the only ships still afloat the next day were a dismasted frigate, four corvettes, six brigs, and four schooners.* It was the worst Turkish naval defeat since the Battle of Lepanto in 1571.[6] There was an urgent need for rehabilitation; with Britain, France, and Russia having been responsible for the debacle, the United States seemed the only available source of help. Without this disaster Turkish dallying might have lasted indefinitely.

The first of the negotiators had been Luther Bradish, a well-traveled, well-educated, urbane Manhattan lawyer of thirty-seven. At Hampton Roads on April 28, 1820, Bradish quietly slipped aboard the U.S.S. *Columbus,* a seventy-four gun ship of the line under the command of Commodore William Bainbridge (who, it will be remembered, had visited the Mediterranean under different circumstances twenty years earlier). At Gibraltar Bradish transferred to the brig-of-war *Spark* and was joined by Charles Folsom of Boston, detached for the purpose from his duties as Bainbridge's private secretary. Bradish was to make arrangements for Bainbridge to follow with the *Columbus* to Constantinople. The *Spark* arrived at Smyrna in October, where Bradish and Folsom conferred with Offley. Bradish then went on alone to Constantinople and arrived to discover that his supposedly secret mission was common knowledge. (It turned out later that the leak had come from within the State Department itself,

* An English missionary at Alexandria, who witnessed the arrival of the Egyptian survivors there, gave a somewhat more liberal estimate: "Yesterday the remains of the Pasha's fleet arrived from Navarino. I think there were three or four Corvets, 3 or 4 Frigates of which two are yet outside [the harbor], and a very considerable number of Brigs and Sloops of War." John Nicolayson to Isaac Bird *et al.* (in Beirut), Dec. 29, 1827. MS letter in possession of Mr. Gordon Torrey, Washington, D.C. Quoted by permission.

much to Adams' chagrin.)* This was unsettling, but just as discouraging was an indication that the *Columbus* and the *Spark* would not be welcome at the capital. The Greek Revolution having broken out, the Turks were being unusually cautious about receiving armed foreign vessels. In the end Bradish cooled his heels for several months in the Porte's drafty, opulent corridors of decaying power and came away with nothing to show for it. He wrote Adams that it might be possible to negotiate a treaty, but only if the dealings were kept absolutely secret, to avoid interference by European powers (mainly Britain), and only if the United States were willing to part with about $50,000 in the way of gifts to officials, including $7000 for the reis effendi, or minister of foreign affairs, "to preserve [his] opinion the same as at present." [7] After a tour of the Holy Land Bradish returned to the United States.**

The rebellion of the Greeks evoked strong sympathy all over Europe and America, and it became very difficult for Secretary Adams to deal openly with the Turks. Publicly, in

---

* As part of the effort to maintain secrecy, the passport drawn up by Adams for Bradish certified that he was about to visit foreign countries "with the view of gratifying a commendable curiosity." The Bradish passport has recently been cited in the Supreme Court of the United States in support of the thesis that Americans have historically been allowed to travel freely abroad. Justice Goldberg, dissenting in *Zemel* v. *Rusk*, 381 U.S. 1, 27 (1965). See also Louis L. Jaffe, "The Right to Travel: The Passport Problem," *Foreign Affairs*, 35, no. 1 (October 1956), 17. Whatever the merits of the passport issue, it is respectfully submitted that the Bradish case probably is not ideal as a precedent because it involved a subterfuge.

** Bradish left no account of his travels after leaving Constantinople, and there is almost no reference to them in his voluminous uncataloged papers on deposit at the New York Historical Society. (For the patient and unrewarding research required to establish this fact, I am greatly indebted to Elliott B. Nixon, Esq., of the New York Bar.) At all events Bradish did not take part in the Egyptian campaign on the Nile in 1820–21, as has recently been asserted. See John A. Wilson, *Signs and Wonders upon Pharaoh: A History of American Egyptology* (Chicago, 1964), pp. 22, 25.

fact, Washington took a strong line of virtuous disapproval of any assistance to them by private citizens.* Adams was enough of a politician to realize that he must work quietly. In April, 1823, he picked another secret agent, George Bethune English, a rather flamboyant young Harvard graduate ('07) with several abortive careers behind him, including command of the Egyptian artillery in 1820–21. (See Chapter 6.) English presented himself to Adams as well suited for the job: he had traveled in the East, spoke some Turkish, and claimed personal acquaintance (on the basis of a brief meeting six years before) with Khosrew Mehmet, the capudan pasha, David Offley's valuable contact. English arrived in Constantinople in November, 1823, spent several weeks renting and furnishing a suitable house in the old part of the town, and adopted native dress. He then set about making contacts, including — oddly enough — the Sultan's librarian. With characteristic confidence he really seems to have thought at first that he could pass for a Turk, but soon he had to abandon this pretense. He got little support from Offley, who regarded English with dark suspicion; Offley wrote Adams: "It is proper that I should inform Your Excellency that this person about six years ago when at Cairo became a Mahometan and of course a subject of the Grand Seignor." [8] English himself reported to Adams: "I came here in a very unobtrusive manner. I am, I understand, at present considered by the

---

* Secretary of State Henry Clay to William C. Somerville, appointing him as special agent to Greece, Sept. 6, 1825. By this time Adams was President, but he retained a special interest in the Turkish treaty problem. Clay wrote Somerville: "Information, which, it is hoped, is not correct, has reached this Department, of one or two American merchantmen having engaged in the Turkish service, to transport military men or means. If any such instances should fall within your observation, you will acquaint the parties concerned with the high displeasure of the President at conduct so unworthy of American citizens, and so contrary to their duty, as well as their honour." United States, National Archives, Records of the Department of State, Special Missions, pp. 31–33.

Europeans here merely as one who has heretofore travelled in
the East and who visits Constantinople in an oriental dress to
have the greater facility to observe what is worthy of notice.
Indeed under favour of this garb I penetrate almost every
where, and have opportunities of learning the mode of trans-
acting public business at the Ottoman Porte which the European dress would infallibly exclude me from. Among my
neighbors I pass for an American musselman who has come
from a far distant country to visit the Capital of Islam. By
encouraging these ideas I have thus far got on pretty well;
but my situation is full of danger and disquietude; and nothing but my determination not to disappoint by my fault your
expectations with regard to me is able to countervail the
anxiety the singular task I have imposed upon myself occasions me, as in passing different guards of Janissaries I frequently hear myself denounced as a Greek spy in disguise, and
my own servant when I go out of doors will not follow me except on the other side of the street, in order as he says not
to partake of a shot meant for me."

After some delay English saw the capudan pasha and
reached an understanding with him that the United States
would send out a negotiator, preferably the commander of
the navy's Mediterranean Squadron, to meet with the capudan pasha privately somewhere in the Greek archipelago.
Back in Washington in May 1824 English urged President
Monroe and Secretary Adams to follow through with this
plan. All summer and into the autumn he badgered Adams,
volunteering himself time and again as the most suitable agent
for carrying it out. (Among other things, he had no other
employment and was short of money.) In January Adams
appointed Commodore John Rodgers as his third negotiator
and assigned English to go along as interpreter.[9] Rodgers, a
hero of the War of 1812, was now (at fifty) the senior officer

in the navy and the new commander of the Mediterranean Squadron. He spent the rest of the winter fitting out his flagship, the brand-new *North Carolina*, a seventy-four-gun ship of the line. (The ship was most impressive: three hundred eighty feet long, two hundred eighty feet to the top of the main mast. She carried nine hundred sixty men, including a ship's band in Moorish costume.)[10] Rodgers, with English aboard and accompanied from Gibraltar by three other ships of the squadron, reached Smyrna August 20, 1825, and inquired after the capudan pasha. Rodgers' instructions from Adams included a warning to "be especially careful, that neither the meeting nor any movement contingent upon it shall be made susceptible of any unfavorable operation upon the cause of the Greeks."[11] So when he discovered that the pasha was off fighting the Greeks, Rodgers thought it wise not to pursue him. David Offley used this opportunity to impress Smyrna with the American naval presence and the navy with Smyrna's hospitality. For three weeks the town sparkled with a constant round of parties and balls. Many Smyrniotes visited the grand ships from the New World, including, it was reported rather breathlessly, veiled Turkish women with eunuchs. The officers paid a formal visit on the governor. And on one occasion men from the ships put out a dangerous fire in the town, for which they were thanked by a letter from the principal merchants.[12]

In October Rodgers repaired to Port Mahon, Minorca, for the winter. George English helped him write a nice note to the capudan pasha, expressing the hope of seeing him soon, and the following June Rodgers and English were back in Smyrna. The meeting finally took place on July 5, 1826, at Tenedos, an island near the entrance to the Dardanelles. In a very cordial conversation, the capudan pasha promised to talk to the Sultan about a treaty and to let the Americans have a reaction within three or four months. (Offley, who had come along from Smyrna, replaced English as interpreter, at Rodgers' request.) Business over, the fun began. The pasha was feted aboard the *North Carolina*, and the American delegation aboard the Turkish flagship. Rodgers got some presents: a pipe, a shawl, two silk gown patterns, two handkerchiefs, and a small box of sweetmeats, which, the pasha allowed, had been fashioned in his own harem. The Commodore also acquired a splendid portrait of the Sultan. In return he parted with a diamond ring, a diamond-studded snuffbox, and sundry firearms which the pasha admired. Upon leaving Rodgers put on a real show for the Turks: "The squadron got under way, and after making a tack to windward, each ship bore up in succession and ran down through the Turkish fleet, and on coming abreast of the flag of the Capudan Pasha, manned her rigging, the crew dressed in white, and gave three cheers, the band at the same time playing 'Hail Columbia!' " [13]

Alas, the promised message from the Sultan did not come. Rodgers was puzzled and discouraged; he suspected that the Turks were irritated because of the increasing tempo of American assistance to the Greeks. In a gloomy and defensive mood he wrote the Secretary of State in February 1827: "in justice to myself permit me, Sir, to say that if I should fail before my return in executing the business which led to my communicating with the Capudan Pasha, it will not be my fault." [14] Regardless of whose fault it was, the Rodgers mission had lasting significance, because the capudan pasha never forgot the impression made on him by the American navy. The quality of American shipbuilding became a matter of urgent concern to the almost fleetless Turks after the Battle of Navarino (October 20, 1827). By this time Khosrew, though he could neither read nor write, had been promoted from capudan pasha to seraskier pasha, the highest position in the

Ottoman armed forces. (An English traveler referred to him as "the Duke of Wellington of Turkey.")[15] Right after Navarino he sent off a "particularly friendly and complimentary" letter to David Offley, inviting him up to Constantinople specifically to discuss the negotiation of a treaty. Now Offley was no fool. Tempted as he was to grab this chance to achieve the aim of a lifetime, he realized at once that the Turks supposed "that, if a treaty of friendship existed between the two nations, they would be allowed to have vessels of war built in the United States, so as to replace those lost at Navarino." [16]

Pro-Greek feeling in America was still high: the news of the Turkish defeat, which reached New York on December 16, was greeted with ringing of churchbells throughout the nation, and a town in Wisconsin was renamed "Navarino." [17] But John Quincy Adams, now President, decided to carry on. He prepared cautious and confidential instructions for Offley and Commodore William Montgomery Crane (Rodgers' successor as commander of the Mediterranean Squadron), giving them full powers to negotiate a treaty of navigation and commerce with the Turks. Crane joined Offley in Smyrna in November 1828; Offley went alone to Constantinople. But after three months of futile haggling he got disgusted and went back to Smyrna. The issues were never very clearly joined, but it was clear to Offley that the main thing the Turks wanted was ships, and in this he was not authorized to accommodate them.[18]

Four days after Offley left Constantinople Andrew Jackson succeeded Adams as President of the United States. His Secretary of State, Martin Van Buren of New York, personally went into the Turkish treaty matter with great care. Warned by Adams about the danger of security leaks, he kept all the relevant papers locked up in his own office.[19]

He soon concluded that a new effort and a new negotiator were needed to get the matter off dead center. He was probably right about this; Offley, for all his skill and experience, had no authority to offer anything new and tempting to the Porte, and his face was becoming all too familiar in Constantinople. But if a new man was called for, Van Buren could hardly have picked a more controversial one than Charles Rhind. A fifty-year-old naturalized Scot, Rhind was a successful New York merchant, prominent in such civic affairs as welcoming General Lafayette (1824) and opening the Erie Canal (1825). He had been engaged in the Mediterranean trade for many years and indeed claimed that Offley owed him his consular post.[20] Van Buren asked his old political crony, James Alexander Hamilton, U.S. District Attorney for New York, for his opinion of Rhind and got this rather chilling response: "I do not think he is a man sufficiently well informed for the employment of which you speak, nor has he address or character to insure reasonable hope of success." Instead, Hamilton suggested Dr. James E. De Kay of New York.[21]

In the meantime, at Van Buren's request, Rhind went over the whole file. Rather superciliously, he told the Secretary of State that Offley had been too rigid in insisting on most-favored-nation treatment on tariffs. (He neglected to point out, however, that State Department instructions had never allowed Offley or any of the other negotiators to accept less than this; the fact that Rhind himself was very casual about the letter of his own instructions was to appear later.) Convinced despite Hamilton's advice that Rhind was the man for the job, Van Buren appointed him. Rhind was to act in consultation with Offley and the new commander of the squadron, Commodore James Biddle, but Van Buren specified that Rhind was to go alone to Constantinople for the first

round of talks with the Turks. Under cover of an appointment as consul at the rather unlikely port of Odessa, Rhind
left New York secretly and met Biddle at Minorca at the end
of November; they traveled together in the U.S. Frigate
Java to meet Offley at Smyrna. As instructed, Rhind went
off to Constantinople alone. To the surprise of all, the reis
effendi agreed to a treaty on the basis of full most-favored-
nation treatment and access for Americans to the Black Sea
trade: "The treaty itself was made in the village of Bebek,
in a little kiosk on the Bosphorus. . . . The American and
Turkish commissioners met here night after night in the time
of Ramazan, and completed their work before those European
powers who might have been disposed to exert unfavorable
influence had any knowledge of what was transpiring." [22]
On May 7, 1830, Rhind signed the treaty for the United
States and two days later sent a jubilant message to Offley and
Biddle, telling them to hasten to the capital. He thoughtfully
enclosed a copy of the treaty he had just signed.

Now Offley and Biddle were understandably surprised that
Rhind had actually signed a treaty without consulting them.
However, on looking the treaty over and finding no serious
fault with it except what Biddle called its bad French, they
proceeded to Constantinople in response to Rhind's summons.

There they were soon sorely disillusioned. In the first
place Rhind had neglected to mention in his letter to them
that he had bought $9000 worth of snuffboxes for the Turkish
negotiators and that he expected to be repaid out of Government funds. Biddle, who as cashier of the mission had been
provided with only $20,000 and saw it dwindling fast,
grumbled because he had not been consulted, but he ultimately reimbursed Rhind without too much fuss. But
Offley and Biddle were staggered when they discovered what
else Rhind had conceded in order to consummate the treaty,

so unexceptionable on its face: he had agreed to a separate secret clause, which (said Rhind in reporting to the Secretary of State) gave the Sultan "the privilege of making contracts for cutting timber in the United States and building vessels, if he pleases." * Worse yet, Rhind was secretive about what he had done; he waited until the morning of the day the other two men were supposed to sign — and four days after they had reached Constantinople — before he broke the news to them. Offley and Biddle, especially the latter, were stunned. Biddle reverted to the $9000 snuffboxes, observing that if he had known about them he would not have come to Constantinople. This, Offley reported, "offended Mr. Rhind to such a degree that both for its violence and long duration appears to me to have far exceeded the cause. . . . Every exertion was made by me to calm Mr. Rhind and I thought to have succeeded. . . . I have been lamentably mistaken." [23] More hard words passed. Rhind stormed out of the house shared by the three commissioners, declaring that henceforth he would not communicate with Commodore Biddle except in writing. Offley, the old diplomat, managed to keep on speaking terms with both and acted as messenger between them. Patiently, he tried to explain to Rhind why Biddle was so incensed. It was not just that Rhind had signed alone without consulting his colleagues, or yet that he had unilaterally disposed of $9000, or indeed that he had agreed to a secret clause. No. The thing that Biddle could not swallow (and Offley was inclined to agree with him) was the *content* of the secret clause. Not only was it recognized United States policy to "establish no relations other than purely commercial with the natives of Europe," as Biddle put it, but the secret provision clearly lay far beyond the scope of authority that Van Buren had granted. Furthermore, it might

* For an English translation of Rhind's secret article, see Appendix I.

impinge on legislation Congress might wish to enact forbidding contracts by foreigners for vessels in the United States: Congress could not enact such legislation without breaking the treaty.

Rhind was not moved. In the first place he seems to have been confident that official Washington would recognize that the secret clause was really a hidden benefit for Andrew Jackson's government; as he wrote the Secretary of State: "so highly is the boon esteemed [by the Turks], that the new Administration have gained great credit by the circumstance." (A year later he had changed his tune; to Secretary of State Livingston he wrote: "the private article . . . being considered as of no importance in itself, I put away among some private papers, and actually forgot until they had consented to sign the Treaty.") He regarded his two colleagues as mere obstructionists. "It evidently had, from the moment they left Smyrna, been their determination to mar the Negotiation (for they even did not bring the money with them, but left it on board of the Java)." He was, he said, "disgusted with this unworthy species of trifling in a case of such importance to the Nation." And he wrote Biddle and Offley a note, saying that they need not sign if they did not want to: Rhind's own signature was enough and he was willing to assume all responsibility. "As their illiberal conduct rendered it necessary for me to sacrifice my individual interests, and return home to America, I forbade their further interference in the matter."

Biddle and Offley conferred. In those days, of course, there was no quick way to refer home for instructions. Failure to sign would surely offend the Turks. In the end Offley persuaded Biddle that in the overall national interest the lesser evil was to sign. This they did, with "very great repugnance" on Biddle's part, on the thirtieth of May. Rhind's own ver-

sion, in a letter to the Secretary of State two days later, is
well worth quoting: "It was necessary to shew the Sultan
that *something* had been granted for the concessions he had
made, and our Turkish Friends suggested the private article.
You will perceive that it is a *perfect nullity*, giving only the
privilege of *consulting* with our Minister about the best mode
of making a Contract to procure Ships or Ship Timber. My
feelings are, at the moment, roused to such a state of excitement by the degraded situation in which my Colleagues have
placed me, that I must crave your indulgence in making my
communication so brief."

Flushed with victory, Rhind then overreached himself. He
demanded that it was he who should have the honor of bearing the treaty back to the President. At this point Biddle and
Offley combined to frustrate him. On the ninth of June they
left Rhind in "an explosion of passion of the greatest violence"
and returned to Smyrna with the treaty in their possession.
Rhind, deprived of his true moment of glory, sulkily took a
quick trip to his nominal post, Odessa, returned to the Turkish capital, and finally left for the United States in September.
He took with him four fine Arabian stallions, the personal
gift of a very grateful Sultan. On their arrival the horses were
summarily seized by the Government and sold at auction for
$1990, which Rhind claimed did not cover the cost of their
transportation.[24]

The greatest authority on the Turkish treaty negotiations,
Professor Wright, summed up Rhind's role this way: "Rhind
behaved as though the treaty which he had negotiated was
something peculiarly holy and not to be questioned in the
slightest detail. . . . Unable in any way to cooperate with
others, humorless, vain, sensitive on imaginary points of honor,
quick to anger and slow to forget, it was his confidence in the
perfection of his own handiwork and his desire to monopolize

all the credit for success which almost succeeded in marring the negotiation." [25]

Yet is this entirely fair? If Biddle and Offley had been in on the whole negotiation, it seems likely that there never would have been a treaty at all. The Turks had been consistent for several years in their insistence on the right to obtain ships. Offley knew this as well as anyone, and he knew that he had no power to accommodate them. At least Rhind got a treaty signed, which is more than anyone else had done and probably more than Biddle or Offley would have permitted to happen had they been with him. There is an arguable case that in the long run it was the rambunctious, unpleasant Rhind who was right.

In the short run Biddle and Offley turned out to be right about the secret clause, for the Senate voted it down twenty-seven to eighteen. In its report to the President, the Foreign Relations Committee made clear its objections: the clause was secret (and there was no precedent for asking the Senate to ratify a secret treaty), it impinged on the government's policy of neutrality (George Washington's still sacred dictum about avoiding "foreign entanglements"), and in any case all available shipbuilding facilities were likely to be needed domestically. The remainder of the treaty, however, was ratified by an overwhelming majority.[26]

CONSPIRACY IN WASHINGTON

Van Buren was now in a difficult spot, for he had to send back a mission to exchange ratifications with some sort of explanation as to why part of the treaty was unacceptable. But Charles Rhind, still smarting over the rejection of his secret article and anxious to redeem himself, had a plan to implement it through the back door. As he explained it to Van Buren, a prominent American naval architect would be made available to the Turks to help them rebuild their fleet. At the same time the first American minister (Rhind frankly fancied himself for the job) would be sent out with instructions to give his "personal" assurance of naval assistance if required.[27]

The naval architect Rhind had in mind was Henry Eckford, a fifty-five-year-old native of Scotland, who had emigrated to the United States and risen to fame and fortune building warships on the Great Lakes during the War of 1812. He had also designed the *Robert Fulton*, one of the first ocean-going steam vessels, and frigates for a number of South American governments. Though indicted in 1827 in connection with the bankruptcy of an insurance company in which he was involved (he challenged the district attorney to a duel!), Eckford retained a circle of sympathetic friends in New York.[28] Rhind proposed that Eckford should sail to Constantinople in a brand-new corvette of his own construction, the *United States* (1000 tons, twenty-six guns), with Rhind as a passenger carrying the ratified treaty back to the Porte. At the same time he prepared to settle in as minister resident.*

President Jackson and Secretary of State Van Buren considered this scheme carefully and at one point were on the verge of using Eckford and Rhind to deliver the ratified

---

* James A. Hamilton had previously mentioned Eckford to Van Buren in connection with Hamilton's suggestion to send out James De Kay rather than Charles Rhind as a treaty negotiator. (See above, p. 58). Hamilton wrote: "Eckford's employment and reputation as a ship builder might be made use of as a cover to De Kay's going out and might be useful in the negotiation not only as affording you the money you will require (which I take for granted you must know) but also *in an other way* to induce the Porte to enter into your views." Hamilton to Van Buren, August 23, 1829. Van Buren Papers, Library of Congress. (Emphasis added; the emphasized words are obviously deliberately ambiguous. Whatever their exact connotation, they at least add to the air of conspiracy surrounding the entire Eckford-Rhind matter.)

treaty. But in the end they accepted Rhind's plan only in part. Instead of Rhind, the President appointed Commodore David Porter to set up the legation at Constantinople. On March 21, 1831, when Porter was first offered the appointment, Van Buren wrote him that Rhind would be bringing the ratified treaty across the Atlantic to meet Porter in the Mediterranean and accompany him to Constantinople, "where his services might be very useful to you." [29] Rhind himself understood that he was to play this role. On April 13 he wrote Van Buren: "I am engaged in a negotiation which will enable me to reach Constantinople in the shortest possible period. The vessel in which I propose to embark may safely be pronounced the fleetest that ever stemmed an Atlantic wave, consequently I shall reach my destination vastly sooner than I ever contemplated." Three days later he added: "Our friend Mr. Eckford is the owner of the vessel to which I alluded in my last letter. He goes to Washington on private business. As he has some idea of taking his corvette to Constantinople, I think it would be a most favorable occasion to forward the ratification, should he thus determine, and I respectfully recommend you to make an arrangement with Mr. E., to carry out the person charged with this duty, as it will unquestionably afford the best and most rapid mode of accomplishing it." [30] In the meantime, however, President Jackson himself decided that a State Department employee named William B. Hodgson, rather than Rhind, would be sent out with the treaty and with instructions about the exchange of ratifications.* In informing Porter of this, Van Buren also

* Rhind was dropped because he persisted in making a public fuss about the horses which had been seized and sold, but he was too insensitive to see the hole he was digging for himself. On March 22 Hamilton wrote a letter to Van Buren which obviously gave Rhind cause for optimism, for a week later Rhind wrote Van Buren: "I am anxiously awaiting your reply on the subject Mr. Hamilton intimated in his letter of 22 inst. and

instructed him to "assure the Reis Effendi . . . that whenever the Sublime Porte may wish to construct ships of war in
the United States, your good offices will be rendered in advice & counsel which your knowledge of the subject and experience may enable you to give it." [31] Though it involves
getting somewhat ahead of the story, it should be noted here
that Porter followed instructions shortly after his arrival and
before the exchange of ratifications. On September 27, 1831,
he wrote the reis effendi a formal note, as follows:

Whereas; a Treaty of Amity and Commerce, has been negotiated between the United States of America and the Sublime
Porte, to which the Commissioner on the part of the United
States, has, without authority, permitted to be added, a Separate
Article, in favor of the Sublime Porte, which it is not in the
power of the Government of the United States to execute, thus
deceiving the Sublime Porte, and causing great embarrassment to
the Government of the United States:

Now I, David Porter, Chargé d'Affaires acting for, and in
behalf of, the United States, near the Sublime Porte, do, in conformity with the orders of the President of the United States,
and as an Equivalent for the aforesaid rejected Separate Article,
hold myself, at all times, ready to give my friendly council and
advice to the Sublime Porte, as to the best manner of obtaining
ships of War, wood for their construction, and timber of every
description, from the United States, and to obtain all the advantages contemplated by the said separate article, without
violating the Laws of the United States, or conflicting with their
engagements with other Nations.

This concession is to be binding on the part of my successors.[32]

---

hope to receive it tomorrow." Rhind to Van Buren, March 29, 1831, DSD.
But it was actually Hamilton who suggested that Hodgson be used instead of Rhind! Hamilton to President Jackson, April 9, 1831, which appears in Hamilton's *Reminiscences* (New York, 1869), p. 204.

Thus the formal record was established, to the satisfaction of all except Charles Rhind, the "Commissioner" referred to by Porter as having acted without authority, who embarrassed the United States government and deceived the Sublime Porte. (This was only the first of a number of singularly undiplomatic choices of phrase which were to be characteristic of Porter's service at Constantinople.)

To return to the spring of 1831: Eckford and Rhind were going ahead with their own plans. Van Buren was aware of them, but he took great pains to tell Porter that Eckford's status was to be completely unofficial. Because of the bearing they had on future events, Van Buren's instructions (April 22, 1831) on this point must be set forth verbatim:

Mr. Henry Eckford, an eminent naval architect of New York, addressed a letter to the President on the 19th of this month, stating that he had lately constructed a fast sailing ship at that Port, with which he proposed proceeding to Europe for the purpose of exhibiting her as a specimen of American Naval architecture, and disposing of her as a legitimate article of mercantile adventure; that it was his intention to make such arrangements as he might find practicable, for extending that useful branch of the manufacturing industry of this country; that in clearing out this vessel upon the contemplated voyage he should conform strictly to the Laws of the United States, and that in the dispositions which he might eventually and ultimately make of her, he should be governed by the same consideration. Upon these grounds, and on that of his having been heretofore exclusively employed as a Naval Architect of the United States, in which service he had reason to believe he had rendered satisfaction to this Government, he requested the President to favor him with some document which might serve to recommend him and his objects abroad, by the favorable opinions which the President might express concerning him.

The President, in his individual capacity, has accordingly written a letter to him in reply, stating, that from the reputation which he sustains in this country, he had no doubt of his being a naval architect of great skill and enterprise, and that he would count with confidence upon a faithful performance of any engagement in the line of his profession, into which he might think proper to enter.

As it is possible that Mr. Eckford may visit Constantinople before his return to the United States with a view to the accomplishment of one or both of the objects of his voyage, and the political situation of the world may be so altered by that time, as to render questionable acts on his part, which in the present state of things would be perfectly allowable, it is the wish of the President, that, in such case, his proceedings there may be observed by you, and that if you discover any attempt on his part growing out of misconception or misapprehension, which may be calculated in the smallest degree to give just umbrage in any quarter, or to occasion the smallest distrust of the sincerity of this Government, in its determined purpose to fulfill with perfect fidelity and exactitude all its neutral obligations, you discourage and repress such attempt.

If circumstances, in reference to the character or interest of the United States, should in your judgement require it, you will take care to let it be understood by the Government of the Porte, and the foreign agents residing at Constantinople, that *this is exclusively and entirely a private and individual enterprise of Mr. Eckford himself, in which this Government has no concern whatever, and with which it is in no way connected.*[33] [Emphasis added.]

In acknowledging these instructions Porter took them at face value.[34] All the same, this is a curious letter. It protests too much. On April 22 when it was written, both Jackson and Van Buren were well aware (from Rhind's letters of April 13 and 16) that Eckford's corvette was heading straight for Constantinople.* In any case, Eckford's preparations to go to work for the Sultan were common knowledge. "His departure created considerable excitement in New York City, chiefly because he took with him a number of American mechanics, who were promised the extraordinary sum of two dollars a day apiece." [35] The unavoidable conclusion is that Van Buren in his instructions of April 22 to Porter was simply being extremely cautious. He, and presumably also the President, wanted the record to show that neither of them had conspired to use Eckford's activities as a device to circumvent the will of the United States Senate when it turned down the secret article.[36]

The skipper of Eckford's corvette was "Commodore" George C. De Kay, whose rank was a matter of courtesy, having been acquired in the service of the Argentine navy.** Also in the party was George's brother and Eckford's son-in-law, James De Kay. Physician, naturalist, graduate of Columbia College, a member of the Bread and Cheese Club made famous by James Fenimore Cooper, this man-about-Gotham let it be known that he "had been sent from the United States as a medical commissioner, to study the new and mysterious disease, the Asiatic cholera." [38] Just what substance there was in this purported medical mission is not clear. At all events, before returning to the United States in mid-1832, he col-

* Hamilton had written the President to the same effect even earlier, on April 9: "He [Rhind] will sail from the first to the fifteenth of May, in a vessel bound directly for Constantinople, if it be possible." He confirmed further details on May 3: "Eckford has built a corvette, and proposed models of the vessels. Eckford and Rhind are to go over in her; she is to be sold to the Sultan, and contracts are expected to be made for other vessels." Hamilton, *Reminiscences,* pp. 204, 216.

** George De Kay was the first American to swim the Hellespont. Later he was offered the command of a division of the Ottoman fleet, turned it down, bought a yacht at Smyrna, and made a tour of the Holy Land. He returned to the United States in early 1833 with the body of his late colleague, Henry Eckford.[37] See p. 73.

lected the material for the really first-rate *Sketches of Turkey*, published the following year. As mentioned previously, James A. Hamilton had recommended De Kay to Van Buren as a suitable negotiator in lieu of Rhind. Perhaps De Kay did not know this; in any case he was full of praise for Rhind, who "deserves great commendation, indeed much more than it was his good fortune to obtain from the public servants of the United States." [39] It was good that there were no hard feelings, for Rhind and De Kay traveled together to Constantinople on Eckford's corvette.

THE SHIPBUILDERS: ECKFORD AND RHODES

Eckford with his *United States* and Commodore Porter on the U.S.S. *John Adams* arranged to come up to Constantinople together (August 8, 1831). One of the first things Porter heard served to confirm how desperately interested the Turks still were in naval aid: an agent was even then on his way to America to buy timber and naval stores. Porter looked forward to assuring the Porte of his "personal" assistance, and at the same time he regarded the arrival of Eckford as "opportune. . . . I shall not fail to make good use of it." [40]

The eyes of the Turks lit up when they saw the corvette anchored off Seraglio Point. They hinted broadly that it would make an uncommonly fine gift for the Sultan. Porter, embarrassed, had to explain that the vessel was Eckford's own property. Eckford was willing to sell it, of course, and after a great deal of haggling managed to do so, at a price of $150,000. The corvette joined the Turkish fleet in April, 1832. Porter, mindful of his instructions, took no part in the matter. He told Washington that "in this affair I have the pleasure of stating that Mr. Eckford has acted entirely to my satisfaction." [41] Typically, Charles Rhind got into a squabble with Eckford over the management of the sale, demanding a commission as middleman between Eckford and the agents of the Sultan. He went so far as to procure the setting up of a Turkish tribunal to adjudicate his claim; when it appeared that the tribunal would go against him, he abandoned his case in a rage. Porter was embarrassed by this washing of dirty linen before Ottoman officialdom, but evidently he felt powerless to stop it. Rhind ultimately left Constantinople on December 9, 1832, having threatened Porter with a suit for slander about the treaty negotiations. (Porter had, in fact, gone out of his way to denigrate Rhind in a formal note to the Porte. See p. 66.)[42]

In the meantime, in a private arrangement with the Turks, with Porter's tacit encouragement, Eckford took over the shipyard of the Turkish navy on the Golden Horn. He put his fifteen American craftsmen to work first on a schooner and a launch and then on a magnificent battleship, the *Mahmud*. At 3934 tons, she was described as the largest vessel in the world.[43] Porter was present when Eckford personally delivered one of the smaller vessels to the Sultan at his palace on July 27, 1832; His Highness, delighted, gave Eckford a snuffbox encrusted with diamonds.[44]

Besides the American craftsmen, Eckford's establishment employed about six hundred Greeks, Turks, and Italians. His operation, according to Porter, "entirely under American control and American regulations, and over which the Turks exercise no authority, occupies a space as large as the Navy Yard at Washington, with work shops, mould lofts, forges, etc., nearly all put up since we have been here." And he added, "It may seem extraordinary, but it does not appear that any of the Diplomatists here have any idea that there is any thing like American influence in operation among the elements of the Marine of this country, and in the way it is managed they can never be certain that I have anything to do with it." [45] (This letter shows, incidentally, that Porter was aware of the informal role he was supposed to play, despite his written instructions from Van Buren.)

The reason Sultan Mahmud fell in so eagerly with the idea of having an American as the head of his navy yard was that he really had little alternative. The Sultan was deeply involved in the painful process of trying to reform his creaky empire and bring it up to date, and his efforts to modernize the army and navy were common knowledge. John Lloyd Stephens noted that "the army wears a bastard European uniform, and the great study of the sultan is to introduce European customs." [46] The British ambassador, Stratford Canning, reported from Constantinople in March 1832: "The great end and aim of the Sultan's exertions is the formation of a military force capable of maintaining his authority at home and enabling him to recover the station which he has lost for the present with respect to foreign countries." [47] The Turks themselves had woefully little in the way of maritime gifts; De Kay wrote scornfully that not a single one of them was capable of starting or stopping a steam engine.[48] Mahmud and his predecessor, Selim III, had long been accustomed to accepting naval advice from Europe, especially from France and England.[49] But the European Powers were hardly to be trusted after Navarino, the effects of which were still to be seen. ("The wrecks of the Turkish and Egyptian ships of war," wrote Robert Curzon in 1833, "stripped of their outer coverings, and looking like the gigantic skeletons of antediluvian animals, gave awful evidence of the destruction that had taken place not very long before in the battle between the Christian and Mohammedan fleets in this calm, landlocked harbour.")[50] The United States, on the other hand, showed no particular signs of having political ambitions in the Mediterranean; American ships even then were world famous for their quality, being ranked with the French and ahead of the British; and Henry Eckford was a distinguished master of his craft. The Sultan was inhibited by anti-Western and anti-Christian prejudice at his court from bringing in as many foreign advisers as he would have liked.[51] It was not only American shipbuilding skill but also her lack of political motives that brought Mahmud to seize on the opportunity created by the American treaty to engage Eckford.* Nor should one forget the impression made by Commodore Rodgers and the Mediterranean Squadron in 1826 upon Khosrew, now the seraskier pasha and a leading figure in the Sultan's military reform efforts.

Henry Eckford's brilliant career ended suddenly with his untimely death from cholera on November 12, 1832, while at work in Constantinople. (News of his death came as a great shock to his friends at home. Preserved in a cask of wine, his body was shipped back to New York in a bark named after him, accompanied by George De Kay; it arrived on February 20, 1833.)[53] But Commodore Porter was confident that American naval assistance to the Turks would continue. "Without appearing publicly in the matter," he wrote a few days after Eckford's death, "I shall endeavor to induce the Porte to continue the plans adopted with respect to Mr. Eckford, and do not doubt that the Sultan will still continue to confide in America for the means of improving the whole Naval System." A month later he reported at length on the arrangements that had been made: "By a little management I

---

* The Sultan's nominal vassal, Mohammed Ali of Egypt, was also interested in naval help from the New World. At the time of Navarino the viceroy had ships on order in France, Italy, and India. But early in 1832 the American consul at Alexandria reported that Mohammed Ali was interested in getting materials from the United States for his own navy. The American firm, Issaverdens, Styth & Co. of Smyrna, arranged for the shipment from the U.S. of lignum vitae (live oak) and mahogany.[52]

have been able to give an impulse to the affair which has induced His Highness to continue the construction under
American superintendence, and on the most liberal terms.
The foreman of Mr. Eckford, under my private council and
advice, conducts the work. . . . A frame of live oak for a
Line of Battle ship is now on its way to Constantinople from
New York and will undoubtedly be got up as soon as the
ship now on the stocks is completed. The men are so well
contented here that there is scarcely a doubt that they will
enter into a new arrangement to build this last ship. . . . The
Sultan under whose personal superintendence this affair is
conducted manifests the most liberal disposition." [54] At the
same time Porter wrote a stilted, official note to the reis effendi:

The undersigned is fully aware of the extensive plans, which
were contemplated by His Highness, for the improvement of the
Imperial Marine, thro' Mr. Eckford, and regrets that it would
be difficult to supply in every respect his place; yet the undersigned, anxious that the enlightened views and expectations of
the Sultan, should not be entirely frustrated, with regard to the
supplies, and other advantages which he may have calculated
on drawing from the United States, thro' the intervention of
Mr. Eckford, seizes this opportunity of tendering his friendly
offices to carry into execution, to its full extent, the agreement
of the 27th day of Sept. 1831, which is annexed to, and forms
part of, the treaty concluded between the U. States Government and the Ottoman Porte, which gives to the latter, all the
advantages of my friendly council and advice in such matters.
The undersigned hopes by this means of convincing His Highness of the kindly interests he feels in all which concerns the
prosperity of his marine, and the honour and welfare of this
Empire, and of the advantages of His Highness, of cultivating
the friendship of a nation, which heretofore has been but little
known to him, and is capable more so than any other, of supply-

ing all the means of improving his marine both in personal [sic] and materials.[55]

Eckford's foreman, who took over from him, was a young man named Foster Rhodes, a native of Long Island who had spent most of his life in New York City. About two years after Rhodes took over, Porter wrote Washington: "Being persuaded of his abilities, I recommended him to the Captain Pacha, and through him to the Sultan, to construct a large frigate on the plan of Mr. Eckford, assuring him of my confidence in his talents. . . . The ship is now nearly ready to launch, and is certainly the finest specimen of naval architecture that I ever met with, and is the admiration of all strangers and naval officers, Russian, English and French, that have visited Constantinople during her construction." He reported that the Sultan and his officials had decided to appoint Rhodes as "constructor in chief to the country." Rhodes, a modest man, sought the advice of Porter, who approved. Rhodes was to be paid about eight or ten thousand dollars a year, a princely salary for the time.[56]

John Lloyd Stephens, who came to Constantinople the following spring, was very impressed with Rhodes: "An honor to our state and country. . . . From a journeyman shipbuilder, all at once Mr. Rhodes found himself brought into close relations with the seraskier pasha, the reis effendi, the grand vizier, and the sultan himself; but his good sense never deserted him. . . . I accompanied him over the ship and through the yards, and it was with no small degree of interest that I viewed a townsman, an entire stranger in the country, by his skill alone standing at the head of the great naval establishment of the sultan. He was dressed in a blue roundabout jacket, without whiskers or mustache, and, except that he wore the tarbouch, was thoroughly American in his appearance and manners, while his dragoman was constantly by his side, communicating his orders to hundreds of mustached Turks, and in the same breath he was talking with me of ship-builders in New York, and people and things most familiar in our native city. Mr. Rhodes cares but little for things that do not immediately concern him; his whole thoughts are of his business, and in that he possesses an ambition and industry worthy of all praise. . . . I have seldom met a countryman abroad with whom I was more pleased." [57]

Though he appears to be entirely forgotten now, Foster Rhodes became something of a celebrity in his own time through the reports sent back by visiting Americans. Stephen Olin, a touring American college president, wrote of Rhodes' ships: "These have been pronounced by the most competent judges to be unsurpassed by any specimens of naval archi-tecture in existence." Edward Joy Morris, visiting Rhodes at work in 1838, reported that he was "dressed *à la Turque,* and both he and his sons spoke Turkish fluently. His vessels were universally admired for their models and sailing qualities, and he introduced such a reform in naval architecture in the dock-yards of the sultan, as to render his fleet, when well officered and manned, a very efficient force. Mr. Rhodes was extremely hospitable to his fellow-countrymen whom accident or curi-osity brought to Constantinople, and he was deservedly esteemed, both by the sultan and all his subjects who had any business with him." In Alexandria some weeks later Morris saw *The American,* a Rhodes-built Turkish ship whose name paid tribute to its builder and his country; Morris was im-pressed with her "sharp, elongated bows, the swelling sides, and the inimitable grace with which the stern was rounded off — and then her very tall masts, which rose to such a height, and tapered off so gently, as to appear lost in air."

Rhodes was also praised in vague but glowing terms by the tourist-socialite Sarah Haight (who knew little enough about naval architecture, to be sure), by Dr. Valentine Mott, and by Cyrus Hamlin, a very mechanically inclined missionary. Also Judith Grant, a missionary bride (1836) wrote: "He has acquired the confidence of the Sultan to a greater degree than any other foreigner — is admitted to personal interviews with him and walks arm in arm with him through the garden of the Seraglio." The American Episcopal missionary, Horatio Southgate, besides complimenting Rhodes for having introduced Sunday rather than Friday as a day of rest in the shipyard, whence it gradually spread to the arsenal and various civil offices, noted that his integrity and ability had "earned for him and his country a very high reputation." [58]

Not only his fellow-Americans praised Rhodes. John Murray's *Handbook for Travellers in Turkey*, the standard British guide of the period, called Rhodes' ships "the astonishment of everyone who beholds them." But Adolphus Slade, an English naval officer, bestowed the ultimate compliment: Rhodes, he said, was not only a "man of talent," but — and this is praise indeed! — "free from many of the peculiarities of his countrymen." [59]

After some delay in getting materials from the United States, the launching of Rhodes' first frigate was scheduled for May 18, 1835. Porter wrote: "A beautiful specimen of naval architecture. We have nothing in any way equal to her in our navy. . . . The whole finish of the ship is in a stile [sic] of excelence [sic] and elegance exceeding every thing of the kind which has ever come under my notice." [60]

John Lloyd Stephens was a guest of Commodore Porter at the launching ceremony (Stephens called it the "launch"), for which the Sultan had kindly provided Porter with an old steamboat to accommodate his friends. Let Stephens tell it: "The waters of the Golden Horn were already covered;

thousands of caiques, with their high sharp points, were cutting through it, or resting like gulls upon its surface; and there were ships with the still proud banner of the crescent, and strangers with the flags of every nation in Christendom, and sail-boats, long-boats, and row-boats, ambassadors' barges, and caiques of effendis, beys, and pachas, with red silk flags streaming in the wind, while countless thousands were assembled on the banks to behold the extraordinary spectacle of an American ship, the largest in the world, launched in the harbor of old Stamboul. The sultan . . . had made a great affair of the launch; had invited all the diplomatic corps, and, through the reis effendi, particularly requested the presence of Commodore Porter; [and] had stationed his harem on the opposite side of the river. . . .

"[Rhodes] had great anxiety about the launch, and many difficulties to contend with: first, in the Turks' jealousy of a stranger, which obliged him to keep constantly on the watch lest some of his ropes should be cut or fastenings knocked away; and he had another Turkish prejudice to struggle against: the day had been fixed twice before, but the astronomers found an unfortunate conjunction of the stars, and it was postponed, and even then the stars were unpropitious; but Mr. Rhodes had insisted that the work had gone so far that it could not be stopped. And, besides these, he had another great difficulty in his ignorance of their language. With more than a thousand men under him, all his orders had to pass through interpreters. . . . Fortunately, he was protected from treachery by the kindness of Mr. Churchill and Dr. Zohrab, one of whom stood on the bow and the other in the stern of the ship, and through whom every order was transmitted in Turkish. . . .

"For a long time she remained perfectly quiet. At length she moved, slowly and almost imperceptibly; and then, as if conscious that the eyes of an immense multitude were on her, and that the honor of a distant nation was in some measure at stake, she marched proudly to the water, plunged in with a force that almost buried her, and, rising like a huge leviathan, parted the foaming waves with her bow, and rode triumphantly upon them. . . . The sultan was so transported that he jumped up and clapped his hands like a school-boy. Mr. Rhodes's triumph was complete; the sultan called him to his tent, and with his own hands fixed on the lapel of his coat a gold medal set in diamonds, representing the launching of a ship. Mr. Rhodes has attained among strangers the mark of every honorable man's ambition, the head of his profession. He has put upon the water what Commodore Porter calls the finest ship that ever floated. . . . The sultan wishes to confer upon him the title of chief naval constructor, and to furnish him with a house and caique with four oars. In compliment to his highness, who detests a hat, Mr. Rhodes wears the tarbouch; but he declines all offices and honors, and anything that may tend to fix him as a Turkish subject, and looks to return and enjoy in his own country and among his own people the fruits of his honorable labors." [61]

Rhodes built other ships as well. Even before the completion of the frigate he had delivered to the Sultan two schooners and a cutter "built by American carpenters and on the American plan," according to Porter. Soon afterwards the Turks accepted Porter's advice to have a corvette built, with a deck one hundred sixty feet long and forty-one feet wide. A schooner similar to the one delivered the previous year was launched in May, 1836. August 21, 1837, saw the launching of a frigate, a twenty-gun brig, and two ten-gun cutters, all within fifteen minutes of each other, to the accompaniment of prayers by the grand mufti and the sacrifice of four sheep. Rhodes found honors heaped upon him: a gift of sixty thousand piasters and a house. Porter described Rhodes' launching methods as "in every way superior to that adopted in the United States," and he commented that Rhodes had taken great pains to instruct the Turks in his methods. A steamer able to make twelve miles per hour slipped down the ways in 1838. It was used by the Sultan to tow his splendid barges upstream against the intractable southern flow of the Bosphorus.[62]

The intensity of the Turkish interest in American naval know-how extended beyond the construction of ships. Late in 1836 the Turks hinted that there was room in the Turkish navy for American officers, to the exclusion of all other foreign nationals. Porter suspected that Washington would take the position that officers holding commissions from the U.S. Government would not be permitted to serve, and he was right. The Secretary of State wrote to him that such officers on active service could not be made available. "There can be no objection, however, on the part of the U.S. to the employment by His Highness of such persons as may have formerly held commissions in our Navy, and have retired from the service, provided they can be induced to engage voluntarily." Porter used Rhodes as an intermediary for bringing Americans into Turkish service, and a number were hired. One was Captain T. B. Tylden, who had been serving in the Portuguese navy. He signed up as captain of a Turkish ship of the line, using a forged letter of recommendation. Tylden, whom Porter did not care for, won a decoration from the Sultan, but he was dismissed after about a year. (The U.S. Government also viewed with favor a suggestion from Porter that Ottoman officers might be trained on American naval vessels. Nothing came of the idea at the time, but it was revived in 1846, when the Porte proposed sending three young officers to the United States to study naval architecture.)[63]

Soon after Commodore Porter returned from leave in the United States in 1839, Rhodes was removed from his post, perhaps as the result of intrigue generated by other powers at the Porte unhappy about the extent of American influence in naval matters. Rhodes told Porter he was resigning voluntarily, but Porter heard rumors that the Turks were dissatisfied with his extravagance. He returned home and became a shipbuilder for the American navy in New York. (There is nothing in the records to show that Porter tried to have Rhodes reinstated, as implied by the Commodore's son and biographer.)[64]

Perhaps Rhodes had been in the East long enough. In the summer of 1839 the entire Turkish fleet, presumably including the handiwork of Eckford and Rhodes, was sailed into Alexandria harbor by its admiral and treacherously turned over to Mohammed Ali. Only the direct intervention of the British navy restored the fleet to the Turks in 1841.[65] Yet it would be wrong to close this episode on a note of anticlimax. From the standpoint of American influence in the Ottoman Empire, the decade of the 1830's was a high point. Through a tedious comedy of ineptitude, persistence, and political maneuvering, the United States did in fact find itself in the important position of developing the Turkish fleet from scratch at a time when the reforming Sultan Mahmud needed a fleet as much as he needed anything. The ships built at Constantinople by Eckford and Rhodes sailed the Mediterranean for many years; most of them must have been in service during the Crimean War. More than the traders, more than the missionaries, these Yankee shipbuilders brought to the East an awesome vision of America's talent and character at a time when the New World was scarcely more than a myth. Henry Eckford and Foster Rhodes deserve to be remembered.

4. David Porter's Constantinople

Soon after he reached Constantinople in the spring of 1835, John Lloyd Stephens called upon the American chargé d'affaires, Commodore David Porter: "Early in the morning we took a caique with three athletic Turks, and after a beautiful row . . . in two hours reached the commodore's residence at St. Stephano, twelve miles from Constantinople, on the borders of the Sea of Marmora. The situation is beautiful, abounding in fruit trees, among which are some fig trees of the largest size; and the commodore was then engaged in building a large addition to his house." Stephens found Porter "small, dark, weather-beaten, much broken in health, and remarkably mild and quiet in his manners. His eye is his best feature. . . . He seemed ill at ease in his position, and I could not but think that he ought still to be standing in the front rank of that service he so highly honored." [1]

Porter's distinguished naval career had been clouded by a court-martial, and he resigned in 1826. After a disastrous three-year stretch as a commander in the Mexican navy, during which his health and finances were seriously impaired, President Andrew Jackson appointed him consul-general at Algiers. On his arrival there in 1830 Porter discovered that this post had disappeared with the successful French conquest of Algeria earlier that year, and he spent the winter at the American naval base at Port Mahon, Minorca, awaiting further instructions. For Porter, a great family man, it was fortunate that his son, Midshipman (later Admiral) David Dixon Porter, was stationed there with the Mediterranean Squadron. It was a restful winter. "I enjoy very good health," he wrote his wife, Evelina, at home in Chester, Pennsylvania, "and I attribute it chiefly to the life of most perfect tranquility which I lead. I have nothing whatever to disturb me." [2] But events were working to interrupt his lassitude and shape the rest of his career and his life. William Brown Hodgson of the State Department had already sailed with orders for Porter to go to Constantinople to exchange ratifications of the new treaty between the United States and Turkey, and to settle in there as chargé d'affaires.

Porter and Hodgson, sharing a cabin in the sloop-of-war *John Adams*, reached Constantinople early in August, 1831, timing their arrival with that of Henry Eckford. (See Chapter 3.) It took about two months of haggling to achieve the exchange of ratifications. To pave the way, Porter suggested that the Sultan be given a steamboat: "The ornamental parts of the boat might be made to resemble a swan, the head and neck fixed to the bow, the wings to the guards of the wheel, and the tail to the stern." While the State Department shrugged off this somewhat pre-Wagnerian proposal, everyone recognized that the question of presents was crucial. Word had reached the Turks of the churlish way Charles Rhind's horses from the Sultan had been seized by the Federal Government and auctioned off; it was made clear that no gifts would be coming to Porter. The vindictive and meddlesome Rhind, back in Constantinople with Eckford, helped muddy the waters; he confided to the Department that Porter was bungling the whole present problem.[3]

At his home the Commodore displayed for visitors what he had bought for distribution among Turkish officials: snuff boxes, watches, fans, spy glasses, coffee-cup stands — all glittering with diamonds and other jewels. On this gaudy treasure he had spent $40,000. The cynical Turks regarded it all with a practiced eye. As James De Kay pointed out: "This identical snuff box, for example, has no doubt passed through the hands of the Sultan, the brokers, and the foreign ministers, upon a dozen different occasions." [4] Word finally arrived that Ottoman officialdom would be pleased to accept. A last-minute tempest over some alleged breach of the etiquette of gun salutes was calmed, and on October fifth all was clear for the exchange of ratifications. Porter's own account of the proceedings is vivid (the Commodore writing anonymously of himself, partly in the third person):

The house of the Reis Effendi is a very ordinary old red wooden house, so near the water in the village of Candalie as to step from the boat into his door. I found some workmen who were making repairs, cleaning out the rubbish. The minister [Porter] went upstairs and found him wrapped up in rather a coarse brown cloak, with his dragoman dressed in a similar manner. There were half a dozen servants standing at the door, and this was the only appearance of state that I witnessed. After rising and shaking hands, he asked the minister to be seated; pipes, coffee, and sherbet were introduced; they talked about the storm and other matters, when the minister mentioned to him the presents were in the bags, and had better be looked to. We all assisted in getting them out, and after we had done so, he examined with great admiration the presents for the Sultan, consisting of a snuff box, costing about $9000, and a fan which the minister paid about $5000 for. He was greatly struck with their richness and beauty, and I have the strongest reasons for believing that from a republican agent the head of the Ottoman empire has received the most magnificent and valuable present of the kind which now is or ever has been in his possession. . . .

The ceremony of exchange was merely rising; the Reis Effendi taking the Turkish treaty in his right hand, and the American minister doing the same with the American, raising them as high as the head, and at the same instant making the exchange.[5]

THE COMMODORE AT SAN STEFANO

David Porter had a hard time finding a suitable place to live. Pera, the diplomatic quarter of the capital, was gutted by fire a few days before he arrived. With the rest of the European community, Porter was forced up the Bosphorus a few miles to Büyükdere, where he rented (for $250 a year) a large villa with gardens and stables; he promptly named it American House. Early in 1832 he moved across the Bosphorus to Scutari. The reasons he gave were financial; he could not afford to keep up with the diplomatic social life and preferred to "retire to a place where, unobserved, I can adopt my own mode of living." He was delighted with the rural charm of Scutari and the splendid view across the busy harbor at Seraglio Point. But Scutari proved too cold in winter, and very reluctantly he moved again, this time to Pera.[6] Rebuilt after the fire of 1831, Pera was once again the Frank quarter, the logical place to carry out Secretary Van Buren's instructions "to cultivate the best understanding and the most friendly social relations with the members of the European diplomatic body accredited to the Sublime Porte." [7] But Porter found the society snobbish and unfriendly, and he

mixed very little. The next year, following a wretched winter
during which he was so ill that he did not leave the house for
five months, he moved south to San Stefano (now called
Yeşilköy: the site of Istanbul's airport). His new home was
right on the sea, next door to a Jesuit college. "I have the advantage of seclusion," he wrote, "without being out of the
world, and of doing as I please; two very great advantages to
a person who is inclined to live within his means, and who
loves retirement. I do not dislike company, when it is such
as I can choose; but I dislike it forced on me whether I like
it or not." To one of his sons he confided: "Months pass
without my seeing a human face except those of the family." [8]

Until Porter's death in 1843, his home at San Stefano served
as the American legation. At first it was hardly more than a
cottage, but in 1835 Porter enlarged it greatly. Elizabeth
Dwight, a missionary's wife of austere habits by necessity, observed the construction in progress and sniffed at what looked
like a "gentleman's house in America." The Commodore succinctly dubbed his residence The Palace. It had these parts:
(a) Porter's private five-room suite; (b) the "Harem," occupied by Mary Porter Brown, the Commodore's widowed
sister, who arrived in 1834 to be a companion to him, and by
her youthful son, John Porter Brown; and (c) a wing given
over to such diplomatic entertainment as could not be avoided,
and also serving as quarters for George A. Porter, another of
the Commodore's nephews.

The Commodore's son, David, approved: "The larger reception chamber was furnished in Turkish style, with a rich
carpet and a divan covered with Damascus satin. The curtains were of the same material. In the center of the divan a
mirror extended from the pier table to the ceiling. Around
the room stood small tables inlaid with mother-of-pearl, and
containing choice books, or ornamented with landscapes.

. . . The windows overlooked the sea, with hundreds of vessels continually passing to and fro. The view included the island of Marmora. . . . Away to the left is seen the dark red houses of Scutari, relieved only by the cypresses of the Greek cemetery, while the city of Constantinople, with golden minarets, handsome palaces, and private edifices ornamented in fanciful style, rises from the rich frame of the landscape like a great brilliant in a golden setting. It was a view such as cannot be imagined."

In the garden was a tall flagpole, upon which the Stars and Stripes was hoisted each morning precisely at eight o'clock. Every American vessel that passed saluted by dipping her own colors. In his household the Commodore enforced discipline as though he were still in command of a ship. Mrs. Brown, a patient and loving soul (known to the other Americans as "Lady Brown"), would read to him for exactly two hours each morning. "At the appointed time," wrote his son, "he was in his seat, clad in a dressing gown, and with a magnificent Angora cat by his side. As he listened patiently to the reading, he would smooth the fur on the Angora's back, often no doubt meditating over the events of his past life. . . . At the conclusion he would retire to his room for several hours, where no one ventured to disturb him." Midday dinner was formal and strict, with no sloppy dressing even *en famille*. Two waiters were in attendance, one of whom served only the Commodore. Afterwards an English carriage drawn by Hungarian coach horses would be found waiting at the stately Grecian entrance, and the Commodore would be driven alone down the long arcaded drive, past the porters' lodges flanking the gate in the high stone wall, and forth into the countryside.[9]

In his mid-fifties Porter was already an old man. His health was indifferent and grew steadily worse; money worries consumed an inordinate amount of his limited energy; his earlier zest for explosive action and adventure had dwindled to a petty querulousness that found its chief outlet within the legation itself. A plain man in some ways, he was all too ready to show his contempt for the conventional courtesies of the Oriental capital. "Salaams are an infernal nuisance," he grumbled after one encounter. "Why the devil can't the man be satisfied with a decent salute!" [10]

"The gentlemen of the different embassies seemed to regard Constantinople as an honorable exile," wrote Elizabeth Kirkland in 1832.[11] Porter had hoped for some other appointment from his good friend, President Andrew Jackson. Perhaps Jackson could say he had tried, having offered Porter the governorship of a naval hospital at Philadelphia, the naval agency at Gibraltar, collectorship of one of the American ports, and the post of marshal of the District of Columbia. Porter had turned them all down. "I want," he wrote, "an office of honor and trust, and a salary not dependent upon any contingency." On the salary point, Porter ran afoul of Jackson's plain-spoken, tobacco-chewing first Democratic Congress. The Senate Finance Committee voted a salary of $9000 plus expense money (called an "outfit" in those days) of an equal amount. But by the time the appropriation got through the House, the salary and "outfit" had been halved. Not only that, but the original idea of making Porter a minister plenipotentiary had been abandoned; his appointment was merely as chargé d'affaires.[12]

Few found Commodore David Porter lovable, and to some he was downright impossible. He was an expert at picking and nursing quarrels over trifles, a master of injured dignity and heavily righteous sarcasm. In response to speculation in Congress as to what presents he might have received from the Turks in connection with his official duties, he listed formally for the Secretary of State: seven lambs, thirteen chickens, a basket of cherries, and a bunch of flowers. William Churchill, smarting from his dismissal from his consular duties at Constantinople in 1833, said Porter had a "quarrelsome temper that nothing more or less than an angel can satisfy." [13] Most of Porter's associates would have agreed with that judgment, though few had the temerity to say so.

One who did was William Brown Hodgson. Born in 1800 into a well-to-do Georgia family, Hodgson had begun his career in government as a "pupil-interpreter" at Algiers in 1826. This appointment was part of the first attempt of the State Department to develop a cadre of Orientalists. Secretary of State Henry Clay decided to put "a midshipman or some other youth" under the care of each of the four consuls to the Barbary States (Tunis, Tripoli, Algiers, and Tangier) for several years to learn Turkish, Arabic, and other languages. Hodgson was the first such appointee, and he did very well. By the time he left Algiers in 1829 he had laid the groundwork for the first scholarly study of the Berber language. Martin Van Buren, then at the State Department, wrote him a glowing commendation, citing "the very laudable and commendable use, which, from the concurrent reports of all, you appear to have made of the opportunities afforded to you." [14]

Thus Hodgson's star was already on the rise when he was assigned to bring Commodore Porter's first instructions to him in the spring of 1831 and to go with him to Constantinople. Van Buren commended Hodgson to the Commodore as knowing both Turkish and "Arabick" from his residence at Algiers; Porter was advised to use Hodgson to bring back the ratified treaty to Washington. At first the old sea dog and Van Buren's young protégé got along very well; Porter was delighted with Hodgson's performance and asked to have him assigned to Constantinople as dragoman, or interpreter. (Among other things, Hodgson had pleased the Commodore and titillated the Turks by conversing with the reis effendi in Turkish, a performance, as Hodgson himself observed, "rather unique in Stamboul diplomacy.")[15]

Having returned to Washington with the ratified treaty, Hodgson received the appointment as dragoman and came back to Constantinople in the summer of 1832. In August Porter stated that Hodgson was fulfilling his duties "to my entire satisfaction." [16] But Hodgson had been there only five months when he asked the Department for a transfer, preferably back to Algiers. His chief complaint was that the Commodore was ignoring him and was running the legation with the help of his two nephews, John Brown and George Porter, who had just arrived in response to their uncle's summons. "They have no classical and but an imperfect English education," Hodgson complained. "Without early discipline in the Latin and Greek languages, no man can attain a competent knowledge of Turkish. The only dictionary of this language is in *Latin*. Our Universities furnish young men as highly educated as the *jeunes de langues* (young linguists) sent here by European Governments, and unless such be sent by ours, we shall never have qualified Dragomans." * Besides, he wrote, "there are several things in the administration of the chargé's mission, done with honorable motives, but which I do not believe to be right." He hinted to the Department that the Commodore was using his expense money illegally to main-

* Ironically, modern experts are dubious about Hodgson's own linguistic claims. Though he is recognized as a pioneer in the study of Berber (and received two honorary degrees from Princeton), the State Department concluded in 1930 that he had lied in describing his own translation of the American-Turkish treaty as being "from the original Turkish"; actually it was from a French version. Hunter Miller, *Treaties and Other International Acts of the United States of America* (Washington, 1933), III, 588–592.

tain his two nephews and that Porter was profiting from his position as local administrator of Henry Eckford's estate. After March, 1833, the two men were not on speaking terms; in May Porter formally relieved Hodgson of his legation duties. (Forgetting his earlier praise, Porter declared that Hodgson's services "have never been of any use.") Hodgson, saying he had "never been so unhappy," asked once again for a transfer.[17]

As soon as the State Department got wind of the bitter quarrel, orders were dispatched removing Hodgson from the scene; but the orders did not arrive for over a year. In the meantime, Hodgson and Porter were unwillingly locked in a desperately unpleasant embrace which soured the whole atmosphere of the American colony at the Turkish capital. Hodgson would not leave Constantinople without further instructions; Porter could not make him go. Furthermore Porter, though long overdue for leave, felt he could not stray from his post even temporarily for fear of the evil that Hodgson might contrive in his absence. Both became more and more free with their blasts and counterblasts, charged with the heavy-handed oratorical irony so characteristic of the time. Hodgson must have worked hard polishing this letter: "A second Dragoman is not required for the ordinary services of this legation. If, however, it shall be established, that our chargé d'affaires may contract with the Sublime Porte to supply munitions of war and to construct ships, and, as in the case of the late Mr. Eckford, may become the Executor and Agent of American citizens, then we shall want a second and a third Dragoman, as well as two nephews for secretaries."[18]

In October, 1833, the pasha of the Dardanelles entrusted a horse to Hodgson to deliver to the Commodore as a gift; whether through a misunderstanding or otherwise, Hodgson took it to the bazaar and sold it. Porter took this tale to Com-

modore Daniel Patterson, then visiting Turkey as commander
of the Mediterranean Squadron; Patterson, of course, refused
to take jurisdiction over Hodgson, much less punish him.
Porter saw fit to forward the whole embarrassing correspondence to Washington.[19]

Serving as a midshipman on Patterson's flagship, the *Delaware,* was none other than young David Dixon Porter, the
Commodore's favorite son. On the night of November 18,
1833, Hodgson was a guest aboard the *Delaware,* then standing off Seraglio Point. After dinner he was rowed ashore in a
barge under the command of Midshipman Porter. Having
stepped onto the pier, Hodgson heard his name, turned around,
and was greeted with a blow on the temple — "for the trouble you have given my father!" In the ensuing struggle,
Hodgson's fine thirty-five-dollar coat was torn beyond repair. As a token of his indignation, Hodgson insisted on de-
positing the tattered remains with the American consul.
Hodgson failed in his efforts to have Midshipman Porter punished, but he was reimbursed for the loss of his jacket.[20]

When Hodgson was finally withdrawn from the Constantinople mission he was assigned to make a brief recon-
naissance of Egypt and return to Washington. Porter, delighted though he was to be rid of him, thought the mission to
Egypt was a poor idea: he considered that the intelligence he
had been receiving from the American consul at Alexandria,
John Gliddon, and was forwarding faithfully to Washington,
was perfectly adequate.[21] Actually, Hodgson went about his
assignment in Egypt very intelligently. His excellent report,
which contained much useful information about commercial
opportunities in Egypt, concluded wisely that a direct treaty
with the viceroy, Mohammed Ali, would be impracticable
because of the latter's equivocal position vis-à-vis the Porte.
Hodgson indeed saw himself as consul-general (Gliddon was

only a consul), and he even specified what his salary should be ($3000).[22]

Commodore Porter confided to his wife that "my mind is more at ease; I have not that puppy Hodgson to vex me." Yet he kept hearing rumors: that Hodgson was to be appointed consul at Constantinople; that he was in Morocco to negotiate a treaty and then come to the Turkish capital. His fears were not realized: Hodgson was posted to London in 1836, to Washington in 1837, and finally to Tunis as consul-general in 1841. He resigned from Government service in 1842, married well, and settled down in Savannah, where he pursued a life of quiet scholarship until his death in 1871.[23]

The inventory of the Constantinople consulate in 1835 included "fragments of a coat deposited by William B. Hodgson as per receipt." [24] Who knows — maybe it is still there!

PORTER AS A DIPLOMAT

Because, as Commodore Porter put it, America's interests did not require much communication with the Porte, his withdrawal from diplomatic society and his rather paranoid preoccupation with "that puppy Hodgson" interfered very little with his duties. But even when proper legation business came his way, he was all too inclined to slough it off. In 1834 the first minister to the Porte from the independent Greek Government approached Porter for help in getting accredited. Many a diplomat would have regarded such a request as a compliment and a challenge; Porter side-stepped "what I apprehended would be a very troublesome and disagreeable affair." He seems never to have considered visiting Syria, Palestine, or Egypt — all within his jurisdiction for almost twelve years. Regretting the difficult political conditions in Syria in 1835, which were troubling the Americans there, he wrote resignedly, "Complaints from me, so far from remedying the evil, might provoke the authorities of Syria, and make things worse." And he had some rather gentle advice for his consul at Beirut: "Leave to others to contest points in which the interests of Americans are not the only ones concerned." [25]

Still, the reconstruction of the Turkish fleet under Eckford and Rhodes gave him an opportunity to play a useful role. The Sultan took a keen personal interest in the progress of his navy. Though protocol forbade a formal audience because of Porter's inferior rank, he and the Grand Seigneur could meet unofficially at San Stefano, where His Highness came often to visit his powder works or the military camp near the Commodore's estate. The Sultan instituted American army drill for some of these troops and also had his guard of honor fitted out with dragoons' caps modeled on some which Porter ordered from the War Department in Washington (they were very unpopular). On a more informal level, Porter sent off to Boston for rocking horses for children of the Sultan's harem.[26]

Porter himself considered that relations with the Sultan and his government were excellent, largely because of the naval assistance. "I do not believe," he wrote in 1835, "that any nation stands so high with the Turks, at the present moment, as the United States." He flattered himself that he was largely responsible for this happy state of affairs: "I have succeeded notwithstanding every obstacle, in establishing the most intimate, and indeed friendly, connection with the Sovereign, and all the higher officers of the government. . . . It is to my character as an officer in the Navy, and my knowledge of naval affairs, by which I have been able to make myself acceptable to the Government. No other person of my diplomatic rank, not possessing such information, could have acquired the influence with the Sultan that I have." And this despite his inferior status: "Had I the talent of a Metternich or a Talleyrand, with the rank only of a chargé d'affaires, I would not be permitted to stand higher in the estimation of the diplomatic corps of Constantinople, than I do now." [27]

On the other hand Porter's relations with his superiors in Washington were never entirely harmonious. One constant problem was money. Throughout his career in Constantinople the Commodore was in debt; his promotion to minister resident was held up pending a provisional settlement with the Government, and he died owing more than $6000.[28] There was continuing irritation over communications. The Department complained relentlessly that Porter's reports were messy, on the wrong kind of paper, improperly numbered (or not numbered at all), and it observed that he really was not required to write quite so often. ("It would make the performance of my duties more pleasant to me," Porter wrote tartly to the Secretary in a letter dated the thirty-first [sic] of June, "if I could always receive instructions before I am compelled to act.")[29] Porter did indeed send a lot of dispatches, often with voluminous attachments. The total came to about six hundred in a little less than twelve years. On the other hand, letters of instruction from the Department were very rare: only fifty-eight over the same period, or less than five a year. Of these a majority (thirty-four) dealt with administrative matters such as staff appointments, routine circulars, and the like; eleven had to do with Porter's own appointment, finances, leave arrangements, and the like; and four enclosed formal courtesy letters from the President to the Sultan on his accession and the birth of his children. Only the other nine are of any substantive interest:

1. Porter's original instructions. (No. 2, April 15, 1831.)

2. The role of Henry Eckford. (No. 3, April 22, 1831. See p. 67.)

3. The possibility of a steamboat for the Sultan. (No. 5, April 3, 1832. See p. 83.)

4. Instructions to deal with an unspecified "gross outrage" to a U.S. merchant vessel at Smyrna. (No. 25, Dec. 2, 1836.)

5. Views about how the United States might meet the Sultan's desire for naval assistance. (No. 27, May 16, 1837. See pp. 80–81.)

6. Instructions to close down most of the consulates in the Ottoman Empire. (No. 41, April 9, 1840. See pp. 254–255.)

7. Instructions to protest alleged "atrocious cruelties" inflicted upon Jews in Damascus and Rhodes. (No. 42, August 17, 1840. Porter replied that he would do so "when necessary," but expressed hope that he would not have to.)[30]

8. A rebuke from Secretary of State Daniel Webster for alleged inattention to the interests of American missionaries. (No. 52, February 2, 1842. See Chapter 5.)

9. Advice about diplomatic protection due to naturalized former Ottoman subjects. (No. 54, August 26, 1842.)

That was all the guidance David Porter ever got.*

While on leave in Washington in 1839 Commodore Porter was made minister resident. Besides a most welcome pay increase (to $6000), his new status entitled him to an official reception by the Sultan, to whom he must present his credentials. President Van Buren's official letter was carefully

---

* The State Department may have had its own problems. At this time its entire staff consisted of the Secretary, the chief clerk, and about a dozen other clerks, some of whom were assigned to certain domestic chores (like registering patents) which the Department had not yet succeeded in shucking off. For correspondence with some twenty diplomatic missions and about one hundred fifty consulates around the world there were just five clerks, and they only worked from ten o'clock till three. In regulations issued in 1833 it was stipulated that regular *weekly* correspondence with each diplomatic mission was to be maintained, but such a lively rhythm was never even attempted as far as Constantinople was concerned. Gaillard Hunt, *The Department of State* (New Haven, 1914), pp. 201–219; Graham H. Stuart, *The Department of State* (New York, 1949), pp. 79–80.

put into a rose-colored satin bag, richly embroidered with gold five-pointed stars. On May 23, 1840, the Commodore, looking aged and tired, clambered unsteadily aboard the legation's new caique (painted red, white, and blue, with bargemen dressed to match) and was rowed to the Sultan's palace, where his reception was totally formal and very brief.[31]

From then on his health sank rapidly. Toward the end there were just occasional flashes of the old temper from the bed-ridden old man. The faithful nephew, George Porter, would take his feeble dictation and then prop him up long enough for him to scratch his signature. When Daniel Webster blasted him in 1842 for his idleness in the face of harassment of American missionaries, Porter was no longer fit to fight back. He died of pleurisy at San Stefano on March 3, 1843, surrounded by various relations and friends.* As he had requested, his body was preserved in spirits in a leaden coffin and buried near the flagpole in his garden. Later, when the remains were exhumed to be returned to the United States, a visiting American journalist named Stephen Massett was on hand (October 14, 1843):

Having received an invitation from the American consul to attend the celebration of the disinterment of the remains of Commodore Porter . . . I went on board the steamship 'Eni Dunia' chartered by the resident Americans for that purpose . . .

The U.S. brig *Truxton* had been sent by the Government expressly to carry the remains of the gallant Commodore to his native land, and now lay in the Bosphorus for that purpose. The party assembled on board the steamer was very numerous, comprising the foreign ministers of the different countries, the officers

* Not including his wife, Evelina, who (for reasons that are nowhere explained) remained in Chester, Pa., throughout Porter's career in the Mediterranean. He wrote her often mainly on family matters and had a monthly allowance for her deducted from his pay. Porter Papers, *passim*.

of H.B.M. ship *Devastation* and the U.S. brig *Truxton* with the Commander, Lieutenant Upsher, and the resident American and English merchants. We left Stamboul about 11 o'clock. It was a glorious day, and after a two hours' trip, we anchored at St. Stephano. We walked in the direction of the late Commodore's dwelling. The old mansion looked gloomy indeed, shaded as it was by tall dark cypress trees. The house had been closed some time, the portion of his family residing with him at the time of his death having left for Galata. . . . Flowers of all kinds were growing near his grave.

Twenty sailors from the *Truxton* were detailed to hoist the heavy leaden coffin and carry it aboard the steamboat. A great ceremonial procession followed: representatives of the various legations, some American marines, a band playing a funeral march, Protestant clergy, Porter's relatives, merchants, English and Russian officers, and American sailors. A splendid sight. Back at Constantinople, the coffin was transferred carefully from the steamboat to the *Truxton*, to the thunder of a seventeen-gun salute.[32]

JOHN PORTER BROWN

After Commodore Porter's death his nephew, John Porter Brown, took over the legation pending the appointment and arrival of a new minister. Brown, a native of Ohio, had lived at Tunis with relatives for three years before he was called by his uncle to Constantinople in 1832, at the age of nineteen. The Commodore set him to learning Turkish, while secretarial chores were generally handled by George Porter. Despite only lukewarm approval from Washington, Brown was appointed acting consul in 1834.*

* Brown replaced Frederick E. Bunker, a New York merchant, who was appointed January 1832 and resigned July 1833. Porter appointed William N. Churchill, Bunker's English business partner, to succeed him but induced the Department to dismiss him at the end of 1833, thus clearing the

Brown received no pay except an annual allowance of $60 from his uncle, and his appeals to the Department about this are somehow rather touching. He conceded that he was receiving consular fees, but in the first four months of 1835 they came to only twenty-one dollars.** "This sum is inadequate to my support," he wrote the Commodore, who willingly passed his plea along to Washington; "and was it not for your kind permission to dwell in your family my circumstances would be painful indeed. Whenever my presence is required in Pera to fulfil my consular duty, I must necessarily walk a distance of between twenty and thirty miles, which I am compelled to do for want of means to procure a conveyance. The small sum of three or four hundred dollars per annum would supply all my expenses and fit me for serving the government with ability." Brown got so discouraged that he resigned in mid-1835 and went home to the United States; once there he had better luck, for in April, 1836, he was appointed first dragoman (at $2500).[34] The post of dragoman at the Turkish capital was important. He was much more than an interpreter: he was a foreign legation's principal contact with the Porte. Many of them had great power; most were natives of the Empire and multilingual. As a class they were such a byword of intrigue that they gave rise to the little jingle:

> In Pera sono tre malanni —
> Fuoco, peste, dragomanni.

Brown was assisted by one Joseph Asker, a local Armenian, until 1840. By then Brown had lived in Turkey almost eight

---

way for Brown. George Porter was appointed consul in 1837 and second dragoman (under his cousin John Brown) in 1840, but he served without pay until 1841.[33]

** By contrast, in 1842 consular fees at Havana came to $9231; at Liverpool $8400; at London $2286. Graham H. Stuart, *The Department of State* (New York, 1949), p. 99.

years and had enough confidence in the language to agree that he could do the job alone.* In a minor sense this was a historic moment. For the first time one of the foreign missions at Constantinople was without a native dragoman. From now on it was John P. Brown who carried the full burden of direct day-to-day contact with the Porte. Even the British, who had spent years trying to train young Englishmen up to the level of fluency required, had not yet succeeded in doing so.[35]

As chargé after Porter's death, Brown moved the legation to Pera, where it should have been all along. The new minister, Dabney S. Carr, was delighted to discover on his arrival in January, 1844, that the United States was the only nation that had one of its own nationals for a dragoman, and he was full of praise for Brown. But Carr, a somewhat mercurial and splenetic character, soon changed his mind. When he went home on leave in 1845 he left Brown once again in charge (he had no other choice), but he took the extraordinary step of sealing up the legation's correspondence files while he was away! Brown, of course, was incensed.[36]

During Carr's absence Brown achieved another "first." Perturbed by reports that a British-flag steamer was plying between Constantinople and Trebizond, carrying an estimated twelve hundred Circassian boys and girls each year to the capital as slaves for transshipment to various parts of the

* Ironically, Brown's appointment ran into a snag because of conflicting interests within the Porter family itself. Dr. Samuel D. Heap, married to Porter's sister, Margaret, was named dragoman (replacing Brown) in 1841. A physician, he had served as consul at Tunis since 1824, but he knew no Turkish. Brown regarded his Uncle Samuel's appointment as a "reproach," as he wrote the Department, but could not complain to the Commodore because of the latter's increasingly bad temper: "The peculiar state of his mind renders it necessary for me to act with the utmost conciliation and prudence towards him." Fortunately for all concerned, Heap soon resigned, recognizing that he was not competent, and Brown was reappointed.

Empire, Brown screwed up his courage and mentioned the matter to the eminent and awesome British ambassador, Sir Stratford Canning. He came away with "reason to think" that Canning would take steps to stop slave trading in British vessels in the Black Sea.[37] A minor démarche perhaps, but one of some significance to Brown's own government, struggling at the time with the crushing problem of slavery at home. This is the first recorded instance of an official American approach to the British Government on a matter of policy in the Middle East. Characteristically, the issue Brown raised was a moral rather than a strictly political one; in this respect it accurately foreshadowed American Middle Eastern policy for almost a century.

In 1868 Brown published a book on the dervishes; its merit is still recognized.[38] Although steadily advanced in the Foreign Service, Brown fell upon hard times. When he died in Constantinople in 1872, his widow was so poor that she had to accept money from the Sultan to enable her to return home.[39]

THE MISSIONARIES AT CONSTANTINOPLE

As elsewhere in the Middle East, Constantinople had its quota of American missionaries. The first to arrive were the William Goodells, who came to Constantinople in June 1831, just a few weeks before Commodore Porter himself. They had been at Malta since their evacuation from Beirut in 1828. (See Chapter 7.)

Goodell was born in 1792 in Templeton, Massachusetts, in a "small house on the side of a hill, containing two small rooms and a garret." The family bedroom was "nine feet by seven, and contained one window, a bed, a small table, a Bible, a hymn book, and two or three chairs." Under the bed was a trundle bed that could accommodate three little Goodells. (There were twelve of them in all, including Jotham, the youngest, of whom eight lived to grow up.) Austere though his boyhood may have been, Goodell later remembered moments of high, almost Tom Sawyeresque, pleasure, such as the time he undertook to mix a rum toddy for a visitor: "On tasting it I thought it too strong, and put in more water, with sugar to match. Tasting it again, I thought it was too weak and too sweet; and therefore made another change, and still another. . . . After he had gone, I thought within myself, Now, what shall we do with all this toddy; for we should be ashamed to have our parents come home and see it, and to throw away any of the 'good creature' would be quite wicked. So, taking counsel with my brothers and sisters, all but one younger than myself, we sat down in high earnest, to see what we could do towards reducing the fearful amount. And we drank and drank till our heads turned round. . . . Those were the days of darkness." "In those days," he explained, "everybody drank, old and young, rich and poor, male and female; and our whole country seemed rapidly descending on the steep and slippery side of the hill towards ruin. But New England at length arose in the greatness of her strength, and, in the firmness of her principles, signed the temperance pledge; 'and the land had rest for forty years.' " [40] One of the disarming things about this very human man of the cloth was his gentle gift of catching the pious and pompous off balance; some people never could be quite sure when he was joshing them. He liked to tell a tack-room story about an order received by a pasha in Syria to take a census of all the Jews in his district. It seems a fly spot on the paper changed the sense of a word; "the order thus changed, purported that the Jews were to submit to a severe operation allied in some degree to their customary natural rite, and several were operated upon, before the mistake was discovered!" [41]

"My family," wrote William Goodell soon after his arrival

at Constantinople, "is said to be the first that has ever visited this place; and Mrs. Goodell, Mrs. Smith, wife of our captain, and Miss Reynolds, who came with us from Smyrna, the first American ladies ever seen here." Settled first at Pera, they were forced to vacate in the middle of the night by the great Pera fire, losing almost all their possessions, and they moved with the other Franks to Büyükdere. There they took rooms in a house near Commodore Porter's American House, shared by other refugees, including James De Kay, Henry Eckford, and Charles Rhind.[42] De Kay, the naturalist, described it in loving detail: "Our palace is delightfully situated on the water's edge, and from the terrace we may amuse ourselves with angling. The large court is filled with oranges, lemon and rose trees, and that universal favorite of the Turks, the oleander. . . . Connected with this is a garden of about ten acres, beautifully laid out in walks shaded by hornbeam and myrtles, the whole forming a succession of terraces, from the uppermost of which we look over our palace and enjoy a superb view of the Bosphorus. In the evening the bushes and groves resound with the notes of nightingales."[43]

Despite their differing backgrounds and temperaments, Porter and Goodell became good friends, and the Commodore was particularly fond of Mrs. Abigail Goodell. Goodell became Porter's unofficial chaplain. Invited to conduct services for the first time at American House on August 21, he wrote: "All the American travelers and visitors who happened to be in the village attended, among whom were a Jew, a Quaker, an Episcopalian, Socinians, and Congregationalists." *

---

* Trying to match these denominations with the Americans in the vicinity at the time is tricky. Porter was a nonbeliever, perhaps nominally Episcopalian; the Congregationalists were the Goodells and probably Mary Reynolds; the Quaker may have been one of David Offley's sons, whom Goodell mentioned as being a clerk to William Churchill. Some of the shipyard workers may have attended. "Socinians" was a pejorative term for Unitarians.

A month later the Goodells' fourth child was baptized at American House. Apparently at Porter's suggestion, the boy was christened Constantine Washington, in honor of his being the first American child born at Constantinople. The bond with the Commodore became even closer when he invited the Goodells to move in with him. They were Porter's guests for five months, and according to Goodell, "no unpleasant word has ever passed between us." [44]

But the main collaboration between the cantankerous, free-thinking Commodore and the ebullient missionary was in a project that brought great satisfaction to both. When the Sultan heard about the missionary schools being set up in the villages along the Bosphorus, he asked for help in organizing similar ones for his own largely illiterate troops. Goodell and Porter were only too glad to oblige. Before long two army schools were established, one on either side of the Bosphorus, catering to about a thousand students. Goodell furnished books and other materials. Courses included reading, writing, arithmetic, geometry, topographical and military drafting, and astronomy. Porter, who had lent the weight of his prestige, was delighted with the "progress of the schoolars [sic]." The idea took hold; soon there were schools in many Turkish towns and villages, organized along New England lines. They all, said Porter, "had their origins in the American gentlemen sent out here by the missionary board. . . . It has been astonishing; perhaps among the greatest benefits which the Empire has derived from the alliance with the United States, is the means she has acquired of giving instruction to the people." [45]

Ultimately the Goodells had six children. One of Commodore Porter's more amiable quirks was his insistence that all resident American children must attend his annual Fourth of July party in the garden at San Stefano, where he was wont to deliver an uplifting patriotic address for their benefit. What a satisfaction it must have been each year when the Goodell family arrived!

Harrison Gray Otis Dwight arrived at Constantinople in 1832. Since his return from Persia the previous year (see Chapter 8), Dwight and his family had been at Malta. In Constantinople Elizabeth Dwight bore three sons and also found time for a wide correspondence illuminating her life in Turkey — and also, incidentally, her own firm New England character. "The customs of society," she once observed, "are totally the reverse of good American ways of living. Every family of respectability must have a train of miserable, lazy, proud servants." And again, "There is no American lady here whose society we can permanently enjoy, and only two or three English ladies, who move in a different circle from ourselves." [46]

Tragedy hit the Dwights in June 1837, when two-year-old John was suddenly struck down by plague. Dwight called the barber, who bled the infant in the foot, but it was no good. Within two days he was gone. [47] As usual, the Dwights and the other missionary families were summering at San Stefano, at Commodore Porter's standing invitation; there they could (Porter observed) "enjoy the fresh air under the American flag, without coming into contact with the populace." [48] It is easy to see why they accepted. In those days the dreaded plague swept across the entire Middle East with a terrible and insistent rhythm. No one knew what caused it, but the most common view was that the plague came from contact with infested persons. "A lazy, lounging, and filthy population," John Lloyd Stephens called the people of Constantinople; "beggars basking in the sun, and dogs licking their sores; streets never cleaned but by the winds and rains; immense burying grounds all over the city; tombstones at the corners of the streets; graves gaping ready to throw out their half-buried dead." [49] When walking in the street one carried a stick to keep other pedestrians at bay. The schools and other works of the missionaries were suspended — and plague could appear as often as every year and last several months before it ran its course. Until the danger was past most prudent folk stayed home as much as they could. Special arrangements were made for visitors. Horatio Southgate described Constantinople hospitality in 1836: "A wooden structure, in form resembling a sentry-box, and sufficiently capacious to admit one person standing upright, is placed close by the entrance to the house. Elevated a few inches from the bottom is a wooden grate. Before anyone is admitted to the house, he must enter the box and take his stand upon the grate. A pan of coals, with a few sprigs of cypress, or some other odoriferous wood, is placed beneath. The door is shut, and the sufferer, to save himself from suffocation, thrusts his head through a hole made in the door for the purpose. For half a minute he undergoes the fumigation of the smoking cypress, and is then admitted into the house. But still he is not supposed to be free from suspicion. He finds the carpets taken up, the sofas divested of their coverings, and the windows of their curtains. The friend, who was wont to meet him with a cordial shake of the hand, receives him at a cold distance, points him to a chair in the middle of the room, and talks to him about — the *plague*!" [50]

Deaths, known euphemistically as "accidents," occurred most often among the Muslim population of cities like Constantinople and Smyrna; this was commonly ascribed to the Muslims' fatalism in refusing to take reasonable precautions.

Various remedies were tried: bleeding, emetics, purgatives, "cold effusion," mercury, cinnabar fumigation, ether, laudanum, wine, opium, bark camphor, brandy, caviar, vinegar, and frictions with olive oil. None did much good. Josiah Brewer confessed: "It seems we are little wiser than preceding generations." James De Kay leaned toward alcohol as a remedy. "The Franks," he wrote, "who live upon the fat of the land, and wash it down with copious draughts of wine, are rarely affected." Actually, De Kay almost had the answer without knowing it: listing, "to exhibit their absurdity," a number of animals suspected as being carriers of plague, he included cats, crows — and rats.[51]

Stephens wondered glumly if Constantinople would ever be free from "that dreadful scourge which comes with every summer's sun and strews its streets with dead." But there was one thing that seemed to keep the plague in check, annoying as it was: quarantine. With the introduction of quarantine stations, or lazarettos, in the 1830's, plague began to vanish from the Mediterranean. It was scarcely known at Constantinople after 1838.[52]

But in the meantime the plague claimed its second American victim. Within a fortnight of her son's death Elizabeth Dwight herself was struck down. Her bereaved husband, forced into solitary confinement, moved into a tent lent him by Porter, while the three remaining boys were boarded with a compassionate and courageous German couple. During his isolation Dwight occupied his time by writing letters to his fellow-missionaries (all carefully fumigated by the recipients). Published three years later, they ran to one hundred thirty-two pages.[53]

In 1832 the Dwights and Goodells were joined by William Gottlieb Schauffler, a German-born missionary of the American Board, assigned to labor among the Jews. A gifted fellow, he was said to be a master of nineteen languages and to play the flute like a professional. Before long he met Mary Reynolds of Longmeadow, Massachusetts, who at thirty-three was helping Josiah Brewer in his educational work at Smyrna. (See Chapter 2.) After some doubt as to the propriety of forsaking such useful labor for love, she accepted Schauffler's suit. They were married at Porter's house; the pious bridegroom had qualms about the venue, fearing that the atmosphere would be too lively, and asked the tactful Goodell to intimate his reluctance to the Commodore. Porter told Goodell: "No, no! Mr. Schauffler must be married under the American flag. You tell him he shall have his own way at my house; I will invite no guests; and you may sing and pray as much as you like." Praying there well may have been, for the guest list consisted of the Goodells, Dwights, Schneiders, Johnstons, and Perkins — all Board missionary couples, the last three on their way to open up stations at Brusa, Trebizond, and Urmia, respectively.[54]

Except for Schauffler, the American missionaries at Constantinople labored mainly among the Armenians. William Goodell's great work was translating the Bible into Armeno-Turkish — Turkish with Armenian characters, the form most readily understood by Armenian Christians, who spoke Turkish fluently but cherished their ancient script.

In 1839 came a crisis in the mission work which was to contribute to great changes in the role of Protestants in the Ottoman Empire. On March 3 the Orthodox Armenian patriarch, whose authority and interests were being directly challenged by the Americans, issued a bull forbidding the reading of the work of Goodell and his colleagues. This was followed by an Imperial *firman* requiring Christian patriarchs to guard their flocks against foreign influence and by another patriarchal bull threatening anathemas against anyone found dealing with the missionaries. But this critical situation for the mission was suddenly eased by the Government's desperate military plight; with the Egyptian army approaching Anatolia and threatening the very existence of the Empire, each *millet* was abruptly ordered to deliver up several thousand men for the army — a measure never before contemplated. The squabble among the Christian sects was forgotten in the general consternation. Despite these desperate measures, the Turks were decisively beaten at Nazib, near Aleppo, on June 24, 1839. The Empire appeared about to topple. Sultan Mahmud died on July 1, mercifully ignorant of the disaster at Nazib, and was succeeded by Abdul Mejid, an ineffectual stripling of seventeen. At this point the European Powers forced the Egyptian viceroy to call off his campaign and intervened physically in Syria. The Empire was saved once more, but at great cost to its independence. The young Sultan made a formal pledge, on November 3, 1839, in the presence of all the foreign ambassadors,* that henceforth he would guarantee the "liberty, property, and honor of every individual subject, without reference to his religious creed." This edict was followed by a written pledge that no person should be persecuted for his religious opinions. In 1847 the Grand Vizier issued an imperial decree specifically recognizing native Protestants as a *millet*, and in 1850 this was confirmed by a *firman* of the Sultan himself.[55]

These developments were greeted by the American missionaries as a sign of the hand of God working among them. Under the umbrella of these decrees new works were begun. In 1846 the legation reported that nine American missionaries were in residence at the capital (including three Episcopalians).[56] A school was started in 1840 at Bebek, near the capital, by Cyrus Hamlin, who had been sent out by the Board the previous year. Brought up as a farm boy in Maine, Hamlin was regarded as "a little quick in temper, and sometimes disposed, in a land of turbulence like Turkey, to take

* Porter was too ill to attend; he sent Brown to represent the U.S. legation.

the law into his own hands." At Bowdoin College he had
built with his own hands the first steam engine ever seen in
Maine; in Turkey he was equally enterprising. The school
prospered, and eventually Hamlin resigned from the American Board to continue it in his own way. It developed into
Robert College, which still thrives. Hamlin became its first
president.[57]

CASUALS AT CONSTANTINOPLE

Other Americans came and went. There were tourists, of
course, and officers and crews from the Mediterranean squadron. Besides, in this first flowering of the American industrial
age, inventors and promoters saw Europe as a profitable outlet for their ingenious gifts, and some ventured as far as the
East in search of wealth or patronage. John W. Cochran,
lured no doubt by reports that the Sultan was keen on modernizing his army, arrived early in 1835 with a small-scale
model of a cannon with "two calibers and receiving chambers
for the discharge of balls." Porter arranged for him to meet
the seraskier pasha, who asked him to build a working model.
Cochran spent the summer on the project, assisted by another
American named Warren Hidden, and by the end of August
it was finished. The Sultan, obviously pleased, paid Cochran
50,000 piastres (about $2400). Cochran left rather suddenly,
apparently to avoid his creditors, but he was back three years
later to peddle a "bomb" he had invented.[58]

Sam Colt, inventor of the revolver, showed up in 1849
looking for a market for his firearms. The Sultan gave him a
diamond-studded snuffbox worth $1250.[59]

Then there was the wealthy Mellen Chamberlain of Philadelphia, a close associate of Samuel F. B. Morse. Chamberlain
came in 1839 to demonstrate Morse's telegraph to the Sultan,
hoping to get a patent from the Turkish Government. Ac-

cording to Cyrus Hamlin, who helped in the demonstration, the instrument failed to work properly, and Chamberlain set off for Vienna to get a new one. He was drowned when his boat capsized at the mouth of the Danube. Morse's telegraph was successfully operated for the Sultan in 1847, however, and Morse was awarded a decoration (*nishan* with diamonds), the first ever conferred by a Sultan upon an American citizen.[60]

Captain Rufus Page of Bangor, Maine, crossed the Atlantic and toiled up through the Dardanelles in his own steamboat in 1842, proposing to run commercially between Constantinople and Salonica. Meeting resistance from the Turks on the ground that his vessel was old and dangerous, he was prevailed upon (somewhat inconsistently) to sell it to the newly formed Ottoman Steam Navigation Company. Her name was changed from *Bangor* to *Yeni Dunia*, or *New World*, and her run was changed to Beirut.* Page's son, William Rufus, arrived in 1846 with another steamer, the *Marmora*, which plied for a time to Smyrna and Syria.[61]

An even more ambitious project took shape in 1846, when Brown reported that the Sultan was anxious to retain two or three experts on the culture of American cotton. The State Department willingly cooperated and engaged Dr. James Belton Davis of South Carolina and Dr. James Lawrence Smith of Nashville. Davis organized an experimental farm for the Sultan near San Stefano, manned by American slaves brought from his own plantation. (It failed.) Smith, evidently a versatile fellow, doubled as the Turkish Government's geological consultant and also assisted at the successful demonstration of Morse's telegraph.[62]

---

* She was chartered for Commodore Porter's disinterment. See above, p. 97.

Might as well attempt to convert bricks into bride-cakes as the Orientals into Christians. It is against the will of God that the East should be Christianized.

—*Herman Melville*[1]

5. *Missions*

WITH THE DEPARTURE OF John Lloyd Stephens by steamboat for Odessa in May 1835, we lose sight of him (as far as the Middle East is concerned) until he reappears at Alexandria in December. Let us take the opportunity to look more closely at the missionaries, who far outnumbered the other American residents in the East in Stephens' time. Stephens himself, the debonair Gothamite, had little enough in common with these zealous men of the cloth except (as we have noted) an admiration for their wives. Yet even he granted them a healthy respect. He found them gentlemanly, well educated, well informed, generous with their conversation and their libraries, and he made many warm friends among them. The missionaries Stephens met were a true reflection of a vital aspect of the America they had left.

The early nineteenth century was an age of Protestant vigor such as America had not known for generations. Tocqueville saw religion as the foremost institution of the country. This was the time of camp meetings, revivals, conversions, the "anxious seat." The Bible was paramount; only faith in what God had done through Christ as divinely re-

corded in Scripture could assure salvation; punishment for-
ever in Hell was the alternative. This basically is what Christianity had always meant to Protestants, and this is what it
meant — par excellence — to the New England Congregationalists, the direct spiritual descendants of the original Puritans.

Tenets like these concerned not just the theologians. New
England society at large was still firmly in the hands of the
Calvinists. Until 1827 the clergy in Massachusetts were
charged by law to inspect and license schools and teachers;
many of the teachers were in fact clergymen. Until 1834
everyone was required by law to contribute to the churches'
support. Nine-tenths of all college presidents were ministers,
and so were most of the faculties.[2] People lived and thought
in Biblical terms. Edward Robinson, explaining why he was
irresistibly drawn to study the archaeology of the Holy Land,
wrote from Palestine in 1838: "As in the case of most of my
countrymen, especially in New England, the scenes of the
Bible had made a deep impression upon my mind from the
earliest childhood. . . . Indeed in no country in the world,
perhaps, is such a feeling more widely diffused than in New
England; in no country are the Scriptures better known, or
more highly prized. From his earliest years the child is there
accustomed not only to read the Bible for himself, but he
reads or listens to it in the morning and evening devotions of
the family, in the daily village school, in the Sunday School
and Bible class, and in the weekly ministrations of the sanc-
tuary."[3]

The first American missions were to the Massachusetts
Indians, who had John Eliot's Bible in their own language
as early as 1663. But the idea of *foreign* missions seemed
strange to many, both in Europe and in America. In 1796 the
General Assembly of the Church of Scotland warmly ap-
plauded one of their number who allowed that "to spread

abroad the knowledge of the gospel among barbarous heathen nations . . . reverses the order of nature. Men must be polished and refined in their manners, before they can be properly enlightened in religious views." Another pronounced foreign missionary societies "highly dangerous in their tendencies to the good order of society." Reaction within New England's Congregationalist Establishment was at first hardly more encouraging; a group of eager young Williams students who broached the subject in 1808 were told that their proposals smacked of "infatuation," and that there was more than enough work to be done at home.[4]

But the pressures proved to be irresistible. A sympathetic and perceptive modern commentary puts it succinctly: "The pioneers were moved by the disturbing sense that many in Asia had not so much as heard the Gospel: millions of souls, believed to be in danger of eternal death, might be given the opportunity of life; there was but one way, the way of Christ. There was need for haste."[5] By 1810 enough influence and money had appeared to organize the American Board of Commissioners for Foreign Missions. In 1813 the first missionaries were off for India. Nominally nonsectarian, the American Board with its headquarters in Boston was dominated by Congregationalists. Its sponsors were prosperous, remarkably self-assured, imbued with a conviction that they were instruments of Providence. The American Board had an aura of Yankee efficiency and rectitude: America was God's country and the Protestants of New England knew it. Piety was somehow intimately linked with civic virtue, right social conduct, and sound accounting practices. (According to the authoritative *Encyclopaedia of Missions* [1891], "no banking house in the world has a wider or more substantial credit in business circles" than the American Board.) The distinction between religion and manners was deeply obscured in the missionaries' own marrows. Rigid as they were about the Gospel as the only means of salvation, they adopted observance of the Sabbath, teetotalism, decorum, and thrift almost as additional articles of faith. Scornful of ritualism in other churches, they were thus imbued with an unconscious ritualism of their own. Calvinism and Islam had this much in common: neither was just a religion; both were social systems.

Take the Sabbath for instance. In New England nobody traveled on Sunday if he could avoid it; missionaries in the Middle East risked hardship or danger, as well as the ridicule of the people they were trying to influence, by rigid adherence to this custom. Here are Eli Smith and Harrison Dwight, describing a Sabbath among the Christians of Armenia in 1830: "Though labor was suspended, nothing was thought of the sacredness of the day. Some were going to a distant village on business; others were meeting with their friends to amuse themselves with music, and carouse over a bowl of punch; and others still were lounging away their time with their pipes, or in sleep. How lamentable their condition!" The particularly virtuous Sarah Smith, Eli's first wife, once firmly declined a Sunday invitation from the British consul at Tyre, "enlarging a little on my principles."

As for the "bowl of punch," the rule among missionaries was simple: abstinence. They were invariably dismayed at the waywardness of their Asian fellow-Christians in this particular. In Bursa, Asia Minor, the Benjamin Schneiders began a temperance society. Smith, who found little to admire in the Muslims, had to concede that abstinence was "a really commendable precept of their religion." He flung this challenge to his American Protestant readers: "How long shall the indulgencies of the cup give us just cause to blush before the followers of Mohammed?" [6]

Others among them disapproved of people's clothing — or

lack of it. William Thomson was appalled at pilgrims bathing in the Jordan: "Many of the men were in a state of shameless nudity, and the females, in changing their scanty dress, were shockingly exposed." The tourist Stephen Olin, a Methodist clergyman (not however a missionary), wrote from an Egyptian river boat in 1840 that the fellahs (peasants) "seem not to be endowed with a sense of shame. Our sailors, as well as the people whom we saw along the banks of the Nile, raised their clothes as high as their arms, or threw them off entirely, whenever it was convenient either for the purpose of wading to the shore, for climbing into the boat, or for any other purpose. The presence of countrywomen, or of Frank ladies and gentlemen, operated no restraint upon them. I never entered a village without meeting the most disgusting spectacles." * Worse was to greet the eye of this good Wesleyan divine: in Cairo he was called upon to witness a very traditional spectator sport of the country, the belly dance; peering nervously through his glasses he could discern that "the chief part of the performance consists in a succession of attitudes, contortions, and gestures performed by the muscles of the thighs, abdomen, and loins." William Thomson, the missionary, was equally graphic: "We see little to admire in their performances. They move forward, and backward, and sidewise, now slowly, then rapidly, throwing their arms and heads about at random, and *wriggling* the body into various preposterous attitudes, languishing, lascivious, and sometimes indecent." [7] Thomson wisely included a picture to show why he was so offended (see the illustrations).**

* It was reported recently that the Egyptian Government has decreed that citizens may no longer bathe naked in the Nile. This, to the London *Times*, "seems a pity. . . . The only response they are likely to stir among tourists is envy." The *Times*, July 6, 1966.

** A versatile Princeton sociologist has analyzed the belly dance in detail, together with some later American reactions to it. Morroe Berger, "The Oriental Danse du Ventre," *Princeton Alumni Weekly*, December 8, 1961, an article abridged from *Dance Perspectives*, Spring 1961.

Aversion to the local folkways must have made the missionaries' task even harder than it otherwise might have been. The leading theorist of the American Board, Rufus Anderson, recognized this, in a way, after half a century of foreign operations: "The higher civilization of the Christian church," he wrote in 1870, "as compared with that of modern heathen nations . . . has tended to confuse our conceptions of the religion we were to propagate. From our childhood our idea of the Christian religion has been identified with education, social order, and a certain correctness of morals and manners; in other words, with civilization." [8] What he was advocating in 1870 was to preach the Gospel and let manners take care of themselves. But he was almost two generations late as far as the missionaries in the Middle East were concerned.

By modern clerical standards the early Protestant missionaries in the Middle East would be considered somewhat narrow. Their Biblical upbringing was reflected in their Christian names: scattered among the Williams and Johns were Elnathan, Isaac, Josiah, Simeon, Abel, Daniel, Levi, Azariah, Asahel — to name a few. Most of them came from the smaller towns or farms of New England and upstate New York: places like Catskill, Marshall, Manlius, Kinderhook, Canaan (New York); Salisbury, Farmington, Torrington, Northford, Middletown, Windsor (Connecticut); Conway, Shelburne, Templeton, Plainfield, Hawley, Monson, Goshen, Topsfield, Phillipston, Reading, Haverhill, Woburn (Massachusetts); Waterford and New Castle (Maine); Lebanon, Eaton, Hillsboro, Wilton, Unity (New Hampshire). If you plot these places on a map (some of them are hard to find nowadays) you find that most of them form a band sweeping across Massachusetts, northern Connecticut and lower New Hampshire into the Hudson River valley — a sort of early Bible belt. "On its secluded little farms," wrote Vernon Parrington, "New England was living a narrow parochial life, cooping up its mind in a rigid theological system and disciplining its character by a self-denying ordinance." [9]

On the other hand the Board missionaries were almost invariably well educated by the standards of the day. Most had spent four years at college and three more at a theological school — in an era when only about two percent of Americans went to college at all. Yale, Amherst, and Dartmouth, all firmly under Congregationalist control, claimed about two-thirds of them; there was a sprinkling from Williams, Middlebury, and Bowdoin. Most went on to Andover Theological Seminary, founded at Andover, Massachusetts, in 1808 by Congregationalists appalled at the turn of events at Harvard, where a Unitarian had just been installed as professor of religion.

Andover was the focal point of missionary activity. The young seminarian had full exposure to the idea of spending his life in a remote non-Christian land. Here too he began to adopt the vocabulary of the missionary; if he "felt a call" he was to seek an "opportunity for service" and become a "laborer." "Fields" were to be "occupied"; "stations" would be set up. The "heathen" included not only pagans but Jews, Mohammedans, and "nominal Christians." The receptive among them were "inquirers," and those who tarried became "hearers." A precious few were "hopefully converted"; and some even became "native helpers." To return at last to the United States was to "retire from the field"; to die was to "ascend the throne of grace."

THE HUMAN ELEMENT

In the twenty-five years beginning with 1819, about sixty missionaries were sent to the Middle East from the United States, all but a few by the American Board. Three or four were non-ordained spinsters acting as teachers; almost all the men were either married or got married soon afterwards. Most were in their twenties when they started out (the youngest was 21, the oldest 36). Many lived to retire in America. But a tragic number of them, and their wives and children, were cut down prematurely by the rampant and incomprehensible diseases of the Orient. Here are some informal statistics based on the missionary literature: The median lifetime of all these missionaries was sixty-seven years. Not bad. But about a third died in the Middle East, and *their* median age was only thirty-nine; and this allows for old Elias Riggs, who ended his extraordinarily uneventful life of quiet study in Constantinople in 1901 at the age of ninety-one. Consider the Syria mission: of the eighteen adults who had arrived by 1836, eight were dead before 1842, and at least three more had retired for health reasons. (For the eight who died, the average time in Syria was less than three years.) Taking the area as a whole, thirteen missionary wives out of forty-six were dead by 1842, and ten more had had to be shipped home. Mortality among the children was even higher.* "It is my settled conviction," said Eli Smith in a sermon in 1832, "that enfeebled health and shortened life are among the sacrifices necessary to the work of the missions." [10] No one seems to have disagreed with him.

Among the missionaries in the Middle East there was a great sense of solidarity ("fellowship"). As was the custom among pious folk of the time, they addressed each other as "Brother"; wives, of course, were "Sisters," but they were known officially as "Assistant Missionaries" and were counted

---

* Of the three boys of the Isaac Bird family, one died in 1825 and another a year later, in infancy, in Beirut. Their elder brother, William, survived to become a missionary himself; he was buried in Beirut in 1902 at the age of seventy-nine, near the other two in the old Protestant cemetery. Henry Harris Jessup, *Fifty-Three Years in Syria* (New York, 1910), II, 713.

on to lend meaning to the title. Often the families shared quarters in a "Mission House." (When the William Goodells got a house of their own after five years, they confessed, "We bless God!") Ordinarily they dressed alike, in the thrifty, no-nonsense black of their calling. In the East, where a hat was the infallible mark of a Christian, the missionaries of the 1820's and 1830's wore the stovepipe or the spade. William Thomson was known to village children of Syria as "Abu Tangera," or, loosely, "The father of all cooking pots," in honor of his headgear. Jonas King, however, excited comment from his brethren by wearing a turban and a beard among the Arabs; and the missionaries of northern Persia, after some hesitation, decided to let their beards grow as a professional measure, having learned that among the Persians no man without whiskers could claim to be a sage.[11]

For many years Rufus Anderson was the link between the individual missionary and the Board's Prudential Committee, whose functions were to raise and allocate funds, select missionaries, and keep a watchful eye on "missionary policy." A man of stern countenance and strong principles, Anderson was regarded (one suspects) as much with awe as with affection among the men and women under his purview. Each missionary, said Anderson, went as an individual messenger of the Gospel. He was not a "servant" of the Board or of the church of which he was a member; on the contrary they were his "helpers." [12] And a great deal of "help" was forthcoming. Among Anderson's duties, to which he brought great energy and skill, was drafting "Instructions" to the missionary to be read aloud at the last service before he left. These were often polished works, full of eloquence after the fashion of the day, crammed with detailed good advice — for instance, in laying out the route to be traveled to the field. These "Instructions" would be followed up from time to time by further words of wisdom — such as Anderson's advice to James Merrick, last heard from in the dusty outskirts of Isfahan: "I beg of you not to undertake hazardous journeys into Persia *alone*. The Saviour does not require it." [13] Anderson toured the Middle East twice (in 1828–29 and 1843–44), and each visit was shortly followed by far-reaching changes in the organization of local mission work. An austere man, famed for his own frugality, he was well known for his advocacy of what came to be known as "missionary economy." Until 1843 the missionaries were paid no salaries. They lived on expense money dealt out charily by the Prudential Committee against itemized accounts. (This had at least the advantage, as pointed out by the well-to-do American tourist, Elizabeth Cabot Kirkland, that they were never in debt.) But sometimes expense money was short, notably during the Panic of 1837, when even the wealthy backers of the Board began to feel the pinch. "We sympathize with the Board in their present distress," wrote William Goodell cheerfully from his post at Constantinople. "We find many little things, yea, and some great ones, which can easily be dispensed with." It was well known that Anderson regarded horses as an unnecessary luxury (and hence a vice). So when he was in Syria in 1844 the men of the mission, tongue in cheek, took him on a rocky nine-mile walk among the villages of Mount Lebanon. The effect was beneficial: from then on the laborers in Syria were permitted to keep horses if they wished (though the Board paid only for the barley to feed them).[14]

MISSIONARY POLICY

Overshadowing these human problems were thorny questions, the answers to which were by no means obvious, as to what the missions were trying to achieve, and how they ought to go about it. To Rufus Anderson the key objective was the formation of local churches with native pastors. (All other activities — preaching, travel, translations, "visiting," medical aid, education — were secondary.) To promote this aim, word went out in the 1850's that in missionary schools teaching was henceforth to be entirely in local languages. Until then it was the practice in the Middle East to teach in English; boys at the school in Beirut in 1835 who slipped into Arabic went without their supper.[15] "Those best in English seem farthest from embracing the Gospel," Anderson complained; they become vain: "denationalized." These unsatisfactory scholars "longed for more cultivated hearers than they found in the village, and for larger salaries than they could receive, or ought to receive, and shrank from pastorates in obscure places, among low-caste, ignorant people; and sometimes they were impatient of advice and wholesome restraint from their missionary fathers. In some quarters they were tempted to contract business relations with the world, and thus the labor and money bestowed on their education were in great measure lost to the cause." [16]

All this may have been sound doctrine from Anderson's point of view, but the modern observer (perhaps swayed by his own ideas about the role of the West in the East) may inquire whether the people of a country like Syria or Turkey would be so ill served by the education of young men able to "contract business relations with the world" — in other words, to use their education to raise the standards of their countries and help them to develop. After all, in whose interest (besides the missions' themselves) was it to keep potential future leaders content with "advice and wholesome restraint from their missionary fathers"?

Once Anderson had spoken, contrary views were unwelcome. After a period of vigorous controversy the missionary ranks split wide open. A number seceded from the

Board so as to be able to continue to teach in English, and this led directly to the establishment of Robert College in Constantinople and Syrian Protestant College — later American University of Beirut, possibly the outstanding Western cultural institution in the Middle East today.

Very early it was decided that no direct attempt should be made to convert Muslims. The practical reason for this was that under Islamic law as applied in the Ottoman Empire and Persia the penalty for apostasy from Islam was death. (The punishment sometimes took the form of a particularly thorough kind of beheading, whose ritual included placing the severed head between the legs of the corpse and displaying it to public view for several days.) There was less objection in theory to proselyting among the so-called Eastern Churches. These Christians, while sneered at and humiliated by the meanest Mohammedan porter ("infidel dog" was the least of the epithets), had achieved a sort of recognition and acceptance under the *millet* system, which gave the religious leader, or patriarch, wide civil jurisdiction over his own people. The patriarchs wielded immense power of course. The Eastern Churches were ancient and some of them wealthy, and they had scarcely been affected by the upheaval of the Reformation in Europe; their liturgies were for the most part in dead languages. As viewed by American Protestants, the clergy were inept, often personally corrupt, and the laity were illiterate, responding by long habit to outworn, incomprehensible rituals. If these "nominal Christians" could be reached and reformed, the missionary theorists felt, there was a good chance that they could then indirectly effect a change for the better among the Muslims. The fact that in the seventeenth and eighteenth centuries the conversion of some from these groups to Roman Catholicism had led to no visible weakening in the hold of Islam was accounted more a sign of the falseness of Catholic doctrine than an indication that the theory was no good.

It was to these minority groups that the American Board missionaries directed their main efforts. The most important from the Board standpoint were the Greek Orthodox, Armenian Orthodox, and the Nestorians. The Board was also not averse to trying to win away from Rome members of those ancient churches who in the past had embraced Catholicism, such as the Maronites of the Lebanese mountains and the so-called Chaldeans of northern Mesopotamia, ethnically akin to the Nestorians.

As might be expected, the patriarchs of these groups (as a modern commentator neatly puts it) "did not share American convictions concerning the innate superiority of Calvinism to Eastern Christianity." [17] They were prone to take a dim view of efforts to subvert their congregations — and, incidentally, cut into their revenues. The missionary annals are full of accounts of their zealous resistance. Awful anathemas and curses poured forth; people were forbidden to fraternize with the Americans, and merchants were told not to deal with them, under pain of excommunication or even physical punishment. The Maronites of Mount Lebanon, where Isaac Bird was stationed in 1827, were forbidden even to utter the word "Bird," a difficult injunction to enforce (at least in winter) since "bird" comes very close to the Arabic word for "cold"! [18]

Sometimes the patriarchs invoked official Ottoman support; in 1824 for instance the Porte issued a decree forbidding the importation and circulation of Bibles in Syria, on the ground that they had caused the people "apprehension, disputation and disturbance." [19] In such a case the only recourse for the Americans was intervention by some foreign power. In the absence of United States diplomatic relations with Turkey (until 1831) and Persia (until 1883), the American missionaries generally turned to the British.

In 1820, when the first American missionaries appeared in the East, the War of 1812 had been over for only five years, and the American Revolution was far less remote in time and memory than World War I is today. Official relations between the two governments were still very cool. (Stratford Canning, sent as British ambassador to Washington in 1819, had only one directive: to keep peace with the Americans — and this rather overbearing and impatient man had a hard enough time maintaining his diplomatic aplomb and a courtly smile in the face of the anglophobia that still prevailed in the former colonies.)[20] But the missionaries really had no choice. The other Powers with any influence were France, Russia, and Austria: France and Austria were Catholic countries whose ambassadors and officials pursued a policy of support for some of the very leaders who were creating the difficulty; the same was true of the Russians as far as the Orthodox communities were concerned. These Powers became in effect patrons of the respective *millets* as a matter of official policy. The British, on the other hand, had no *millet* to support (until 1850).

At all events British officials and American missionaries got along very well. Assistance went far beyond passports and other formalities. One American wrote from Beirut in 1823: "The English Consul and his Lady have treated us as if we had been their own children; and by taking us under the wing of their protection, and as it were identifying our interests with their own, have given us an importance and respectability in the view of the natives, which we could not otherwise have enjoyed." The British ambassador to Persia wrote the missionaries in 1835 that their work was "a matter of deep and serious interest" to His Majesty's Government.[21]

Without British support the lot of the American missionaries would have been much more trying; faced with British antagonism, mission work in the Middle East probably would have been impossible.

In 1844 protection of all foreigners — including Americans — was stopped by the British embassy in Persia on orders from London. (The missionaries thereupon turned to the Russian ambassador.) But British protection continued for some time at isolated missionary locations within the Turkish Empire, under the personal influence of H.M. Ambassador Stratford Canning.[22]

Why were the British so helpful? Mainly common humanity, bolstered by common language and tradition. Many Americans, particularly New Englanders, still thought highly of the British, and this was flattering. (Harriet Martineau, herself English, grumbled: "In New England, the veneration for England is greater than I think any one people ought to feel for any other.")[23] And in the Americans the British knew they had no political rivals, as they had in the French and the Russians. As long as Americans did not clutter up the path of British policy in the Middle East (and the first to do so was really Woodrow Wilson), they were welcomed as friends, entitled to the privileges of the house.

Paradoxically, after American-Turkish relations were established in 1831 the missionaries sometimes fared less well. Most American consuls and consular agents in the Ottoman Empire were not Americans at all, but simply local men of affairs, often members of those same Christian sects that were the prime missionary targets. More important was the equivocal attitude of Commodore David Porter, in charge of the American legation from 1831 to 1843. Porter was on splendid terms personally with the missionaries he knew, and he often went out of his way to lend them a hand. But if a request for help involved intervention at the Porte, Porter was much less inclined than some of his European colleagues to take energetic action and more likely to think up reasons why nothing could be done.

A major test came in 1841, when the Maronite patriarch made a serious effort to expel the Americans from Mount Lebanon on the ground that they were trying to induce people to change their religion. The patriarch petitioned the Sultan, whose foreign minister wrote Porter: "The Sublime Porte . . . takes leave in a friendly manner to request that you will adopt measures for their removal." In his reply Porter regretted that he lacked authority to have the missionaries removed. But he added: "The Constitution of the United States allows to all its citizens the right of free exercise of their religious opinions, but no article of the Treaty of Commerce and Navigation between the United States and Turkey gives them authority to interfere in any way with the rites and religion of any person living under the authority of Turkey; therefore after this correspondence has been made known to the American citizens residing in the vicinity of Mount Lebanon, any attempt to excite the minds of the inhabitants to change their rites and religion must be done at their own risk, and on their responsibility."

In forwarding this correspondence to Washington, Porter expressed the hope that "the steps which I have taken on the subject may not give offense to the religious zeal of the persons implicated, and that they may not trouble the Department with their complaints." A few weeks later he amplified his position for Secretary of State Daniel Webster: "Although it has been hinted to me that complaints will be made to the Government unless I take some measure in violation of the Treaty to ameliorate the condition of missionaries in Turkey, that may place me in the condition of the Consul

of the Sandwich Islands, of whom the complaints of the missionaries was [sic] the cause of his removal from office, still
I shall adhere strictly to the Treaty unless I am instructed
to act in variance with it."

But he hardly anticipated the storm that followed. When
news of Porter's attitude got back to Lebanon, the patriarch
lost no time in proclaiming that the missionaries had been denounced by their own government as troublesome, mischief-
making proselyters and would not be protected. Alarmed by
this propaganda, the missionaries protested to Porter that the
patriarch's charges were false; their work was mainly among
the Druzes, who were not even Christians: "to make prose-
lytes from other Christian sects to our own has never
been the object to which we have aimed." They reminded
him, not too subtly, that American property interests were
involved: "This property, should it be illegally sacrificed,
would not fail to be inquired after by those whom it concerns." Porter replied, "I cannot see that I can do anything
further in the matter."

But the missionaries themselves could, and they did. They
reported the whole story to Rufus Anderson and the Prudential Committee, which in turn passed it on to Washington.
Secretary Webster pinned Porter's ears back: "It has been
represented to this Department, that the American Missionaries, and other citizens of the United States not engaged in
commercial pursuits, residing and traveling in the Ottoman
Dominions, do not receive from your Legation that aid and
protection to which, as citizens of the United States, they feel
themselves entitled, and I have been directed by the President,
who is profoundly interested in the matter, to call your
immediate attention to the subject, and to instruct you to omit
no occasion, where your interference in behalf of such persons may become necessary or useful, to extend to them all

proper succor and attentions of which they may stand in need, in the same manner that you would to other citizens of the United States, who as merchants visit or dwell in Turkey." Porter replied weakly that he had never refused to extend such aid and protection as the missionaries had a right to expect; and he enclosed (somewhat irrelevantly) an affidavit from his nephew and dragoman, John Brown, attesting to Porter's kindness to the missionaries at Constantinople — which no one had ever challenged.[24]

The missionaries were not expelled. Porter died a few months later, and the controversy died with him. With copies of Webster's letter in their pockets, the missionaries were on strong ground. Porter's successor, Dabney Carr, told the consul in Beirut: "The missionaries themselves know that I will protect them to the full extent of my power, not only through you but, if need be, by calling the whole of the American squadron in the Mediterranean to Beyrout." Washington thoroughly approved.[25]

THE MISSIONS AND POLITICS

Unlike the missionaries of the European powers generally, and of France in particular, those from the United States were never used as instruments of foreign policy. European diplomats could hardly bring themselves to believe this, but in 1888 the French consul general at Beirut was at last convinced: "For a long time," he wrote to his chiefs in Paris, "I have sought to determine the objective of the Americans in coming to evangelize here. At long last I am persuaded that their sole motivation was religious propaganda. I simply do not perceive any ulterior political motive." [26]

Yet the missionaries had their own political bias. Like most Americans then and now, they were good republicans, and they were inclined to take a dim view of Ottoman statecraft on ideological grounds. They also saw in the Turkish regime an obstacle to the progress of their work. As long as the authorities remained stubbornly Islamic, the Protestant branch of Christianity could hardly be expected to thrive. Outwardly they remained judiciously neutral; but if they could not work for political change, at least they could pray for it. Jonas King wrote from Syria in 1823: "Possibly some great political revolution is to open the door for the free preaching of the Gospel to the followers of the False Prophet." From Persia Justin Perkins observed that one could not "reasonably anticipate permanent quiet in these lands until they shall yield to the dominion of the Prince of Peace." Evidence of an improving political climate was regarded by some as divinely inspired. Perkins wrote in 1840: "The English are rapidly extending their conquests in Afghanistan. This opens an encouraging prospect to the churches. . . . And the tide of European light which will roll up the Indus, as English political influence prepares the way, cannot fail to do much to civilize the inhabitants of central Asia and facilitate the progress of the Gospel. How instructive to watch the hand of Providence, in the political changes in these Eastern countries!" Rufus Anderson, looking backwards with satisfaction in 1866 on almost half a century of missionary work in the Middle East, listed the factors without which no progress could have been made: "That England should secure a predominant influence in the governments of both Turkey and Persia . . . Only the hand that moves the world could accomplish all this." Anderson even detected divine intervention behind Clive's victory at Plessy in 1757, after which Britain had routes to India to protect: "Were it not for this, the whole political influence in Turkey, if not the absolute dominion (so far as we can now see), would have been divided between France and Russia, — the one Roman Catholic, the other of the Greek Church, and both hostile to Protestant missions." [27]

In 1841 Edward Robinson, not a missionary but a good New England Calvinist, took the British to task. The rise of Protestantism, he concluded, was being checked only by the fact that there was no Protestant *millet*, and this was Britain's fault: "That England, while she has so deep a political interest in all that concerns the Turkish empire, should remain indifferent to this state of things in Syria, is a matter of surprise. . . . The English Government needs to take but a single step, and that unattended by danger or difficulty. It needs simply to obtain, for native Protestants, the same acknowledgment and rights, that are granted to other acknowledged Christian sects. Such a request, earnestly made, the Turkish government could not refuse." [28] England, in the person of Lord Stratford de Redcliffe (Stratford Canning), did just this in 1850. Under pressure from him, the Sultan granted the Protestants the *millet* status. During the negotiations William Goodell of the American mission was the secret contact between Stratford and the local Protestants at Constantinople. When Stratford finally retired in 1858, Goodell pulled out all the stops: "We love to consider your Lordship's influence as one of the important providential means by which God has been pleased to carry on His work." [29]

Rufus Anderson summed up: "We owe all this, under God, to the providential fact that England had gained an empire in India, and must needs preserve an unencumbered way to it." [30]

THE IMPACT

What sort of impression did the American missionaries make? By the Middle Easterners they were viewed at first with wonder. All travelers and foreigners were looked upon with suspicion unless their objectives were plain. Eastern peasants understood itinerant merchants, but "a man who confesses to traveling without a definite aim, or in search of knowledge, is either a madman or a very clever person masquerading as a madman." Besides, the New World was unknown except by rumor; one Turk, asked where he thought it was, pointed straight up! Eli Smith and Harrison Dwight, traveling in Anatolia in 1830, were told by a traveler that "an ambassador from our country had just been received with great honor at the capital; and added, as if it were news that would give us great pleasure, that the Sultan had granted us a king." (Thereafter, the two missionaries "took pains . . . to make known, not only the name, but something of the character of our country.") Justin Perkins heard the following version of the California gold rush from a young Kurdish chief: "A remarkably strong wind had arisen, over beyond Constantinople, so strong that it laid bare a portion of the bed of the sea, and even swept sand from its bottom, and there revealed a mountain of pure gold! This wonderful locality (the chief continued) is about eight hours, thirty or forty miles, this side of England, and the English had placed a guard over the gold." [31]

Rumors abounded in Constantinople: one was that "the missionaries took a likeness of every one that went over to them, and hung it up in one of their rooms — and if at any subsequent period any one of these should apostize [sic], the missionary would send a ball through his picture with a pistol, and after that the man would soon die." [32] Missionaries in Palestine, measuring the remains of antiquities, were suspected by some of planning to buy land. By others they were credited with rare powers, such as being able to produce money inexhaustibly from their seemingly conventional purses.

The British, while not so awe-struck, were also impressed.

F. V. J. Arundell, an English chaplain at Smyrna, compared Josiah Brewer's work favorably with that of his British colleagues. Brewer's ability to obtain funds from home for schools particularly evoked his admiration. Another British chaplain named Walsh praised the American missionaries in Constantinople in 1831: "I had the pleasure of a long and intimate acquaintance with them; and whatever prejudice I might have imbibed of American society from imperfect or unfavourable representation, it was entirely removed by experience. They were uniformly persons not only of education, pleasing and gentlemanly manners and moral conduct, but also pious and serious beyond those of the same class in England." [33]

Between Protestant and Roman Catholic missionaries there was of course a well-defined and hearty antipathy, and one may be excused for discounting most of the ridicule and innuendo that emerged from Catholic presses of the period. Much of it was excessively personal and centered upon the supposedly luxurious life led by the Americans: their palatial homes, fine stables, vast financial resources, and their reluctance to live in bad climates. Most of this nonsense is best forgotten; it is only fair to add that American Protestant attacks on "Romanism" were just as uninhibited. [34]

The missionaries are credited with introducing many amenities of Western civilization to the Middle East, including the potato (1827), kerosene lighting (1865), the camera (1856), the sewing machine (1854), and the parlor organ (1854). [35] Also, whatever their limitations, these were on the whole gentle, honorable, industrious folk in an area where personal corruption, official malfeasance, and sharp commercial practice were legendary. The role of the mission women was a particular revelation: in a society where women were universally treated as objects of sensual dalliance or as beasts of burden, and in either case could rarely read or write, it was a matter of constant surprise that the mission wives and teachers could be so intelligent and well educated.

But the missionaries and their backers often had to face the skeptical query: "How many converts?" There is no precise answer to this as far as the Middle East is concerned, and the only figures are fragmentary. In 1855 the native Protestant community in northern Persia numbered one hundred fifty-eight. No more than ten Greeks had been converted by 1844. In 1856 there were thirty American-led Protestant communicants at Beirut, but none elsewhere in Syria or Palestine. In 1839 there were about twenty-two Armenian Protestants at Constantinople. Chaplain Walsh was probably not greatly exaggerating when, referring to the Turkish practice of enslaving and circumcising Greek boys, he wrote in 1836, "More converts are thus made from the Gospel to the Koran in a day, than all our missionaries have made from the Koran to the Gospel in a century." [36] By any estimate no more than a few hundred converts had been made in Persia and the Ottoman Empire by mid-century. Virtually all were from other Christian sects. The foremost modern authority, Kenneth Scott Latourette, points out that the missionaries often raised hopes among their converts, giving them a sense of undue confidence; they were demoralized and bewildered when the patriarchs and Moslem authorities cracked down. "In some respects," says Latourette, "the Occidental missions may have weakened the Christian communities. Certainly they added to existing divisions." And he ventures to suggest that at the end of the nineteenth century there were actually *fewer* Christians in the Middle East than there were at the beginning (partly because of emigration), despite all the missionary work in the meantime.[37]

But once again, it would be unfair to end on a negative

note. In the development of America's relations with the Middle East the early missionaries played a unique role. It is straining things a bit to insist that people of Eli Smith's generation had a seminal influence on the development of Arab nationalism, though the case has been made (and refuted).[38] But in terms of American awareness and knowledge of the area, the prime source of information has been — until quite recently — the missionaries who lived and traveled there and who learned the languages out of professional necessity. As late as World War II the U.S. Government drew heavily on the experience of men of missionary background. Even now there are descendants of nineteenth-century missionary stock in posts of importance (especially in the Government and the oil companies), dealing day-to-day with the affairs of the area their grandfathers and great-grandfathers knew so well.

This continuity of specialized knowledge is of course only a by-product of early mission activity. And indeed one is struck by how often the missionaries who most fulfilled themselves, in one way or another, were those who developed by-products: who struck out on their own, away from what their sponsors had in mind for them to be doing. A post-Freudian "Commission of Appraisal" (1932), groping for the roots of missionary motivation, observed: "Although the normal impulse toward missionary work abroad arises from courage, enterprise and a pioneering spirit, there are persons who are driven in the same direction by restlessness and discontent. . . . There are elements in the missionary's life and work which make for nervous tension and instability." [39] It would be a grave disservice to the reckless zeal of Ashahel Grant and James Merrick (Chapter 8), for instance, or to the literary skill of William Thomson (Chapter 7), or the Yankee enterprise of Cyrus Hamlin (Chapter 4), to leave them mired

in the stolid piety which characterized the early missionary
movement generally. Men like these were personalities in
their own right, who owed less to their professional discipline
and training than to their own inner resources. What the missionary organization did was provide them a framework
within which to develop.

6. *Egypt*

One can easily imagine John Lloyd Stephens as he approached Alexandria in December, 1835, "perched up in the rigging of an English schooner, spy-glass in hand, and earnestly looking for the Land of Egypt." Unlike Constantinople, Smyrna, and Beirut, Egypt had no American "colony" — the first American-born U.S. consul did not arrive until 1848, and the missionaries only in the 1850's. But if Egypt attracted few permanent residents from the New World, she more than made up for it in her appeal to adventurers and travelers. The brooding mystery of the Pyramids, the timeless existence of the Nile-dwellers, the splendor of tombs and temples, and the feeling of being on the brink of unexplored Africa — somehow Egypt beckoned not only the tourist but the eccentric and the lone wolf. The first from America was the professional explorer, John Ledyard.

JOHN LEDYARD OF CONNECTICUT

Ledyard was born in 1751 in Groton, Connecticut. He spent a restless year at Dartmouth College, having created a sensation by his arrival through the forest driving a sulky (the first ever seen there) laden with theatrical equipment. With small taste for classwork, he spent most of his time tramping in the New Hampshire wilderness, and he departed as dramatically as he had come — this time by canoe. Then, after a forlorn attempt to buckle down to the study of law, he joined Captain Cook for his celebrated voyage around the world. In 1786 he met Thomas Jefferson and began a correspondence with him that lasted until Ledyard's death. (Jefferson considered him "a man of genius, of some science, and of fearless courage and enterprise.") The same year he set forth on a solitary trek across Russia and Siberia toward the American Northwest, traveling mainly on foot, with a vague idea of organizing a company to engage in the fur trade. Having wandered as far east as Lake Baikal, he incurred the displeasure of Empress Catherine the Great, who had him turned back and hustled out of her dominions.[1]

When Ledyard arrived back in London in May, 1788, somewhat at loose ends, he heard about a new society that was just being formed: the Association for Promoting the Discovery of the Interior Parts of Africa, otherwise known as the Africa Society. This select group of Englishmen (including three dukes, twelve earls, Edward Gibbon, and William Pitt the Younger) were anxious to sponsor an explorer, and it turned out that John Ledyard was just their man. He strode into the office of the secretary of the Society, one Henry Beaufoy, who was struck with "the manliness of his person, the breadth of his chest, the openness of his countenance, and the inquietude of his eye." His manners, "though unpolished, were neither uncivil nor unpleasing." So Ledyard was hired on the spot "to traverse from east to west, in the latitude attributed to the Niger, the widest part of the Continent of Africa." Ledyard said he would be ready to go the next day. "I am accustomed to hardships," he told his sponsors reassuringly; "I have known what it is to have food given to me as charity to a madman." [2]

He left on June 30, 1788, for Alexandria and Cairo, where his expedition was to commence with a voyage up the Nile into Central Africa, a region never before seen by any Westerner. He expected to be gone three years. His first reports were from Alexandria in the first week of August.

"Alexandria at large presents a scene more wretched than I have witnessed," he wrote Jefferson disgustedly. "Poverty, rapine, murder, tumult, blind bigotry, cruel persecution, pestilence! A small town built on the ruins of antiquity." After a few days he took a boat for Cairo; his lively picture of the journey is too fresh to stay buried in the dusty *Proceedings* of the Africa Society: "On board of these boats are seen onions, watermelons, dates, sometimes a horse, a camel (which lies down in the boat), and sheep and goats, dogs, men and women. Towards evening and morning they have music. . . . The villages are most miserable assemblages of poor little mud huts, flung very close together without any kind of order, full of dust, lice, fleas, bedbugs, flies and all the curses of Moses; people poorly clad, the youths naked; in such respects, they rank infinitely below any savages I ever saw."

To Jefferson he wrote: "Nothing merits more the whole force of burlesque, than both the poetic and prosaic legends of this country. Sweet are the songs of Egypt on paper. Who is not ravished with gums, balms, dates, figs, pomegranates, circassia, and sycamores, without recollecting that amidst these are dust, hot and fainting winds, bugs, mosquitoes, spiders, flies, leprosy, fevers, and almost universal blindness."

One thing that nettled Ledyard was the treatment meted out to Christians in Cairo. For instance, they were not allowed to ride horses, but only the inferior asses of the place.

He wrote Jefferson on November 15: "I have passed my time disagreeably here. . . . The humiliating situation of a Frank would be unsupportable to me, except for my voyage. It is a shame to the sons of Europe, that they should suffer such arrogance at the hands of a banditti of ignorant fanatics. I assure myself, that even your curiosity and love of antiquity would not detain you in Egypt three months." Being forbidden to buy slaves, Christians were not even welcome at the slave market; yet it was important to Ledyard professionally to go there, where the caravans from Upper Egypt set down their human cargo, for he needed to pick up knowledge of where he was going and perhaps begin to learn the strange tongues he would have to use.

As it turned out he never left Cairo at all: "A bilious complaint, the consequence of vexatious delays in the promised departure of the caravan, had induced him to try the effect of too powerful a dose of the acid of vitriol; and the sudden uneasiness and burning pain which followed the incautious draught impelled him to seek relief from the violent action of the strongest tartar emetic. A continued discharge of blood discovered the danger of his situation, and summoned to his aid the generous friendship of the Venetian consul, and the ineffectual skill of the most approved physicians in Cairo. . . . He was decently interred in the neighborhood of such of the English as had ended their days in the capital of Egypt." [3]

When Sarah Haight, the tourist from New York, was in Cairo forty-seven years later, she thought John Ledyard's death there worth mentioning in a letter home. How many present-day Americans have ever heard of him?

BARTHOW OF THE RED SEA

After Ledyard we skip a quarter century to early 1813, when an American named Barthow was engaged as an interpreter for the visit to Egypt of two Englishmen, Thomas Legh, M.P., and a Reverend Mr. Smelt. Barthow, according to Legh, had lived and traded in the Red Sea for many years and spoke Arabic fluently.*

On the way back down the Nile from Upper Egypt, the travelers pulled ashore at a place called Manfalout about two hundred twenty miles south of Cairo in order to visit the village of Ma'abdeh, where there was a cave said to contain some interesting mummies. Legh, Smelt, and Barthow were led by three local Arabs to a pit in the desert, ten feet in diameter and about eighteen feet deep. Having lowered themselves into the pit, they crept forward with torches through a small, stinking passage and found themselves in a chamber about fifteen feet high, littered with crocodile mummies and swarming with bats. Shortly their passage was stopped by a broad trench, which they were able to jump across only with difficulty. From then on they were forced to crawl on hands and knees through a long, stuffy, sinuous tunnel. Here we will let Legh take up the narrative: "The heat became excessive; — for my own part I found my breathing extremely difficult, my head began to ache most violently, and I had a most distressing sensation of fullness about the heart. We felt we had gone too far, and yet were almost deprived of the power of returning. At this moment the torch of the first Arab went out; I was close to him, and saw him

---

* Legh said nothing more about Barthow's background and did not mention his Christian name. But there is no doubt that he existed: "Captain Barthod [sic], an American" was seen by the Swiss explorer Burckhardt on March 1, 1813, coming down the river while Burckhardt was going up. John A. Wilson, *Signs and Wonders upon Pharaoh* (Chicago, 1964), p. 23. One Francis Barthow owned a bakery in Alexandria in 1852. Lenoir C. Wright, "United States Policy toward Egypt, 1830–1914," unpub. diss., Columbia University, 1954, p. 32. An American vice-consul at Alexandria in the 1860's was named Victor Barthow (d. 1872), reportedly born in Egypt, the son of an American naval officer. Charles Hale, "Consular Service and Society in Egypt," *Atlantic Monthly*, XL (1877), 280–290.

fall on his side; he uttered a groan — his legs were strongly convulsed, and I heard a rattling noise in his throat — he was dead. The Arab behind me, seeing the torch of his companion extinguished, and conceiving he had stumbled, past me, advanced to his assistance, and stooped. I observed him appear faint, totter, and fall in a moment — he also was dead. The third Arab came forward and made an effort to approach the bodies, but stopped short. We looked at each other in silent horror. The danger increased every instant; our torches burnt faintly; our breathing became more difficult; our knees tottered under us, and we felt our strength nearly gone. There was no time to be lost — the American, Barthow, cried to us to 'take courage,' and we began to move back as fast as we could." Leaving the third Arab to fend for himself, they threaded their way back through the tortuous narrow passage. Exhausted with fatigue and terror, they reached the edge of the trench. Legh leaped, followed by Barthow and Smelt. Waiting sailors from their boat hauled them to the surface.

But their troubles were not over. People demanded to know what had become of the three Arab guides. Being generally suspected of having done the Arabs in, they were brought before the local governor. Widows and children of the lamented guides also appeared, stark naked and plastered with mud in token of their grief. Suddenly the third Arab staggered into the tense assembly; he had found his way out after all. Asked for his account of the proceedings, he asserted that his two comrades had been killed by the Englishmen's magic. Fortunately, the magistrate considered this so absurb that the guide was laughed out of court. Barthow settled with the three Arab women for two dollars each, and the incident was declared closed. The travelers hastened to their boat and left.[4]

GEORGE ENGLISH, RENEGADE

George Bethune English, who appeared on the scene a few years later, followed next in the Ledyard-Barthow tradition. The son of a Boston merchant, English was a graduate of Harvard ('07), where he was known as a gifted student of languages. After an abortive stab at the law and an unsuccessful try for an army commission, he went back to Harvard for a degree in divinity. The study of theology soon persuaded him that the New Testament was entirely without merit, and publication of his views introduced a lively pamphlet battle with the young Edward Everett, a Harvard contemporary.[5] Later he worked on a newspaper and got involved briefly with the New Harmony Movement, the utopia on the Ohio River. His first exposure to the East was as a Marine lieutenant with the Mediterranean squadron, a post secured for him by John Quincy Adams. After about three years' service he resigned his commission, embraced Islam, and changed his name to "Mohammed Effendi." * He was an arresting and perhaps an engaging figure. "I still recollect with pleasure," wrote a fellow-countryman several years later, "the fund of anecdote and information which his various wanderings in different parts of the world had furnished him with. He had adopted completely the Turkish immobility of features, and would frequently set the table in a roar by some amusing anecdote, while not a single muscle of his own face would be discomposed." [6]

In 1820 English, now thirty-three, found himself in Cairo ready for a new career. He discovered that the young Ismael

---

* English may have been the first American ever to become a Muslim of his own free will. During the imprisonment of the crew of the U.S.S. *Philadelphia* in Tripoli in 1804–05, a number of seamen "turned Turk," but this was under duress. See Glenn Tucker, *Dawn Like Thunder* (Indianapolis, 1963), p. 241.

Pasha, third son of Mohammed Ali, was being fledged by his father with the responsibility for an expedition to the remotest parts of the Nile to pacify some Nubians who were disrupting the caravan routes. Through the influence of Henry Salt, the British consul-general, English was made Ismael's general of artillery.

He was a bit late getting started but caught up with the expedition at Wadi Halfa, eight hundred miles up the river from Cairo, where Ismael and his four thousand troops were already assembled. Here he had the bad luck to fall ill: "In two days . . . my eyes were closed up and incapable of supporting the light, and occasioned me such acute anguish that I could get no sleep but by the effect of laudanum, and for a time placed me in the miserable condition of a blind man." [7] Because of his affliction English had to stay behind while the army pressed on up the river, but he had company. "I had with me two soldiers, one Khalil Aga, an American of New York, and the other Ahmed Aga, a Swiss by birth but an American by naturalization, both excellent swimmers." For recreation the two agas fashioned their leader a raft and fell to towing him to and fro in the Nile. Far from resenting this duty, they seem to have been exhilarated by it, for English reported: "In the hilarity of the moment we cheered our passage by singing 'Hail Columbia,' which was probably the first time that the wilds of Africa ever re-echoed to a song of liberty."

Soon after resuming pursuit of his command, English ran into two Englishmen, George Waddington and Bernard Hanbury, who were traveling independently in the train of the pasha's army and who later wrote a book about their adventures. They found him "a pale, delicate-looking man, of above thirty, and he has been successful in acquiring the grave and calm look of the Turks, and the slow motion of the head and roll of the eyes." The acquaintance never ripened into friendship. English, visiting Waddington's boat one morning, ate the next-to-last piece of bread and then complained severely that he had been offered no breakfast. Waddington touched a nerve when he implied that English's apostasy was a sham and that he was apt to change his religion as circumstances indicated.* They saw little of each other thereafter.[8]

About the middle of December English finally caught up with his commander in chief, whose march had been slowed down somewhat in the meantime by the fighting of two battles. English sought an audience. After two days the pasha saw fit to receive him. English entered Ismael's tent, sat down ("there were very few in the camp who had this privilege"), and made haste to apologize for his tardy arrival, which, he observed to the pasha, meant that "I had not arrived until there was apparently nothing left to do." Ismael assured him that there was indeed much left to do, to which English countered that in that event he would find it easier to serve his commander with efficiency if the pasha would be so gracious as to provide him with enough horses and camels to mount himself and his staff. Ismael promised the animals.

Nine days later, when the pasha's army was packing up to move on, the horses and camels for English had not come. Ismael said he was sorry, but he had no spare animals at present, and he thereupon vanished across the desert with his army, leaving the unmounted English to fend for himself. It was apparent that "without camels to carry my tent and baggage, I could not accompany it by land." He had no choice but to continue in the boat that had brought him thus far.

After a few days English was able to catch up once again,

* English demanded a retraction from Waddington's publisher, and he exacted a promise that this "account of me, not a little fabulous," would be stricken from future editions (but there were none). English, *Narrative*, p. 47.

and this time Ismael Pasha expressly asked him to stay with the main body of troops. Heartened by this show of confidence, English sent a messenger with two camels back to the boat to collect his staff and baggage. The next morning the army was ready to leave, but where were the artillery general's camels? He soon found that one of them had died under its burden (it was carrying, among other things, an immense antique stone inscribed in Greek, which English had found along the way) and that the other would have to return for a second load. It took English all day to get this problem straightened out. By this time the pasha's army again had such a head start that it took English eight more days of forced march across the desert before he was able to catch up.

So far General English, by his own account, had done little to affect the course of the campaign. Now, however, the pasha had a job for him. He ordered English to go ahead of the march and select a suitable camping place for the next halt. English set eagerly about his task: "I chose a fine position on the river, about two miles above Halfya, in the rear of which was plenty of grass for the horses and camels. The pasha, however, did not chuse to come so far, but pitched his camp on the low sand flats before Halfya, near which there was no grass for the camels (who, consequently, during the five days following, perished in great numbers)." Thus was the advice of Mohammed Effendi turned aside, on the sole occasion, as far as we are told, when it was asked.

On May 24, 1821, the army reached the junction of the Blue Nile and the White Nile, where Khartoum was founded four years later by Mohammed Ali. English stooped to drink from the White Nile (he thought he was probably the first Westerner to have done so), and the moment filled him with patriotic feeling: "I stood upon the banks of this great and hitherto secluded river, and drank its waters from my joined hands, to the prosperity of the great and liberal republic of the United States." Three weeks later, on June 14, the army arrived in Sennaer, its final goal, the headquarters of the caravan traffic from central Africa. It was a hard trip, this last leg: "I was reduced to great extremity. The camel, carrying my provisions and culinary utensils, and several other articles, was lost by the carelessness of a domestic. I was consequently left without anything to eat." He averted starvation by throwing himself on the bounty of friends, but he does not say whether or not he found it odd that a general's commission in the Egyptian army did not include rations among its perquisites.

Sennaer, a miserable village of some four hundred grass huts, unexpectedly gave up without a shot being fired, and the campaign was as good as over. The Egyptian troops vigorously overran the place and settled in. But to English it seemed like anything but a garden spot. "The houses are full of lizards [he complained], which if you lie on the floor, you may feel crawling or running over you all night." The people he found "detestable," in that they were given to catching, cooking, and eating cats, rats, and mice. "The females are, almost universally, the ugliest I ever beheld." The conduct of Ismael's troops likewise depressed him: "Thirty or forty soldiers are engaged in driving, with repeated strokes of heavy mallets, sharp pointed pieces of timber, six or eight inches square, up the posteriors of some luckless insurgents."

In short, English decided after about a week that he had seen enough of this army. Pleading ill health — for his ophthalmia had returned — he was relieved of his duties at his own request. His return across the desert to Cairo was excruciating: ten of the twenty-two camels in the caravan died, and all the time English's eyes were "running with pus." [9]

September, 1821, found him again in Alexandria, where he fell in with the Reverend Joseph Wolff, a converted German Jew, now a Church of England missionary. Together they took the boat up the canal to Cairo, and for several days the two men, both able and tireless debaters, argued non-stop the very foundations of Christianity. Wolff wound up persuaded that his companion's apostasy was real. (Wolff also met Khalil Aga, "in a very distressed state," and gave him a Bible.) For several weeks Wolff and English boarded with the British consul-general. The argument continued. By the time they parted in December Wolff really thought he had made some progress. English promised to examine Christianity further and proposed that they keep in touch.[10]

George English went home to the United States in the spring of 1822 but returned to the East twice more: once as Adams's secret emissary to sound out the Turks about a treaty and again as an interpreter for Commodore Rodgers on a follow-up mission. (See Chapter 3.) Back in Washington in 1828, English was about to go out once again when Adams suddenly dismissed him. In his diary Adams wrote of a great shock: "Life is full of disappointments, and among the most mortifying of them to me has been the misconduct of persons whom I have peculiarly befriended. The case of English is one of the most mortifying that have occurred. I have repeatedly procured employment for him in the public service, and, notwithstanding his eccentricities, approaching to insanity, have continued to favor him till now. I can now no longer sustain him." [11]

What "misconduct" had George English committed, that the normally unflappable Adams found so unmentionable and so shattering? English was certainly a strange fellow, and one could believe almost anything about him. At all events, the end of the road had come for this rebellious, feckless, lonely man, whose "longing for the East" was perhaps his outstanding characteristic. Discredited and in despair, he died suddenly in Washington, on September 20, 1828, at the age of forty-one. The *Daily National Intelligencer* duly recorded his passing, but the cause of his death was not mentioned.

PARSONS AND FISK

When the Muslim George English left Egypt in the spring of 1822, chance threw him together on the voyage with the keen young American missionary Pliny Fisk. "It is a great trial," wrote Fisk bitterly in his journal: "if you speak of religion at all, the conversation will often take such a turn that you will wish you had not mentioned it." He told English: "Obstinate hostility to the truth is the prevailing temper of your soul. I consider your case as one of the most deplorable and dangerous that I have ever known." [12]

If this heavy judgment upon English's character seems to reflect in Pliny Fisk an emphasis on Faith at the expense of Hope and Charity, one should perhaps allow for the fact that Fisk was staggering under a burden of grief greater than any young missionary ought to have to bear. For he had just come from burying his oldest and dearest friend, Levi Parsons, in Alexandria.

Fisk and Parsons were the first two American missionaries in the Middle East. The career of each was short and relatively unproductive in the professional sense, except that they became important in death as the first American martyrs to the mission cause. (One of the main buildings at the American University of Beirut is called Pliny Fisk Hall.) Parsons, born in 1792 in Goshen, Massachusetts, was moody, introspective, and suffered from indigestion. While at Middlebury College in 1814 he was seized with missionary zeal and wrote his parents: "This spring the subject has become more solemn than ever, and often I am in the center of Asia, listening to the groans of the eastern world, which are wafted to heaven for deliverance." Unable for the present to venture so far, he tried out his talents one day by calling on a gathering of young ladies, all strangers, at the home of one of them near the college. "At first," relates his biographer, "he hesitated whether to introduce religious conversation, fearing it would be unwelcome. But reflecting on his covenant vows, and that he must meet these young immortals in judgment, he tenderly and faithfully recommended to their consideration the importance of early piety." The ladies' reaction to this friendly advice is shaded by a certain ambiguity: "When he departed, all were solemn, and some in tears." It is not stated whether he was asked to come again.

Whatever his reception in Middlebury society, Parsons found plenty of missionary spirit at Andover. In the early spring of 1815, news came that the war with England was over: "The period of peace [he wrote his brother] was ushered in by the ringing of bells, the roaring of cannons, and shouts of joy. . . . For about two hours we did nothing but shake hands." Amid all this rapture he was able to observe that "the countenances well expressed the language of the heart. One observes, 'we can now go to India'; another, 'we can now distribute Bibles'; and all say, 'Zion will now prosper!'"

Accepted for foreign service by the American Board, Parsons was first assigned to preach in Vermont and along an extended route through upper New York State that somehow has a decidedly early-American ring: Herkimer, Sangerfield, Madison, Verona, Cazenovia, Pompey, Marcellus, Auburn, Bloomfield, Rochester, Lewistown, Niagara Falls, Buffalo. From Buffalo he took a steamboat — this was June, 1819, —

to Painesville, Ohio, a trip marked not only by a severe storm, but also by a lively dispute over whether the tiny cabin was to be used for saying prayers or playing cards. "The improper conduct of many of the passengers," he said, "added not a little to my sorrow and anxiety." Back at Andover to say goodbye before leaving for the Mediterranean, "the parting scene was mournfully delightful." [13]

Pliny Fisk, from Shelburne, Massachusetts, and just Parsons' age, had a particular aversion to the study of ancient languages. He was somewhat better at mathematics and sciences, but was reluctant to grapple with them, for "he feared the influence which intense application to the sciences might have on his piety." However, he managed to get through Andover in 1818, was accepted by the Board, and took a preliminary tour of the American South. In Washington he was received by Secretary of State John Quincy Adams, who provided letters of introduction and protection.[14]

The American brig *Sally Anne*, Captain Edes, brought Fisk and Parsons to Malta the day after Christmas, 1819. A fortnight later they were off for Smyrna. As a parting gift some English missionary friends sent along a basket of fine oranges and ("for the improvement of our Missionary Character") the memoirs of Henry Martyn, an English missionary who had died of fever at Tokat, in the remote interior of Anatolia, some years before. They also got some homely advice: "Go in the character of literary gentlemen, make the circulation of the Bible the ostensible object of travelling, exercise in the morning, eat sparingly of fruit at first, dress warm, wear a turban when on the passage to Jerusalem." [15]

It was Parsons' poor health at Smyrna that brought the two young men to Egypt in January 1822. His doctor having specified a sea voyage, they sailed for Alexandria. When they arrived, Parsons was so weak that he had to be carried ashore in a chair. Subject to constant chills in the Alexandrian winter, he kept to his bed. Brother Fisk read aloud to him, and they prayed a good deal, on one occasion for "every Missionary Station, beginning at China, including India, Cape of Good Hope, Sierra Leone, Malta, Astrachan, etc." Parsons died on February 10. His funeral, arranged by the British consul, attracted all the Englishmen in Alexandria (six or seven in all) and several visiting ship captains. He was buried in the court of the Greek convent; for many years his pious countrymen derived inspiration from visiting his grave. Back home, an undergraduate's elegy was read at the commencement exercises at Middlebury College:

> Thy spirit, Parsons, lur'd by seraph's song,
> Spreads its untiring wing and upward flies . . .
> Who now like him shall toil for Judah's race?
> And who like him destroy Mohammed's sway? [16]

Pliny Fisk himself died in Beirut in 1825. On his return from a trip to Palestine he felt poorly and was not able to pray as long as usual. Anxious colleagues of the mission applied leeches to his forehead. An Italian-speaking doctor, summoned from Sidon, ordered mustard poultices for his feet, warm wet-cloths for his stomach, and frequent draughts of rice-water. All to no avail. Fisk died in agony. The consuls flew their flags at half-mast.[17] His gravestone, still to be seen in the Protestant Cemetery at Beirut, reads simply: "Rev. Pliny Fisk. Died Oct. 23 1825. AE 33 yrs."

STEPHENS IN EGYPT

Alexandria affected Stephens very much as it had Ledyard almost fifty years earlier: "All the illusion of the distant view was gone. . . . Between ambling donkeys, loaded camels, dirty, half-naked, sore-eyed Arabs, swarms of flies, yelping dogs, and apprehensions of the plague, one thinks more of his own movements than of the pyramids." [18] The only friendly face in Alexandria was John Gliddon, the American consul.* Gliddon, one of Commodore Porter's first appointees, was an English merchant, a resident of Alexandria since 1818.[19]

Without even spending the night Stephens embarked on a canal boat for Cairo, a trip that still took five or six days, as it had for John Ledyard almost fifty years before. In Cairo he again looked up the American consular agent, who was George Robbins Gliddon (1809–57, son of John Gliddon), a very able and energetic bachelor with a thorough command of Arabic and a flair for archaelogy.** George Gliddon invariably made a great effort to accommodate American tourists in Egypt and was mentioned in glowing terms by many of them. He was also responsible for the importation of American cotton-ginning machinery for Mohammed Ali in 1837, and he obtained the services of Alexander Marshall of New York to supervise rice and oil-manufacturing equipment imported from the United States at Rosetta from 1838 to 1841; Marshall had three other American engineers with him. After the Cairo consulate was closed in 1840, George Gliddon

* John Gliddon's commercial duties were light. During the first six years of his tenure he saw only two American merchant ships; both arrived in 1835 from Boston with cargoes of rum, cigars, candles, fish, and sugar. The first American ship to carry Egyptian goods (linseed and two camels) to the United States crossed the ocean in 1838. L. C. Wright, "United States Policy toward Egypt, 1830–1914," unpub. diss., Columbia University, 1954, pp. 155–156. Appointed first as consular agent, Gliddon was elevated to consul in 1835. On his death in 1844 he was succeeded by his son-in-law, Alexander Tod, a Scotsman resident in Egypt since 1830. Daniel S. Macauley, an American, was appointed consul-general at Alexandria in 1848.

** George Gliddon was appointed consular agent in 1832 and was made consul in 1836.

made his living traveling about Europe and America as a lecturer on Egyptian antiquities.[20]

Gliddon took John Lloyd Stephens along to see Mohammed Ali, with whom Stephens discussed the feasibility of steam navigation on the Nile.[21] He also helped with arrangements for a trip up the river. By this time no great adventure attached to such a journey; Commodore Patterson, U.S.N., reported in 1834 that "traveling now in the Nile is safe as on the Hudson, but not so comfortable or expeditious." [22] Stephens set forth on the first day of January, 1836: "At about twelve o'clock, the hour when at home my friends were commencing their Newyear visits, . . . I embarked; and with a fair wind, and the 'star-spangled banner' (made by an Arab tailor) floating above me, I commenced my journey on the Nile. It is necessary here for every stranger to place himself under the flag of his country, else his boat and men are liable to be taken at any moment by the officers of the pasha. It was the first time I had myself ever raised the banner of my country, and I felt a peculiar pride in the consciousness that it could protect me so far from home." [23]

This patriotic outburst was characteristic of early American visitors to Egypt and to the East generally. Except for the antiquities most of them could find little to praise, and invariably they drew invidious comparisons with their native land. Americans were known for a zealous and often immoderate attachment to the United States and all it represented to them. One Englishman wrote in 1810: "The national vanity of the United States surpasses that of any other country, not excepting France." [24] And there is a delightful passage in Mrs. Trollope's *Domestic Manners of the Americans* (1832): "I shall never forget the gravity with which a gentleman . . . showed me, past contradiction, that the whole of the British dominions did not equal in size one of their least important states; nor the air with which, after the demonstration, he placed his feet upon the chimney piece, considerably higher than his head, and whistled Yankee Doodle."

And so it was with many an American in the Middle East. George English floated on a raft in the Nile singing "Hail Columbia! happy land!" in 1820, and drank from its waters "to the prosperity of the great and liberal republic of the United States." Edward Joy Morris gleefully ripped down the Union Jack from the summit of the Great Pyramid in 1838 and substituted the Stars and Stripes. It was John Ledyard's patriotism, perhaps, that led him to describe the Nile as no bigger than the Connecticut River, and Cairo in August as cooler than Philadelphia.

Unworldly missionaries were not immune from the warm glow of patriotism. After visiting Lebanon's exiled Emir Beshir in Cairo in 1823, Pliny Fisk reported, "He knew something of America, and when we told him we were Americans, he gave us a salutation, and an expressive look, which flattered our national pride."

Morris observed: "There is a feeling of nationality among Americans abroad that I think belongs to no other people. The English shun each other, and the French are much more cordial to strangers than to their countrymen; but the Americans, I have observed, abroad, always seek out and associate with Americans." And here is Sarah Haight of Smithtown, Long Island, writing from Alexandria in 1835: "Bless me! How the barometer of one's *patriotism* rises as the distance increases from one's fatherland!" [25]

The ordinary traveler came to Egypt for the antiquities. Stephens described them, too, while confessing that "I know nothing of architecture, and never measured anything in my life." For him it was enough that the Great Pyramid of Giza, for instance, had a base as large as Washington Square and rose three times as high as the steeple of Trinity Church; and we can note that these particular comparisons are just as meaningful to a modern New Yorker as they were to Stephens' original audience.[26] But his interests took him far beyond physical description and into human experience. Here is his harrowing account of a visit to the governor at Cairo for the purpose of getting some necessary travel documents: "I found the little governor standing at one end of the large hall of entrance, munching, and trying causes. A crowd was gathered around, and before him was a poor Arab, pleading and beseeching most piteously, while the big tears were rolling down his cheeks; near him was a man whose resolute and somewhat angry expression marked him as the accuser, seeking vengeance rather than justice. Suddenly the governor made a gentle movement with his hand; all noise ceased; all stretched their necks and turned their eager eyes towards him; the accused cut short his crying, and stood with his mouth wide open, and his eyes fixed upon the governor. The latter spoke a few words in a very low voice, to me of course unintelligible, and indeed, scarcely audible, but they seemed to fall upon the quick ears of the culprit like bolts of thunder; the agony of suspense was over, and, without a word or look, he laid himself down on his face at the feet of the governor. A space was immediately cleared around; a man on each side took him by the hand, and, stretching out his arms, kneeled upon and held them down, while another seated himself across his neck and shoulders. Thus nailed to the ground, the poor fellow, knowing that there was no chance of escape, threw up his feet from the knee-joint, so as to present the soles in a horizontal position. Two men came forward with a pair of long stout bars of wood, attached together by a cord, between which they placed the feet, drawing them together with the cord so as to fix them in their horizontal position, and leave the whole flat surface exposed to the full force of the blow. In the mean time two strong Turks were standing ready, one at each side, armed with long whips much resembling our common cowskin, but longer and thicker, and made of the tough hide of the hippopotamus. While the occupation of the judge was suspended by these preparations, the janizary had presented the consul's letter. My sensibilities are not particularly acute, but they yielded in this instance. I had watched all the preliminary arrangements, nerving myself for what was to come; but when I heard the scourge whizzing through the air, and, when the first blow fell upon the naked feet, saw the convulsive movements of the body, and heard the first loud piercing shriek, I could stand it no longer; I broke through the crowd, forgetting the governor and everything else, except the agonizing sounds from which I was escaping; but the janizary followed close at my heels, and, laying his hand upon my arm, hauled me back to the governor. If I had consulted merely the impulse of feeling, I should have consigned him, and the governor, and the whole nation of Turks, to the lower regions; but it was all important not to offend this summary dispenser of justice, and I never made a greater sacrifice of feeling to expediency than when I re-entered his presence. The shrieks of the unhappy criminal were ringing through the chamber, but the governor received me with as calm a smile as if he had been sitting on his own divan, listening to the strains of some pleasant music, while I stood with my teeth clinched, and felt the hot breath of the victim, and heard the whizzing of the accursed whip, as it fell again and again upon his bleeding feet. . . . I thought the governor would never make an end of reading the letter, when the scribe handed it to him for his signature, although it contained but half a dozen lines; he fumbled in his pocket for his seal, and dipped it in the ink; the impression did not suit him, and he made another; and, after a delay that seemed to me eternal, employed in folding it, handed it to me with a most gracious smile. I am sure I grinned horribly in re-turn, and almost snatching the letter just as the last blow fell, I turned to hasten from the scene. The poor scourged wretch was silent; he had found relief in insensibility; I cast one look upon the senseless body, and saw the feet laid open in gashes, and the blood streaming down the legs. At that moment the bars were taken away, and the mangled feet fell like lead upon the floor. I had to work my way through the crowd, and, before I could escape, I saw the poor fellow revive, and by the first natural impulse rise upon his feet, but fall again as if he had stepped upon red-hot irons. He crawled upon his hands and knees to the door of the hall, and here it was most grateful to see that the poor miserable, mangled, and degraded Arab yet had friends whose hearts yearned towards him; they took him in their arms and carried him away.

"I was sick of Cairo . . ." [27]

At Aswan in Upper Egypt Stephens ventured into the market place. "I began to bargain for the costume of a Nubian lady, and, to use an expressive phrase, though in this case not literally true, I bought it off her back. One of my friends in Italy had been very particular in making a collection of ladies' costumes, and, to a man curious in those things, it struck me that nothing could be more curious than this. One of the ele-ments of beauty is said to be simplicity; and if this be not a mere poetical fiction, and beauty when unadorned is really adorned the most, then was the young Nubian girl whose dress I bought adorned in every perfection. In fact, it was im-possible to be more simple, without going back to the origin of all dress, the simple fig-leaf. She was not more than six-teen, with a sweet mild face, and a figure that the finest lady might be proud to exhibit in its native beauty: every limb charmingly rounded, and every muscle finely developed. It would have been a burning shame to put such a figure into frock, petticoat, and the other et ceteras of a lady's dress. I now look back upon this, and many other scenes, as strange, of which I thought nothing at the time, when all around was in conformity. I remember, however, though I thought nothing of seeing women all but naked, that at first I did feel somewhat delicate in attempting to buy the few inches that constituted the young girl's wardrobe. Paul [his Levantine servant and interpreter] had no such scruples, and I found, too, that as in the road to vice, 'ce n'est que le premier pas qui coûte.' In short, I bought it, and have it with me, and to the curious in such matters I have no hesitation in saying, that the costume of a Nubian lady is far more curious than any thing to be found in Italy, and would make a decided sensation at a masquerade or fancy ball." [28]

And here is some remarkably frank and sensitive self-analysis by Stephens at the majestic, half-buried temple of Dendera: "It is strange how the organ of mischief develops itself when it has something to work upon. I sat down upon the sculptured fragments of a column, which perhaps at this moment forms the abutment of some bridge, and, looking at the wreck around me, even while admiring and almost reverencing the noble ruin, began breaking off the beautifully chiseled figure of a hawk, and, perhaps in ten minutes, had demolished the work of a year. I felt that I was doing wrong, but excused myself by the plea that I was destroying to preserve, and saving that precious fragment from the ruin to which it was doomed, to show at home as a specimen of the skill of the Old World. So far I did well enough; but I went farther. I was looking intently, though almost unconsciously, at a pigeon on the head of Isis, the capital of one of the front columns of the temple. It was a beautiful shot; it could not have been finer if the temple had been expressly built to shoot pigeons from. I fired: the shot went smack into the beautifully sculptured face of the goddess, and put out one of her eyes; the pigeon fell at the foot of the column, and while the goddess seemed to weep over her fallen state, and to reproach me for this renewed insult to herself and to the arts, I picked up the bird and returned to my boat." [29]

TOURISTS IN EGYPT

On his trip up the Nile Stephens did not happen to run into any of his countrymen, though several other American tourists came to Egypt that year. In fact, by this time the Eastern Mediterranean was becoming a rather well-traveled tourist attraction, not only for Europeans but also for visitors from the New World. Mohammed Ali, the viceroy, was busily carving out his independence from the Sultan, and he made a point of encouraging Westerners to come and see his considerable achievements.

In the 1830's regular steam navigation was introduced in the Mediterranean, and then on the Atlantic; for the first time the voyage from the New World to the Old became more nearly a pleasure than an ordeal. By 1838 the trip from New York to Alexandria could take less than a month.* Besides, America was growing up a bit; more people were beginning to find that they had both the means and the taste for foreign travel.

Eastern travel still had its hazards. Many travelers, if not most, suffered at one time or another from disease. Shipping schedules were erratic; red tape, especially the quarantines, could be vexatious and frustrating; and parts of the interior

* With luck Jerusalem could be reached in thirty-three days, via Bristol, Paris, Marseilles, Syra, and Jaffa. *North American Review*, 48 (January 1839), 184.

were often unsafe because of bandits. An American couple named Potter are said to have been stoned by an angry crowd in Damascus for walking arm-in-arm through the bazaars, a display of affection regarded as the height of indecency. Hotels were invariably wretched; the best of them, like Key's at Alexandria, and Mrs. Hill's and Munday's at Cairo, were run by English expatriates. (In Jerusalem there were no hotels at all.)[30]

A few of the hardy early travelers are worth a word or two. Perhaps the first American woman tourist was Elizabeth Cabot Kirkland, who at forty-four undertook a three-year foreign trip in 1829–32 with her husband, John Thornton Kirkland, a Unitarian minister who had just resigned as president of Harvard College. The Kirklands reached Egypt in April 1832 as guests of Captain (later the renowned Commodore) Perry aboard the U.S.S. *Concord*. Her letters show her to have been an acute observer and a pretty good writer. On horseback between Nazareth and Jerusalem: "I wore my Frank dress, except my hair all put back, a turban on my head, and over this a white cotton sheet which covered a considerable part of my face and was fastened around my waist like the friar's robe. I mounted my horse astride with a pair of yellow Turkish boots on my feet."

In a street in Cairo "we perceived a man lying stretched before us, the head severed from the body and placed between the legs to indicate that he was a Christian. They were just sewing a label on his breast to notify the people that he came to his fate by expressing his opinion too freely on politics. . . . I can scarcely write about it without a giddiness in the head."[31]

Sarah Haight arrived in Egypt two or three years later. She was a plucky and observant traveler with a gift of gab, and her letters contain much that was missed by her male

contemporaries. Mrs. Haight was born Sarah Rogers of Smithtown, Long Island. Her husband, Richard, was in a family
drygoods business that had brought the Haights prosperity
and social position in New York, where Sarah was regarded
as "a very elegant woman." [32] After several business trips to
Europe with her husband, in 1836 he took her on a grand tour
of the East.

The Haights enjoyed having a good time and could afford
it. Among their many servants on their travels was a French
chef. In Cairo they chartered the best boat on the Nile, with
a crew of sixteen, to sail to Upper Egypt. This boat, which
had been built to the specifications of George Gliddon, was
considered so superior that it did not require preliminary total
immersion in the river to float away vermin; Mrs. Haight was
told that two other Americans who had overlooked this pre-
caution got smallpox. (Richard Haight later repaid Gliddon's
kindness by financing his American lecture tour.)

Except for this expansive scale of living, Mrs. Haight acted
very much like other American tourists before her and since.
At the Great Pyramid of Giza she did not feel quite strong
enough to climb with her husband to the top, so she asked
him to carve her name along with his on the summit so that
she could feel that she had made it. She was proud to have
her national flag flying above the Nile boat "to command
respect from the natives." She shared the general nonchalance
of the day about preserving antiquities; true, she criticized
desert travelers for using the wrappings of mummies to water-
proof their drinking-water skins, but only because she found
it repugnant. She made her husband carry their water (much
more expensively) in casks.

Sarah Haight enjoyed remarkably good health during her
travels in Turkey, Palestine, and Egypt, but she was laid low
in Athens by "Greek fever," and was so ill that for a time

her husband despaired of her recovery. In due course they reached Trieste, where they engaged the royal suite in the best hotel. Her husband bought an English post chaise for the trip to Paris, and there we take leave of her — a spunky, garrulous, rather conventional socialite who would require little more than a drip-dry wardrobe, traveler's checks, and sensible shoes to become a familiar modern caricature.[33]

David Bushnell was not a tourist in the conventional sense; he was more in the Ledyard tradition: a restless, lonely wanderer. In Cairo and out of money in 1840, he was generously offered a trip up the Nile by a wealthy Bostonian, George Sumner. At Beni-Hassan he distinguished himself for posterity by scrawling "David Bushnell, Ohio, U.S." in charcoal across the magnificent paintings in one of the tombs. Bushnell had the misfortune to cross paths with Mr. James Ewing Cooley of New York, who in 1842 published a very successful book about his experiences called *The American in Egypt*, in which Bushnell is thinly disguised as a dim-witted backwoodsman named "Nebby Daoud." (Cooley's book, incidentally, is pretty awful; it has been described as the first of the "funny school" of American travel-writing, a vein which Mark Twain exploited so successfully a generation later in *The Innocents Abroad*.)[34]

Finally, there was John Lowell "Junior" (his uncle was named John, his father Francis Cabot), scion of the wealthy and prominent Massachusetts cotton-manufacturing family, who left for Europe and the East in 1832, fleeing his home out of intense grief over the recent death of his young wife and two daughters of scarlet fever. Goaded by true *Eothian* sorrow, the thirty-two-year-old widower proposed to travel by land and sea as far as China, "not coming home till I see the circle of the earth." In Italy he fell in with a young Swiss artist, one Gabriel Charles Gleyre. Upon reaching Smyrna late in 1834, Lowell invited Commodore Porter to join them on the Greek brig *Bellerophon* for a trip to Egypt. (Porter replied that he was tempted, but felt he was a bit too old.) Gleyre drew a picture of the interior of the brig, showing much of the cargo: casks of wine; fresh vegetables; boxes of bacon, macaroni, and cheese; live turkeys and a pig on the hoof. Calmly surveying the provender was an Arabian horse.

Lowell and Gleyre reached Alexandria in December. On the Nile they crossed paths with the viceroy, Mohammed Ali, who granted Lowell an audience on February 18, 1835. The viceroy, besides discussing the possibilities of steam navigation on the Nile (as he did with John Lloyd Stephens the following year), suggested that Lowell might want to continue his journey across the desert from Upper Egypt to the Red Sea, rather than returning down the river to Cairo.

Soon afterwards, the two young travelers had a serious falling out; Gleyre vanished in the company of a Nubian mistress. Lowell consoled himself by appropriating all of Gleyre's paintings, including a portrait of himself in Turkish costume, which eventually wound up in Boston's Museum of Fine Arts. (See the illustrations.)

At Luxor, then as now the center for visiting the ruins of Upper Egypt, Lowell pitched his tent on top of a derelict palace and began to collect antiquities on a grand scale. His acquisitions have been called "the largest collection of Egyptian antiquities ever up to that time collected by an American, perhaps by any individual for his own account." He also sent home instructions for endowing the Lowell Institute, a beacon of Bostonian adult education to this day. After leaving Luxor, Lowell adopted the viceroy's well-intended advice; he crossed the desert by camel to the Red Sea. There he chartered an Arab schooner for Mocha, the coffee port of southern Arabia. Six days later he was shipwrecked. Rescued, but exhausted by fatigue and fever, he took one of the new steamers of the P & O line to Bombay, where he died on March 4, 1836. "He died," says a modern chronicler of the Lowell family, "as he had long lived, in loneliness." [35]

Dozens of other American tourists visited Egypt in the decade surrounding Stephens' visit.

In 1832 Colonel Mendes Cohen of Baltimore returned from Egypt with 680 antiquities, which were eventually donated to Johns Hopkins. Lewis Cass, a former governor of Michigan, future Secretary of War, visited Egypt and Palestine in 1837 on leave with his wife and family from his post as minister to France; an imposing figure, he made such an impression in Palestine that even twenty years later he was referred to as "Sultan Cass." Commodore Daniel Patterson brought a large party of officers from the U.S.S. *Delaware*, and his own wife and daughters, in 1834. Others were Dr. Valentine Mott, an eminent New York surgeon who was called upon to remove a growth from the Sultan's head, and General Josiah Harlan, who passed through Cairo on his return from many years in India, where he had won fame as the governor of the province of Goozerat. From the educational world came Nathaniel Fish Moore, a classical scholar who returned to America to become president of Columbia College; and Stephen Olin, president of Wesleyan, who wrote a pair of uncommonly dreary books about his travels.[36] Most of the others were prosperous and well-educated citizens from the Eastern seaboard. (A list of all those who took the trouble to register with the American consuls in Egypt from 1832 to 1842 appears in Appendix II.)

By the winter of 1838–39 it was said that there were more American travelers in Egypt than any other nationality but

English. A bit later they began to come in droves. While only twenty or thirty American tourists were officially reported in Egypt in 1850, the number approached five hundred at the outbreak of the Civil War.[37] Among the distinguished American visitors to the Middle East in the 1850's were Herman Melville, William Cullen Bryant, and Commodore Vanderbilt — who toured the Mediterranean in his yacht in 1852.

7. Palestine and Syria

AFTER RETURNING FROM Upper Egypt to Cairo Stephens set out by camel for Suez, Sinai, and Akaba, a route rarely traveled by Westerners. As before, his account is enlivened by the human touch: his rapacious, garrulous, filthy yet somehow noble Bedouin traveling companions, the indolent but dedicated and hospitable monks at St. Catherine's Monastery, and the bored, suspicious Turkish garrison at Akaba — all of them come alive. His own discomforts continue to amuse him; here is a scene near Akaba: "We pitched our tent in the open valley; the thunder was rumbling, and ever and anon bursting with a terrible crash among the riven mountains, and the red lightning was flashing around the hoary head of Sinai. It was a scene for a poet or painter; but under the circumstances, I would have given all its sublimity for a pair of dry pantaloons." [1]

He was the first American to visit Petra, the fabulous Roman city carved out of solid rock in the Nabatean Desert, even today one of the most breathtaking splendors of the area. Since the Crusades Petra had been known to the Western world only in legend, until the Swiss traveler Burckhardt stumbled across it in 1812. From then until Stephens' visit Petra had been seen by only about ten other Westerners, and it was not until nine years later that it was crystallized for all time as the "rose-red city — half as old as Time" by an otherwise forgotten Oxford undergraduate.[2] Like many visitors to Petra, Stephens was too overwhelmed by it to do it justice in prose, and his description is not very memorable. And, like other visitors, he was not too prostrated to do the tourist's duty: "I confess that I felt what I trust was not an inexcusable pride, in writing upon the innermost wall of that temple, the name of an American citizen." *

After Petra Stephens became a pioneer in the most literal sense. His chosen route to Palestine led through the dreaded and utterly desolate Land of Edom, which lay under a Biblical curse and through which no one, at least no foreigner, apparently had ever passed before. Yet aside from a strenuous monetary argument with his guides, Stephens came through unscathed, and rather proud of his achievement: "I am the only person, except the wandering Arabs, who ever did pass through the doomed and forbidden Edom, beholding with his own eyes the fearful fulfilment of the terrible denunciations of an offended God." [3]

JERUSALEM

Stephens reached Jerusalem on March 12, 1836. Here he was saddened by the grave of Cornelius Bradford, a boyhood friend who had died there in 1830 at the age of twenty-five.

---

* Within the next three years seven other Americans added their names below Stephens'. — They were Edward Robinson, Eli Smith, Edward Joy Morris, Stephen Olin, H. B. Humphrey, and Mr. and Mrs. James Cooley. Mrs. Cooley was the first Western woman there; Morris, for what it is worth, was the first American to visit Petra *twice*. Morris, *Notes of a Tour through Turkey, Greece, Egypt and Arabia Petraea to the Holy Land,* (London, 1843), pp. 132-135.

This young American had been a merry fellow, well known in Parisian society and a particular pet of the family of General Lafayette, who had recommended him to Martin Van Buren as a treaty negotiator with the Turks. Lafayette's suggestion was politely turned down, but Bradford was appointed U.S. consul at Lyons in 1829. After six months he applied for leave to come home to America; this being granted, he unaccountably turned up several months later in the East. Stephens had traced Bradford's path by the places where he had scratched his name on antiquities. "Years had rolled away since I bade him farewell in the streets of our native city," he wrote. "I had heard of him in the gay circles of Paris as about to wed with one of the proudest names in France; again, as a wanderer in the East, and then as dead in Palestine. . . . I could not but ask myself who had buried him, and who had mourned over his grave. The inscription on his tombstone afforded but vague answers to my questions, and they were of a painful character. It ran thus:

D. O. M.
Hic jacet,
C******** B*******, ex Americae,
Regionibus
Lugduni Galliae Consul Hyerosolomis tactus intrinsecus sponte
Erroribus Lutheri et Calvini abjectis,
Catholicam religionem professus synanche correptus
E vita decessit IV. nonas Augusti, MDCCCXXX, aetatis suae
XXV.
Amici moerentes posuere
Orate pro eo.

"He had died at the convent, and died alone. . . . The Catholics here are ever on the watch for souls, and with great ostentation had blazoned his conversion upon his tomb. . . . I had known B——— well. I knew that, like most young men

with us, though entertaining the deepest respect and rever-
ence for holy things, in the pride of youth and health he had
lived as if there was no grave; and I could imagine that,
stretched upon his bed of death in the dreary cell of the convent, with 'no eye to pity and no arm to save,' surrounded by
Catholic monks, and probably enfeebled in mind by disease,
he had, perhaps, laid hold of the only hope of salvation offered him; and when I stood over his grave, and thought of
the many thorns in his pillow in that awful hour, . . . I could
not blame him."

For at least a generation Bradford's grave was a stopping
place on tours of Jerusalem given to American travelers by
the American missionaries. Their interest was partly professional, for they shared Stephens' indignation at Bradford's apparent conversion under duress.[4]

When Stephens arrived in Jerusalem, there was only one
American family living there — the George Whitings, missionaries of the American Board. Whiting gave Stephens a
warm welcome. "I was an American, and at that distance
from home the name of [a] countryman was enough. In the
city of Jerusalem such a meeting was to him a rare and most
welcome incident." Whiting invited him to join in the regular Sunday service at his home the next day. "I found him sitting at a table, with a large family Bible open before him. His
wife was present, with two little Armenian girls, whom she
was educating to assist her in her school; and I was not a little
surprised to find that, when I had taken my seat, the congregation was assembled." [5]

Efforts to establish an American Board mission in Jerusalem
had been dogged with bad luck from the beginning. The very
first missionaries to the Middle East, Pliny Fisk and Levi Parsons, were supposed to settle there, and Parsons actually did
live in Jerusalem for several months in early 1821. Fisk and

Isaac Bird, who were in and out of Jerusalem during 1823 and 1824, achieved some distinction in missionary annals by being arrested and imprisoned for a night by the governor.

The action was taken, they were convinced, on representations from the Latin patriarch, who was becoming increasingly irritated at their attempts to proselytize; Fisk and Bird thus may have been the first among what is surely a very select number of Americans ever to have been imprisoned for their missionary activities. They took their difficulties with great good humor and wrote of them almost jovially: "[The police] probably thought it hard that they must insult us, search our rooms, trunks, and secretaries, seal up and open, once and again, all our doors, conduct us to the Judge and the Governor, and keep us twenty-four hours in custody, and not be paid for all this trouble." [6]

One of their good Anglican friends was reassuring about their work in Jerusalem, and in fact wrote spontaneously to the American Board: "Of the mode of their proceedings in their Mission at Jerusalem, I can speak as an eyewitness. . . . Nothing could be more quiet, harmless, and unimpeachably correct, than their way of preaching the Gospel. . . . There was no crying or lifting-up of their voices in the street, as if they meant to make a party. On the contrary, I think your Missionaries have an admirable way of avoiding party-spirit." [7]

But Pliny Fisk died in 1825, Isaac Bird and his family went to live in Beirut, and Jerusalem was "unoccupied," as the saying went, until the American Board sent out William Mc-Clure Thomson and his bride, Eliza, in 1834. (Thomson was 28, Eliza six years older. They had met while Thomson was at the theological school at Princeton, where Eliza ran a girl's seminary.) There were no other Americans in Jerusalem, and only one other Frank. While Thomson was on a short trip to Jaffa, attending to some problem or other about the shipment of their household goods, rebellion broke out in Jerusalem against the new regime of Ibrahim Pasha, and Thomson was cut off from his wife for two agonizing months. "I have not heard one syllable from Mrs. T. since I left," he wrote, "and have been agonized with all manner of horrid reports. . . . May God soon put an end to all this confusion." Meanwhile, Eliza, in the best frontier tradition, amid the "roar of cannon, falling walls, the shrieks of the neighbors, the terror of servants and constant expectation of massacre," brought forth a son, William. In due course Ibrahim's father, Mohammed Ali, feeling the rebellion had gone on long enough, reached Jaffa with some 12,000 troops and marched on the Holy City. The anxious young missionary followed the army into town and hastened to the side of his wife. "Jerusalem," he wrote, "had been plundered, both by the rebels and the Egyptian army. Repeated earthquakes had nearly destroyed many buildings, including my own." Alas, Eliza Thomson, ill with fever and an eye infection, died on July 22, 1834, less than a fortnight after his arrival.[8]

The death of Eliza Thomson was a setback to the Board's plans for a mission station at Jerusalem, but others were sent to continue the good work. The first were Dr. Asa Dodge and his wife, who arrived in September, 1834. Dodge died the following spring.*

The George Whitings were there from 1834 to 1843. They were joined in 1836 by John Francis Lanneau and his family and also by Betsey Tilden, a teacher. Charles Sherman replaced Lanneau in 1838 and stayed about four years. But in

---

* His widow returned to the United States in 1838, having married a middle-aged clergyman named John D. Paxton, who had come to the East as a tourist in 1836. He had no formal connection with the American Board but helped in the Syrian mission while he was there. John D. Paxton, *Letters from Palestine, Written during a Residence There in the Years 1836, 7, and 8.* (Lexington, Ky., 1839), p. 204.

1843 the Board closed down its efforts and left the field to the Church of England.

Every pilgrim to Jerusalem took a side trip to the Jordan River where it empties into the Dead Sea. Stephens was no exception. He spent the night at Jericho, and he has left a most appealing account of the experience: "I saw at Jericho what I never saw before. It was a beautiful moonlight night, and all the women were out of doors singing and dancing. The dance was altogether indescribable; consisting not of wanton movements, like those of the dancing girls in Egypt, but merely in joining hands and moving round in a circle, keeping time to the music of their own voices. I had never seen so gay and joyous a scene among the women in the East; and though their fathers, and brothers, and husbands, and lovers were away among the mountains, I did not feel disposed to judge them harshly. It was so rare, in that unhappy country, to see any thing like gayety of heart, that if they had been dancing over the graves of their husbands I should have been inclined to join them. And they did not shun us as the Moslem women generally do; they talked with us with their faces uncovered; and I remember a young Arab girl, not more than sixteen, who had a child in her arms, and who told me that its father had fled to the mountains, and she put the child in my arms while she joined the dance. . . . Long after I had lain down on my stony bed, their song and laugh prevented my sleeping." [9]

But not every American traveler found the ladies of Jericho so attractive. Two years after Stephens, Edward Robinson visited Jericho and gave this account: "We overheard our Arabs asking the Khatib [leader of the guides] for a paper or written charm, to protect them from the women of Jericho; and from their conversation, it seemed that illicit intercourse between the latter and strangers who come here, is regarded as a matter of course. Strange, that the inhabitants of the valley should have retained this character from the earliest ages; and that the sins of Sodom and Gomorrah should still flourish upon the same accursed soil." [10]

Edward Robinson may have been a blue-nose, but he was also an intellectual pioneer, a brilliant and tireless scholar who won world recognition at a time when most Americans were too busy carving out a continent to make much of a mark in scholarship. Robinson's field was the archaeology of the Holy Land.

The great attraction of Jerusalem and the Holy Land was their association with the Bible, with which every young American was intimately familiar — much more so, for better or worse, than is now the case. To go to Palestine was to make a pilgrimage rather than an excursion. Even John Lloyd Stephens, not a particularly religious man, was seized with the awe of visiting the actual places where Jesus was born, lived, taught, and died. Yet something was amiss. For eighteen centuries avid and pious Christians of divergent sects had overlaid the simplicity of Biblical scenes with tawdry symbolism, rude commercialism, and pious hokum. Stephens found it hard to take it all very seriously. He laid the blame (perhaps not altogether fairly) upon the Empress Helena, the mother of Constantine, who in the fourth century had come looking for concrete evidence of the places associated with the life of Christ, which had gone unmarked for three or four hundred years. "And the traveler," wrote Stephens, "is often astonished that, with so little to guide her, she was so successful; for she not only found all the holy places mentioned in the Bible, but many more; and the piety of Christians will never forget that it was through her indefatigable exertions the true cross was drawn from the bottom of a dark pit, and is now scattered in pieces all over the world. . . . She always covered a doubtful piece with a handsomer monument, upon much the same principle that a jockey praises a bad horse and says nothing of a good one, because the bad one wants praising and the good one can speak for himself. Besides, the worthy empress seemed to think that a little marble could not hurt a holy place." [11]

Now Stephens, the worldly and amused traveler with no pretensions to Biblical scholarship, could only report his skepticism and disenchantment. Robinson, on the other hand, undertook the gigantic task of sorting out fact from legend in the Holy Land.

He was born in 1794 in Stonington, Connecticut, the son of a Congregationalist minister. After graduation from Hamilton College he worked for a while in a law office and later returned to Hamilton to teach Greek and mathematics. In 1821 he moved to Andover, Massachusetts, where he saw his first book (an edition of the *Iliad*) through the press and began teaching Hebrew at the theological seminary. He resigned in 1826 and went to study in Germany. (In writing of this period of his life, Robinson took care to identify these years, out of scholarly habit, as "A.D. 1826 to 1830.") Robinson returned to Andover for a number of years, but he resigned again in 1833 to begin work on a Hebrew lexicon and a Greek-English lexicon of the New Testament.

For a number of years the orderly and inquiring mind of Edward Robinson had been frustrated and puzzled by the imperfections of modern knowledge about the Palestine of the Bible. He read everything he could find, in all the modern languages and most of the ancient ones (though he was never an Arabic scholar): Scripture, ancient historians, legends, travelers' accounts, from earliest times to the most recent explorers such as Burckhardt. Their descriptions did not hang together. Honest men differed as to the antiquity of buildings, the locations of towns, and the sites of Biblical events. He decided there was nothing to do but go and see for himself.

Some years before, Robinson had discussed with Eli Smith of the Syrian mission the idea of exploring the Holy Land together. Smith was just Robinson's kind of man — a former pupil of his at Andover, himself a scholar, a ten-year resident of the East with a good knowledge of Arabic. Having arranged to tour the Holy Land together, they arrived in Jerusalem from Cairo on Easter Eve, April 14, 1838, almost precisely two years after the visit of John Lloyd Stephens. But unlike Stephens, who found only one American missionary family there, Robinson and Smith were welcomed by no less than eight Board missionaries. It was the custom to have an annual mission convention somewhere in the Middle East, and this year it was held in Jerusalem. As Robinson put it, "They had come up with their families, like the Hebrews of old, at the time of the Passover, to worship in this place, and to consult together on the best measures for promoting the great work in which they were engaged." On Easter Sunday they all joined in a service at the George Whitings'; it was, Robinson surmised, the largest congregation of Protestants ever gathered in the Holy City up to that time. There being no hotels in town, Robinson stayed with the family of John Francis Lanneau, who had recently joined Whiting at the Jerusalem station. This arrangement, as Robinson noted with true Protestant fastidiousness, "enabled us to live aloof from the convents . . . a privilege which all travelers cannot command." (Actually, the Lanneau house seems to have been very comfortable. It was entered from a deceptively dark and narrow street in the Muslim quarter near the Church of the Holy Sepulchre; but inside one found a spacious dwelling with marble floors and an extensive garden. Located next door to the mufti, or chief Muslim religious leader, it was reckoned as one of the finest houses in Jerusalem, yet the rent was only $50 a year.) Rumors of approaching plague soon broke up the meetings of the missionaries; fearful lest they should be pent up indefinitely in Jerusalem by quarantine, the visitors left hurriedly on April 30. Smith and Robinson, however, were not frightened off; they remained and quietly undertook their work. Robinson wrote: "We took measurements within and without the city in all directions, without interruption, and without being subjected to the slightest inquiry or token of suspicion. . . . I am persuaded that neither in London nor New York could anything be similarly undertaken without exciting far more attention, and probably gathering together a crowd of idlers. We just pursued our own course; went where we would, and undertook what we pleased; asked no leave of the government or others, whenever it could be avoided; and thus encountered no opposition." [12]

Here is an example of the famous Robinson method, which won him such renown as a painstaking researcher:

We found it to be the current belief at Jerusalem . . . that a passage existed between the two fountains [Virgin's Fountain and Siloam]; but no one had himself explored it, or could give any definite information respecting it. We therefore determined to examine it ourselves. . . . Repairing one afternoon (April 27th) to Siloam, in order to measure the reservoir, we found no person there: and the water in the basin being low, we embraced this opportunity for accomplishing our purpose. Stripping off our shoes and stockings and rolling our garments above our knees, we entered with our lights and measuring tapes in our hands. . . . At the end of 800 feet, it became so low, that we could advance no further without crawling on all fours, and bringing our bodies close to the water. As we were not prepared for this, we thought it better to retreat, and try again another day from the other end. Tracing therefore upon the roof with the smoke of our candles the initials of our names and the figures 800, as a mark of our progress on this side, we returned with our clothes somewhat wet and soiled.

Three days later they started from the other end.

Having clothed (or rather unclothed) ourselves simply in a pair of wide Arab drawers, we entered and crawled on. . . . Most of the way we could indeed advance upon our hands and knees; yet in several places we could only get forward, by lying at full length and dragging ourselves along on our elbows. . . . There are here many turns and zigzags. . . . But at length, after having measured 950 feet, we arrived at our former mark of 800 feet traced with smoke upon the ceiling. . . . We came out again at the fountain of Siloam.[13]

William Thomson, who substituted for Smith as Robinson's companion on a later tour of Palestine, described him with some awe as "the greatest master of measuring tape in the world." [14] Robinson had a profound skepticism, an inquiring nature that would not let him rest until he had examined a thing as thoroughly and as meticulously as he had traversed the tunnel between the two fountains. This was his unique strength. But he did, after all, have one blind spot; whereas John Lloyd Stephens had reacted with tolerant skepticism, Robinson had nothing but righteous contempt for the legends and idolatry with which (he judged) Jerusalem and its antiquities had been corrupted by the generations of mainly Catholic and Orthodox pilgrims and clergy. He was particularly incensed at the aura of commercialism and humbug that surrounded the Church of the Holy Sepulchre. This church, erected in the early fourth century by the Empress Helena, was supposed to mark the spot where Christ was raised from the dead. To Robinson this was frankly absurd; all the Scriptural reference showed that the Resurrection must have taken place outside the walls of the city. But even more offensive to him was the way the various sects squabbled over the church, sharing the premises (as, indeed, they still do) in an uneasy *modus vivendi* that satisfied none of them. Robinson was disgusted. He admitted that he visited the Church of the Holy Sepulchre — one of the major landmarks of Jerusalem whatever its pedigree — only once, and he never examined it. An American archaeologist of a later generation noted sadly, but with some justice: "Here speaks the Puritan, not the Explorer." [15]

After several weeks in Jerusalem, Smith and Robinson struck out across the countryside. Here Robinson was more at ease, unencumbered by the rigid traditionalism that so offended him. Even later and more sophisticated archaeologists agreed that it was difficult to fault Robinson for his pioneering efforts to reconstruct the map of Palestine. A very thorough man, he "never wasted any time; he never was in a hurry. It may be added that he seldom got excited. . . . No amount of fatigue prevented the explorer from writing up his journal in his tent, sometimes as late as eleven at night." [16] This journal, which was published simultaneously in Germany, Britain, and the United States in 1841 and won for its author a gold medal from the Royal Geographical Society (the first bestowed by that august organization upon anyone from the New World), is undeniably heavy going. It runs 1971 pages, some 600,000 words, marginally longer than *War and Peace*. Though it found a ready audience in its day, it presupposes a far greater interest in and knowledge of the Bible than the average modern reader can muster; and, inevitably, it has been partly superseded by later research.* Yet in the cracks be-

* It is interesting that Robinson and Smith were troubled by a problem that still besets scholars of the Middle East: the transliteration of Arabic into English. After much consideration it was decided to adopt the system already developed by an American missionary named Pickering for the

tween the massive courses of pedantry one occasionally comes across a rewarding flower: a refreshing reminder that Edward Robinson was after all human. Like many another traveler he saw nothing amiss in carving his name in public places — at Petra and Thebes, for example. A salty comment after his return from Petra: "We had now done with camels; and I cannot say otherwise, than that I rejoiced at the circumstance." He scorned exaggerated accounts of hardships of Eastern travelers: describing a severe desert sandstorm he remarks, "For a time the prospect was dreadful . . . yet here there was no danger of life." At Ramleh, a town not far from Jerusalem, Robinson and Smith were welcomed as guests in the home of the American consular agent, an Arab Christian of the Greek Church. "In our large room," wrote Robinson, "we had opportunity to arrange our toilette a little, for the first time, after three weeks of dwelling in a tent and traveling mostly in deserts. . . . Our youthful host now proposed, in the genuine style of ancient Oriental hospitality, that a servant should wash our feet. This took me by surprise; for I was not aware that the custom still existed here. Nor does it, indeed, towards foreigners; though it is quite common among the natives. We gladly accepted the proposal, both for the sake of the refreshment and of the scriptural illustration. A female Nubian slave accordingly brought water, which she poured upon our feet over a large shallow basin of tinned copper; kneeling before us, and rubbing our feet with her hands, and wiping them with a napkin. It was one of the most gratifying minor incidents of our whole journey." [17]

Robinson and Smith, having crisscrossed Palestine diligently

---

languages of the North American Indians, "with such modifications as might be necessary in adapting it to the Oriental languages." Robinson, *Palestine*, I, x. The Smith-Robinson system was later adopted by Orientalists generally and persists here and there to this day, despite modern linguistic developments.

for more than six weeks, reached Beirut on June 26, 1838. Since leaving Cairo they had spent sixty-six days on mule or camel back, an average of eight hours each day, for a total of about a thousand miles. Seriously ill with one of the East's elusive and debilitating fevers, Robinson made his way back, via Alexandria, Smyrna, and Constantinople, and up the Danube to Vienna in September. He spent the next two years writing his famous book and then returned to the immense esteem that awaited him in America. His fame was well deserved. According to the Swiss Titus Tobler, Robinson's greatest competitor, "The works of Robinson and Smith alone surpass the total of all previous contributions to Palestinian geography from the time of Eusebius and Jerome to the early nineteenth century." [18]

Robinson took up a chair at Union Theological Seminary in New York, where he came irreverently to be known as "Old Waddy," an allusion to his frequent references to the wadis, or dry watercourses, of the Eastern deserts. Except for a return trip to the Middle East in 1852 to amplify his earlier work (in the course of which he was again assisted by Eli Smith and later by William Thomson), he taught at Union almost until his death in 1863.[19]

GUESTS OF "THE NUN OF LEBANON"

Like many another traveler in the East, John Lloyd Stephens eventually got very sick. Though he does not say just what was wrong with him, his mention of cathartics and emetics implies some sort of dysentery. At all events, he was laid up in Jerusalem, unable to travel, for a good many days in the spring of 1836. When he finally restored himself, he headed north toward Syria — through Nazareth, Tiberias (on the shores of Galilee), Safed, and then over to the Mediterranean coast. Passing Sidon, he was not too ill to attempt what had become a goal for every traveler: a call upon Lady Hester Stanhope, the "Mad Nun of Lebanon." Lady Hester was a real curiosity: the daughter of the Earl of Stanhope, she lived in a semiruined castle at Djoun above Sidon, attended only by her servants. Tales of her romantic and often violent exploits and religious excesses were common in Europe and America. But she never suffered fools gladly and commonly found no time for the casual lion hunter. This elusiveness, of course, made a call upon her all the more desirable. Lamartine, the French poet, was one of the favored, and so was Kinglake, the author of *Eothen*. Stephens was not, despite his very courteous note, which ran as follows: "Mr. Stephens, a young American, on the point of leaving the Holy Land, would regret exceedingly being obliged to do so without first having paid his respects. . . ." His messenger returned with a brisk negative reply, and Stephens turned regretfully away toward Beirut.[20]

Only a handful of Americans ever succeeded where Stephens had failed as far as Lady Hester was concerned. One was the missionary Jonas King, who spent an afternoon at Djoun in 1823. But even before King, homage had been paid by a middle-aged New Yorker named George B. Rapelje, the first American tourist who wrote for publication about his Eastern travels, and a very engaging fellow in many ways. A prosperous member of an old merchant family, Rapelje left his wife and family to journey to Europe and the East in 1821. "My objects in traveling," he wrote frankly in what is almost a dictionary definition of *tourism*, "were to find amusement, and to gain health and information." He pursued these objects with vigor and acumen in Europe and then found himself alone in Malta in January, 1822. "I turned my attention to visiting Greece, and the great city of Constantinople, as in all probability I shall never again be so near it, being within a thousand miles." Having successfully done the rounds of Constantinople, Smyrna, Egypt, and Palestine, Rapelje reached Sidon on June 22, 1822. His approach to Lady Hester was cautious and deferential. He wrote her the following note: "Mr. George Rapelje, with diffidence, takes the liberty to present his compliments to Lady Hester Stanhope, and, if agreeable, will pay his respects to her while he stops at Seda, a few hours, on his passage from Baruth to Alexandria; he thinks it necessary, and his duty, to give her some account of himself, being from the city of New-York, in the United States of America, of one of the oldest Dutch families, who went from France to Holland in the persecution of the Protestants, and were among the first settlers in that city, which was originally called 'New Amsterdam'; is about fifty, a plain man, of steady habits." Somehow this artfully quaint approach appealed to the remote and majestic Lady Hester, and she invited him to come ahead. They chatted amiably for a long time; she gave him patterns of embroidered gold and silk — no doubt of the sort still produced in Damascus — with a view to seeing if they could be marketed in America. "The time passed so quickly with this superior and interesting lady," he wrote, "that it was only an hour before sunset when I departed; she bidding me an affectionate farewell, giving me her hand, and wishing me a safe and speedy return to my wife and country." [21]

But certainly the most exotic of the successful American visitors to Lady Hester Stanhope was Miss Harriet Livermore. A religious fanatic and professional evangelist, Miss Livermore journeyed to the Middle East in 1836, as she said, "to meet my lot, which I fervently hope, is martyrdom at last, in Jerusalem." She stayed for some time in the castle at Djoun and on one occasion is said to have got the better of her hostess in a very recondite argument whose point would have been apparent only to the two of them.

First, to go back a bit: * Harriet was born at Concord, New Hampshire, in 1788, daughter of Justice Edward St. Loe Livermore of the State Supreme Court and granddaughter of Samuel Livermore, a judge and later a United States Senator. Despite the judicial heritage, she was born with a violent temper, and once clouted a girlhood friend in the face for not agreeing that her father was the most handsome man in the world. Her mother, nee Mehitable Harris, having died when Harriet was four, her father soon married again. The young Harriet was not pleased: "Though generous to a fault," it is said by a Victorian biographer, "from childhood her disposition was wholly uncontrollable; and so much did she dislike her step-mother, that her father boarded her from home most of the time."

Unusually graceful, of medium height, with striking black eyes, she was no doubt both comely and vivacious, but she had a disposition "unfavorable to domestic bliss." While at finishing school she was deeply attracted to a worthy young man named Moses Elliott, who was heading for a career in medicine. When her suitor broke off the relationship, she conceived that his family had swayed him, and "vainly did she strive to remove the prejudices of Dr. E.'s family, by the 'honeyed music of her tongue' and oft-times by little gifts. Kneeling one day at the mother's feet, she besought her to accept the elegant silk and golden chain she brought, and no longer oppose the marriage."

Like so many of her upper-class New England contempo-

---

* Much of the following material is based on some energetic and imaginative research by Mrs. John W. Hennessey, Jr., of Hanover, New Hampshire.

raries, Harriet became a schoolmistress, but her usefulness was impaired by the fact that children were often so afraid of her that they refused to attend. When chided for the severity of her threats, she would say mildly, "Of course, I did not mean to fulfill them!" Her broken liaison with Elliott made her more moody than ever, and she plunged deeply into religious experiment. She toyed with such obscure groups as the Methodist Perfectionists and the Freewill Baptists, the latter requiring total immersion in a New Hampshire lake in January; a hole was cut in the ice for the purpose, at her insistence. At one point she even sought to join the Quakers. John Greenleaf Whittier, a life-long friend, later recalled that she seemed ill-suited to the Quakers: "An unlucky outburst of rage, resulting in a blow, at a Friend's house in Amesbury, did not encourage us to seek her membership." Harriet herself was quick to perceive that "God did not will that I should be a Quaker."

In 1825, now a confirmed spinster of thirty-seven, Harriet Livermore took up preaching, and this, it proved, was her true métier. She soon attracted great renown as a mystical evangelist and won large audiences as far away as New York, Philadelphia, and Washington. Her notoriety even brought her to the floor of the House of Representatives, where in January, 1827, she was honored by being invited to address both Houses of Congress and President John Quincy Adams. In 1832–34 she went west as a missionary to the Indians, whom she regarded as descendants of the Lost Tribes of Israel and for whom she wrote a book of hymns.

Like Lady Hester Stanhope, Harriet was obsessed with the "Great King," a coming Messiah, and this dubious bond led her to Djoun in 1836. (In preparation for her trip to the East, the Secretary of State had sent Commodore Porter a

letter of introduction describing her as a "lady of high character, both moral and religious.") One day while there, it is
related, the two women went to the stables, where Lady
Hester pointed out to Harriet a fine Arab stallion. The following story is told: " '*That* one,' said Lady Hester, 'the
Great King when he comes will ride, and the *other* I will
ride in company with Him.' Thereupon, Miss Livermore gave
a most emphatic 'No!' declaring with foreknowledge and *à
plomb*, that 'the Great King will ride this horse, and it is I,
as his bride, who will ride upon the other.' It is said, she
carried her point with Lady Hester, overpowering her with
her fluency, and assertion."

Some say Harriet Livermore spent months, perhaps years,
wandering among the Arab tribes, by certain of whom she
was thought to be a prophetess. In England in 1841 she tried
in vain to present a box of trophies from Jerusalem to Queen
Victoria. Edward Everett, then American ambassador in London, cautioned her "not to make what has taken place the
subject of remark either in conversation or writing to any
person whatever," but he very helpfully offered to buy the
box and its contents for himself.

Whittier, a kindly man, remained Harriet Livermore's
friend for many years. She stayed with him for a few days in
Philadelphia in 1838, where he organized a lecture appearance
for her. Even more, he brought her immortality by including
her in his long narrative poem, *Snowbound:*

> . . . Under low brows, black with night,
> Rayed out at times a dangerous light; . . .

Miss Livermore went to the East twice more during her
long life. She was admitted to an almshouse in Philadelphia
in 1867 and died on March 30, 1868, in her eightieth year,
in Germantown, where she is buried in a Dunkard cemetery.[22]

WILLIAM THOMSON

When word was received in 1839 of the very serious illness of Lady Hester Stanhope, it was William Thomson of the American mission at Beirut who climbed with the British consul to her eyrie above Sidon to investigate. They arrived about midnight to find her already dead, almost alone in her castle, which had been looted by faithless servants. Thomson wrote:

It was an intensely hot Sabbath in June 1839. . . . The consul decided that the funeral must take place immediately. This vault in the garden was hastily opened, and the bones of General Lousteneau, or of his son, I forget which — a Frenchman who died there, and was buried in the vault by her Ladyship — were taken out and placed at the head. The body, in a plain deal box, was carried by her servants to the grave, followed by a mixed company, with torches and lanterns, to enable them to thread their way through the winding alleys of the garden. I took a wrong path, and wandered some time in the maze of these labyrinths. When at length I entered the arbor, the first thing I saw were the bones of the general, in a ghastly heap, with the head on top, having a lighted taper stuck in their eye socket — a hideous grinning spectacle. It was difficult to proceed with the service under circumstances so novel and bewildering.[23]

This brisk sketch appears in William Thomson's *The Land and the Book*, the most popular book ever written by an American missionary, and one of the best. First published in 1859, it reappeared in many editions and sold almost 200,000 copies, more — it is said — than any other American book of its time except *Uncle Tom's Cabin*. The style of *The Land and the Book* is dignified, yet chatty. Like the *Compleat Angler*, it is cast in the form of a rambling dialogue that seems hopelessly out of date. Yet somehow it is still moving and engaging. Thomson had a streak of human tolerance that was all too rare among his missionary colleagues, many of whom tended toward "that intolerant intensity of faith which in others we call 'bigotry.' " [24] He refers, for instance, to a problem that troubled all the missionaries in the Levant: the fact that people approached them hoping for material gain. "It would not be charitable — possibly not just — to say to every applicant, You seek us, not because you have examined our doctrines and believe them, but for loaves and fishes of some worldly advantage which you hope to obtain; and yet it is difficult for me at this moment to recall a single instance in which that was not the *first* moving motive." Thomson consoled himself by the reflection that this kind of motivation was characteristic of all changes in religion, and indeed was true of Christ's own following. Where a government is corrupt and the people are poor, he points out, they will often change their religion for some extraneous reason such as tax avoidance. "To us, who have always lived under a form of government where our temporal rights and privileges have been guarded by law, this is a monstrous perversion; and we cannot adequately appreciate the pressure which has crowded these people into such mercenary ways." [25]

And William Thomson loved the Holy Land as Walton loved fishing. What distinguishes *The Land and the Book* from, say, Robinson's *Palestine* is Thomson's warmth and enthusiasm for the country in which he lived and traveled for forty years. A certain homely gusto brings Palestine alive: "In our native Cincinnati, a hog walks into a narrow passage on his own feet, and comes out at the other end bacon, ham, and half a dozen other commodites; at the aga's camp, it is a calf or sheep that walks past you into the cauldron, and comes forth a smoking stew." Thomson's contemporaries knew him principally as a traveler. He loved the saddle and the tent, the open air, the evening talks with shaikhs and villagers. "Yes," he wrote, "give me the tent, the open country, and the clear blue sky, at least while spring lasts. And then these nights, so solemn, so sad, and yet so very sweet. . . . It is sort of bliss merely to lie still and breathe." [26]

BEIRUT

Having tried in vain to see Lady Hester Stanhope, John Lloyd Stephens galloped off from Sidon for Beirut. "Her Ladyship," he wrote, "was exceedingly lucky in not having received me; for that night I broke down at Beyroot; my travels in the East were abruptly terminated; and, after lying ten days under the attendance of an old Italian quack, with a blue frock coat and great frog buttons, who frightened me to death every time he approached my bedside, I got on board the first vessel bound for sea. . . . For ten days I lay on the deck of a little Austrian schooner, watching the movements of a pair of turtle doves; and on the morning of the eleventh I was again off the coast of Egypt, and entering the harbor of Alexandria." Here he takes leave of the reader "with thanks for his patient courtesy"; and we would do well to return this courtly sentiment.[27] But we must also come back for a look at Beirut, which Stephens knew only from a sickbed.

Sarah Haight was also in Beirut that spring. "A wretched place," she wrote, "with no one thing in it worth noticing." [28] Others were more favorably impressed. Mrs. Eli Smith, a newly arrived American missionary wife, wrote home in February 1834: "The city itself, which is enclosed by a wall, is small, and not particularly attractive or repulsive; but the environs, where the missionary house stands, and which occupies an extent of country several times larger than the city, present an enchanting prospect, even at this season of the year. The ground rises gently towards the south, and is covered with an uninterrupted succession of gardens, separated by hedge-rows of cactus, or prickly pear, and filled with mulberry trees trained to a low growth. These are now stripped of their verdure; but the sycamore, the kharoob, and here and there a palm and cypress, diversify the landscape, while innumerable almond trees in full blossom enliven the scene, and place its beauties beyond all description. The houses, which are a bright yellow tinged with brown, and unique in their appearance, are scattered at equal distances over the gardens. . . . Some of the terraces of the houses are surmounted with low pointed columns. . . . I can truly say, that Beyroot pleases me more than any spot which I ever saw." [29]

Beirut was just beginning to develop into an important commercial center and port for the interior of Syria. Its polyglot Levantine population of ten or fifteen thousand included some five hundred Europeans. About a score of trading vessels called each year, anchoring in the open roadstead or, in bad weather, at the mouth of the Nahr-el-Kelb (Dog River), a few miles to the north. A flourishing local silk industry drew traders from Marseilles, Leghorn, and the Barbary states. Damascus was coming to depend on Beirut to supply the great desert caravans bound for Mesopotamia and Persia. There were two resident firms of British merchants, though as yet America had no direct trade with Beirut as it had with Smyrna. [30]

The only American residents in the 1830's were several missionary families. The mission was well established, the first families having arrived in 1823. In November of that year, curious idlers along the beach paused to observe a little Greek brig standing off shore signaling for porters. The passengers were Mr. and Mrs. William Goodell, who have already figured in Chapter 4, and Mr. and Mrs. Isaac Bird. (The Birds had with them a three-month-old son, William, born in Malta.) All were carried by half-naked Arab porters through the surf, the ladies clutching their plain but ample skirts and simple bonnets, all but oblivious to the "multitude who ran to witness so novel a scene," as Goodell put it. "We were in the English costume, and the ladies were without veils. The Turkish governor sat with his pipe, and looked on very composedly." The British consul, Peter Abbott, at that time the only Englishman in town, heard the fuss and came down to meet them. To their great relief they were invited to lodge in the Abbott household until they found their own home. After all, the Abbotts' was the only house in Beirut with glass windows, and winter was coming on.

Beirut, in fact, had little to offer in the way of material comfort in 1823. The streets were narrow, crooked, and filthy; no wheeled vehicle had been used in all of Syria since the days of Roman chariots. Beirut was subsidiary even to Sidon, which gave its name to the Turkish *pashalik*, or province, that ran along the Syrian coast. But from the first the town appealed to the missionaries. Goodell noted its advantages as a station: an English consul for protection, good communications by land and sea, and the availability of Mount Lebanon as a safe retreat in times of political disturbance. He reported to the Board that a missionary family would be more comfortably situated there than anywhere else he had seen in Syria.[31]

Among their first converts was a young Syrian of the Greek Orthodox faith named Asaad el Shidiak. When news of his apostasy reached the Greek patriarch, Asaad was clapped into prison. The missionaries were not dismayed: "We entertain high hopes of his future usefulness," they wrote home cheerfully: "Should he be prematurely cut off, [we] will tenderly lament his death." And so, when Asaad died stubbornly in chains in a convent, he became the celebrated

"Martyr of Lebanon," a postmortem sobriquet much used by supporters of missions over the next generation or so. The story of Asaad, countlessly retold, could generally be relied upon to appeal to the heartstrings and pursestrings of the worthy and the wealthy at home.[32]

Because of the hostilities between the Greeks and the Turks, communications with other mission stations and with the United States were a problem, Goodell reported. "All our letters, papers, periodicals, books, clothing, etc., came to us very irregularly. They would, for instance, be collecting at Malta and Smyrna for a considerable time, till there should be an opportunity for Alexandria. At Alexandria they would again accumulate and remain, till there should be an opportunity for Beirut; and then they would all come together. Our letters, that had been accumulating for months, often came with all the correspondence of the merchants, in a bag with a large cannon ball tied up with them. This the Captain did, in order to sink them all to the bottom of the sea, the moment a Greek man-of-war should appear. . . . Our letters and papers, whenever they reached us, would come like a perfect deluge, sweeping away all calm reflection and sober thought, and making us almost crazy for several days." [33]

In March, 1826, twelve Greek men-of-war sailed into Beirut harbor to sack the town. When Turkish troops arrived, the Greeks withdrew, but the cure was as bad as the disease. A group of armed Bedouins, frustrated by the failure of the Greeks to stay and be punished, approached the Goodells' house and demanded entrance. "Some of their more resolute and reckless ones came, and, in their strong guttural manner, called upon me to 'Iftah el Bab' (open the door). I told them I should not 'Iftah hoo' (open it). They saw from my dress that I was not a native." It took the Arabs about half an hour to chop down the door, while Goodell was "reasoning with them from a narrow window above." Once inside, the bandits stormed upstairs. Cleverly, Goodell pointed out that Mrs. Goodell's room was a harem — forbidden, of course, to all true sons of the Prophet. Surprisingly, they accepted this, and while they weren't looking, Goodell was able to slip many of his valuables through the door to Abigail within. Later, after a strong protest through Consul Abbott, the governor paid $300 by way of compensation for this outrage. A sketch (see the illustrations) was done by a local artist, to Goodell's specifications, to present to the governor as evidence, and it was accepted as conclusive proof of the felony.[34]

In 1827 the climactic international events leading to Navarino brought new tension in Beirut. On the advice of Consul Abbott, Goodell sent his wife and children off to stay in a Maronite convent in the mountains, where — curiously, in the light of the general Catholic-Protestant antipathy — they were made welcome. Goodell himself was not, and to keep peace with the Maronites, Emir Beshir, the governor of Mount Lebanon, ordered him to stay away. Nevertheless, "I visited my family several times in their retreat, going up in the evening after dark, climbing in at a back window, staying as a sort of prisoner in Mrs. Goodell's room during the day, and climbing out of the window again in the night."[35] Whether Emir Beshir was ever aware of this flouting of his orders by the uxorious William Goodell it is impossible to say.

Trouble was brewing. On June 23, 1827, Eli Smith wrote to his sister in Connecticut: "We have rumors of an approaching war between the Turkish government, and 3 or 4 of the European powers. . . . We have united with the others here under English protection to send to Smyrna for a man-of-war to come and take us away in case of such an emergency. This letter goes by the messenger whom we send on this business."[36] On October 20 a combined force from the British, French, and Russian navies gunned almost the entire Turkish fleet into the bottom of the Bay of Navarino. (See Chapter 3.) The Turks were stunned. British consuls throughout the Ottoman Empire, fearing reprisals, quietly and prudently stole away. By the spring of 1828 the missionaries in Syria found themselves without the accustomed protection of a friendly government and daily expecting an outbreak of war. Plague had broken out in Beirut, and there was nobody left in town who would cash a check. The plan to "send to Smyrna for a man-of-war" evidently having fallen through, they chartered a "little Austrian trabaccolo of a hundred tons" for Malta, where they would be safe among their missionary brethren under the secure aegis of the Union Jack. They hid their money in the bedding of the five-year-old William Bird, who thus, as someone later archly remarked, became the "treasurer of the Syrian mission." [37]

When the Birds came back in 1830 to reopen the Syria mission, it was said that the entire Protestant community in the Turkish Empire — three persons — came out in a boat to meet them. But things began to improve. The capture of Beirut by Mohammed Ali in 1831 proved a blessing, for the Egyptian viceroy was on his best behavior toward Christians, seeking to gain favor in Europe by way of contrast with his Turkish overlord. Isaac Bird was allowed to buy the plot occupied to this day by the American Community Church. Here he built a mission house, which came to be known as "Burj Bird" (Bird's Fortress). The basement was first set up as a boys' school, with classrooms and a dormitory for six students. One of the objectives was to teach them English, and after two months a boy was allowed to speak no more Arabic. "The penalty was that the delinquent should stand with open arms before the other boys whilst they ate their meals; and should he choose he might eat what they left." [38]

This building, now an American school for girls, has just recently been threatened by the construction of a new highway through what is now downtown Beirut. (When it was built it was the largest building outside the city walls.) To the modern American visitor of whatever faith, Burj Bird and its compound area are still a refreshing, quiet oasis in the heart of one of the world's noisiest capitals — and a historic landmark that it seems a pity to destroy.

While the Egyptian Government of Mohammed Ali was basically tolerant of the missionaries, life in the midst of his troops and local officials could occasionally be unpleasant. Quarantine, to which all newcomers were subjected for several weeks for health control reasons, was carried out under squalid conditions. Only a low leaky shanty of boards without a door was provided; bedding was filthy straw. In winter the quarantine camp became a sea of mud. In August, 1833, a servant of Isaac Bird was beaten and insulted by an Egyptian soldier in the Birds' garden. In the fight that ensued the soldier was knocked down by a stone and the servant fled. Bird, hearing the commotion, came to the aid of the stricken soldier and fell into the hands of his comrades. "They seized my arms and forcefully pulled me out of the garden and conducted me to the plain. . . . They held me fast until we reached the further extremity of the tents, their rabble crowding near me as I passed, beating me from behind with canes and cuffs and from before presenting their guns and bayonets as if to blow or run me through." After about forty minutes Peter Abbott came to Bird's rescue with his corps of guards from the British consulate; there was a skirmish with the Egyptian troops but no loss of life. In due course Bird was released by the American consul, Jasper Chasseaud, supported by civil authorities from the town. Chasseaud, a native of the Levant, was never one to tolerate an insult to his adopted countrymen. He fired off letters of protest to Mohammed Ali and Ibrahim Pasha. And imagine his pleasure several weeks later when a British frigate arrived to inquire whether there was anything further to be done. Chasseaud reported pompously to Commodore Porter that he was given a salute of seven guns and invited to dinner aboard the frigate. He also had the satisfaction of seeing the Egyptian troops tried and sentenced to be bastinadoed; their captain, he reported with evident relish, was to be confined for fifteen days in "a dark dungeon loaded with Iron Chains and living on bread and water." But in the end Chasseaud was denied his pound of flesh. The sentences were never carried out, despite his strenuous efforts, which included calling for the American fleet. Commodore Porter was willing to let well enough alone: "I take the liberty of observing," he wrote to Commodore Patterson, commanding the Mediterranean Squadron, "that application from Consular Agents for the appearance of ships of war on any part of the coast within the limits of this Empire, ought to be acted upon with caution. . . . The zeal of Mr. Chasseaud has outrun his discretion in this affair. . . . It is in vain to hope by a show of hostile disposition to induce the authorities to lay aside the laws, and the decisions of their courts, or change their ancient customs to pacify an American Consular Agent who is a foreigner born in this country." Sound advice indeed, and of course Chasseaud resented it.[39]

ELI SMITH

The outstanding figure of the early Syrian mission was Eli Smith. He was popular, energetic, imaginative, more a scholar than a missionary, and the first true American orientalist. A Connecticut Yankee, born in 1801, he was graduated from Yale and Andover and arrived in Beirut in 1827. Right away he set off for the mountains, where he could study

Arabic undisturbed. The plague that disrupted missionary operations that year did not bother him; he found it "an excellent time for study, free from interruptions."

Written (as opposed to colloquial) Arabic is a hard language to master. Poor old Pliny Fisk had quickly become discouraged by its "thirteen conjugations, and twenty ways of forming the plural, and thirty-three ways of forming the infinitive; with its consonants without vowels, and its unnumbered dialects." [40] But throughout Syria, Palestine, and Egypt, Arabic was the vernacular language, and a cardinal tenet of Protestant missionaries everywhere is that the Bible should be available in the vernacular. This is what Eli Smith set out to provide. Having spent twenty years mastering Arabic, he started work on the Bible in 1848 and continued until his death (of cancer) nine years later. His study was a top-story room of the Beirut mission house, where a plaque now commemorates his efforts. After his death other willing hands took up the unfinished task, and the Protestant Arabic Bible was finally completed in 1864. It was printed on the press originally established in Malta in the 1820's, using type (known as "American Arabic") made to Smith's specifications in Leipzig.*

When Eli Smith was in the United States in 1833 he married Sarah Huntington, of a prominent Norwich, Connecticut, family. The bride was thirty-one and something of a blue-stocking. Her credentials included an eminent grandfather, General Jedediah Huntington, a founder member of the American Board. (Her father's name could hardly have been anything but Jabez, and it was.) Several years before

* Surprisingly, this version of the Bible was adopted by Arab Christians of diverse sects and has been in constant use for over a century. It is now reported that Coptic scholars in Egypt, after having used the American translation for many years, have recently completed a new Arabic translation more to their liking. *Kayhan International* (Teheran), April 12, 1966.

her marriage she had felt the missionary call, though it troubled her that so many missionaries were — well, frankly — not exactly of her own station. In her diary she mused: "If individuals from what are called 'the first families,' of both sexes, were to consecrate themselves to the work, it would give new impulse to the cause. Suppose, for instance, a young lady or gentleman, from the midst of our pleasant circle in Norwich, should go to the heathen. . . ."

Acting on her own suggestion, Sarah became an avid missionary among the Indians near her Connecticut home. "From hut to hut she visited among these degraded children of the forest. . . . When she met in the road a few ragged natives, or a knot of men and women, she would stop her horse, and converse awhile with them, and slip a tract into the hand of each, and with a smile pass on."

The Smiths set up housekeeping in Beirut early in 1834. No more did Sarah have to venture forth along the road, as she had among the threadbare Indians of Connecticut. Just the opposite: "At times, while she was least prepared, and while visits were least desirable, her house would be invaded by a company of five or six women, who would remain a long time, asking questions and prying into a hundred things which did not concern them." She is said to have endured these annoyances bravely, but her letters home reflected certain reservations: "If the people were cleanly in their habits, it would be more pleasant to have them about our persons. I often think of the Savior, surrounded as he was by a multitude of the lower classes. . . ." Again: "I generally feel less at my ease in exchanging civilities with the natives, than I did in any circumstances in which I was placed in America."

Indeed, Sarah Smith's comfortable Norwich upbringing never entirely deserted her in the East. "Looking at our national character at the distance of 5,000 miles, and mingling

with foreigners, I feel myself forming a more impartial estimate than when I was borne along amid the excitement and
self-complacency, to which my countrymen are certainly
exposed. While I see much to admire and love, I also see
faults that I wish might be corrected." Writing home about
the qualities to be sought in a potential missionary, she cautioned, "The plain, independent manners of some of our good
republican citizens, would be offensive to foreign taste."
Sending to America for some new frocks, she explained: "In
our chapel we are seldom without the presence of English
travelers, and not infrequently there are with us English
noblemen. . . . I think that America should send forth her
best to foreign lands." [41]

She soon began a school for girls, and she achieved some
note in missionary circles as the only schoolmistress in all
Syria.* Before long she had persuaded an old friend, Rebecca
Williams, of East Hartford, to join her in the work. (Miss
Williams arrived in November 1835, married the Reverend
Story Hebard of the mission the following year, and then
died in Beirut on February 8, 1840; her husband died in the
quarantine station at Malta, on his way home, in June 1841.) [42]

Sarah Smith's routine was interrupted only rarely. The
most notable occasion was the visit of the U.S.S. *Delaware*
in August, 1834, the first visit of an American warship to the
Syrian coast. (See Chapter 10.) Commodore Patterson, his
wife, and two daughters called upon the Smiths, to Sarah's
patrician satisfaction. Eli was invited to preach aboard the

---

* In the churchyard of the American Community Church in Beirut
there is a column with an inscription that reads: "1835 — Site of the first
edifice built in the Turkish Empire for a girls' school erected in 1835 by
Mrs. Tod, an English lady of Alexandria, for Mrs. Sarah L. Smith, its first
teacher. Here also was begun the first Sunday School in Syria." Presumably "Mrs. Tod" was related to the Alexander Tod who succeeded John
Gliddon as consul at Alexandria on the latter's death in 1844. (See Chapter
6, p. 153 n.)

Delaware; Sarah went with him and gave this report: "It was a most interesting and attentive audience. The numerous crew, standing, formed two compact bodies each side of the speaker. Their clean and simple uniforms, of white shirts and pantaloons, blue collars and cuffs, and a black handkerchief tied around the neck, and their fair complexions, contrasted strongly with the tawny skin and fantastic dress of those whom for a year we have been accustomed principally to see. . . . The Arabs crowded on board, and I suppose that in and around there were more than a thousand souls." (During the *Delaware*'s stay in Beirut, in fact, it was estimated that 40,000 persons visited her.)

The Commodore told the missionaries that he had come to Beirut mainly as a demonstration of their government's support for them, and Sarah Smith found this very gratifying. "Commodore Patterson," she wrote, "is a plain, unceremonious, agreeable American; Mrs. Patterson is the same; and the daughters are intelligent, affable, and polished. I love the manners of my countrywomen. The ladies of no land that I have seen compare with them in that delicacy of feeling and refinement which are the ornament of a female." Sarah was infinitely pleased when Mrs. Patterson sent her ashore a few pounds of black tea and a keg of crackers.[43]

In 1836 Sarah Smith's health began to fail. Alarmed, Eli resolved upon a sea voyage, a highly regarded curative for the intransigent maladies of the Levant. They embarked on a leaky, uncomfortable old coaster headed vaguely in the direction of Smyrna, and things soon went from bad to worse, for "the crew and some of the passengers were anything but agreeable, and horrid profanity was heard, instead of prayer and praise." On the fifth night out the vessel ran upon a reef on the coast of Cyprus and sank like a stone. Having reached shore, the Smiths were rescued in due course by a Turkish lumber vessel, and they eventually reached Smyrna after an agonizing journey of thirty-three days. There Sarah died on September 30, 1836, a martyr to the mission cause, whose life story was published, republished, and anthologized for many years to come. The flags of American vessels in Smyrna harbor, and David Offley's at the consulate, were respectfully lowered to half mast on the day of her funeral.[44]

Eli Smith married twice again. His second wife (Maria Ward Chapin of Rochester) died of dysentery in Beirut in 1842, leaving a three-day-old son, Charles, who grew up to become a Yale professor.* The third Mrs. Smith (Hetty Butler of Northampton) survived him. After his death in 1857, she returned to the United States to raise six children alone.

In 1851 Smith took time out to send to the Journal of the American Oriental Society his translation of a "treatise on Arab Music" by one Mikhael Meshakah of Damascus. In an accompanying note, Smith disclaimed any knowledge of or taste for the science of music. He undertook the task of translation, he said, "in consequence of the necessities of my calling. The mission with which I am connected has not yet succeeded in introducing singing into Arabic worship. . . . Not only do we find the singing of the Arabs no music to us, but our musicians have found it very difficult, often impossible, to detect the nature of their intervals, or imitate their tunes." [45] Many a modern listener to Oriental music can sympathize with the tone-deaf Eli Smith, and all will salute the true scholar in him.

Eli Smith set a high standard for those who followed him.

* An interesting letter by Maria Smith from Ain Anoub, dated July 15, 1841, was published in *Middle East Forum* (Beirut), January 1964, p. 11.

He knew the Syria of the Arabs as well as any Westerner of his generation.* His thirty years in the Levant formed a solid link between the early generations of Americans there.

By the end of 1840 there were no less than eight missionaries attached to the Syria mission, most of them with their families: the Eli Smiths, William Thomsons, Story Hebards, Beadles, Wolcotts, Keyeses, Leander Thompsons, and young Cornelius van Dyck. Another brief evacuation took place during the British attack on Beirut in August 1840. The missionary families were taken to Cyprus by the U.S. navy corvette *Cyane*, Captain Latimer, and they returned to Beirut in October.[46] Teaching, of course, was suspended but was later resumed. The boys' school at Beirut was closed in 1842 for lack of funds, but it was later reopened in Abeih, a nearby mountain village.

The mission schools begun in the 1830's were the forerunners of the American University of Beirut, founded in 1866 as Syrian Protestant College by missionaries who resigned from the Board to do so. These developments fall beyond the scope of this book, but they can be followed up in Dr. Bayard Dodge's *The American University of Beirut* (Beirut, 1958), the *Reminiscences* of Daniel Bliss (New York, 1920), and particularly in the very interesting *That They May Have Life* (Princeton, 1941), by the late Stephen Penrose.

* The contribution made by Smith to Robinson's *Palestine* should not be underestimated. It was he who supplied much of the detailed information that made the book so outstanding. A modern British scholar regards Smith's lists of villages, with notes on the inhabitants, as "unique. . . . No one else (to my knowledge) did anything similar for several decades. . . . As material to be used in building up a picture of the human and economic geography of the country in the 1830's, they are first rate." Letter to the author from Mr. Norman Lewis, October 9, 1964. Quoted by permission.

8. Pioneers of Persia and Mesopotamia

Tucked away in remote Kurdistan, which centers on the area where Turkey, Iraq, and Iran now meet, dwelt some fifty thousand Nestorian Christians in the early nineteenth century. For generations they had lived in poverty and squalor, the clergy inept and corrupt, the laity illiterate. They were an isolated survival of ancient ecclesiastical history. Surrounded by hostile Kurds, Turks, and Persians (all Muslims), the wretched Nestorians eked out a miserable life from ignorant tillage of their mountain soil. Virtually unaware of the outside world, they themselves were almost equally unknown to the West until an English clergyman published some notes about them in 1826.[1] True, the Jesuits and other Catholic emissaries had won some away to Rome, but this was no step forward in the eyes of Protestants.

SMITH AND DWIGHT

In 1830 the American Board of Commissioners for Foreign Missions, having decided the Persian Nestorians might prove a fertile ground for mission labor, sent out Eli Smith and Harrison Dwight to investigate. Smith, a bachelor of 29, was attached to the mission in Syria, then evacuated to Malta (see Chapter 7). Dwight, a native of Conway, Massachusetts, was three years younger and new to the East. Recently graduated from Hamilton College and Andover, he set sail from Boston in January, 1830, with the Board's instructions in his pocket and his bride of two weeks at his side. In April Smith and Dwight set off for northern Persia, leaving Elizabeth Dwight at Malta. For her the honeymoon was definitely over — when Dwight saw her again fifteen months later he belatedly discovered that he had fathered a bouncing boy.

Dwight, according to a fellow-missionary, must have been just about the ideal traveling companion. "He was in his element in the field. If somewhat reserved at home, in touring he was social, genial, and full of good-humor. The discomforts, the strange notions, the unlooked-for obstacles, and the manifold absurdities of the oriental world, as viewed by us, were all met in a spirit that changed dross to gold wherever found." [2] Qualities like these were sure to come in handy. Smith and Dwight were likely to find very few friendly Western faces where they were going; there were no other Americans at all beyond Constantinople, and even the British had consular representation only in Trebizond and Tabriz. "Still," they wrote, "are we never to go any farther from the coast than a European's hat can be seen, or a consul's arm can reach?" [3]

They knew it was going to be a rough trip, and two decisions they made at the outset probably made it more arduous than it otherwise would have been: first, they decided to stay in villages and towns rather than camping in the open and, second, they decided they could move about more rapidly and independently by traveling by themselves than by joining a caravan, generally regarded as the normal and indeed the only rational way of traveling in the area at the time. In retrospect, they thought the advantages outweighed the difficulties: "In a country where no accommodations for comfortable travel exist, there can be only the alternative of furnishing one's self, or of dispensing with them entirely. . . . The [latter] alternative was adopted. Innumerable annoyances, some expense of health, and risk of life even, were among the consequences; but there was the serious advantage, also, of a more thorough introduction to the domestic condition of the people, than otherwise would have been had. . . . If in any case [the reader's] taste is annoyed by a picture drawn offensively naked, it is presumed he will not complain, when he reflects what the experience of the reality must have been." [4] At all events the trip of Smith and Dwight, "the first Americans who have trod the soil of Armenia," does not suffer by comparison with pioneering in the American West in the same era. Their book, *Missionary Researches in Armenia*, is a neglected American travel classic.

They started quietly enough, with the trek overland from Smyrna to Constantinople, where Charles Rhind was engaged at the time in his treaty negotiations. (See Chapter 3.) They were there for several weeks. Through Rhind's good offices they conducted Sunday services for the British colony, who were then without a chaplain. Here they also bought their provisions at the only store where English goods could be obtained. (This store became a rendezvous for English artisans at the Turkish capital: "No missionary could happen in, when they were there, without hearing a great deal of profane and insulting slang, spoken to each other, but really intended for him." [5]) Their trunks being considered too frail, they substituted large bags and valises of Russian leather, lined with wax cloth and provided with padlocks. For bedding they shunned mattresses as too heavy and settled for a carpet and a coverlet apiece. Beyond this their shopping list included copper pans, a mill, coffee pot, cups, knife, fork, spoon, copper drinking cup, and a portable leather table. They changed into loose Turkish robes, turbans, Tartar stockings and boots, and carried pistols. Neither shaved throughout the trip.

They left Constantinople on May 21, 1830, striking eastward on horseback across the northern slopes of Anatolia. This is bleak country even now; in those days the road was only a dusty track, virtually impassable for any kind of wheeled vehicle. Three weeks later, still two tantalizing days short of Erzurum, the first town of consequence on the route, the travelers' horses gave out, and there were no more to be found. "We resorted to the only expedient that offered, and took carts. Not the large, well-finished ox-carts of the United States. They would have been chariots." They rested briefly at Erzurum, got some new horses, and headed east again. On June 24 they wrote: "Our accommodations were not the best last night. The corner of the stable we occupied was but imperfectly defined, and we found a horse among us before morning. . . . We arose unrefreshed and feverish."

Next day they passed through a little Armenian settlement. They paused for evening prayers in the village church, which was "like the houses, underground, and bearing equal marks of poverty with them." Smith wrote: "I had new emotions in first attending divine service under ground." On Sunday, July 4, having slept as usual among the livestock in an underground stable, Smith "awoke with strong feverish sensations. . . . Horrible stench of our room in the night. . . . In it horses, calves, and hens herded with us; and dirt was constantly falling from the terrace in the night; to the great danger of our eyes."

Soon after leaving Tiflis on August 4 Smith fell seriously ill with cholera. Too weak to ride a horse, he jolted along in a kind of rough and exceedingly uncomfortable wagon. On the evening of August 12 they arrived at a post-house just before midnight, where they slept on a "mosquito scaffold, raised ten or twelve feet from the ground, and undefended by the slightest covering." The mosquitoes were a major problem along this road, and the idea of a scaffold was to rise above them: "The bushes . . . were the next morning black with them." But on the scaffold Smith got little rest: "The mountain breeze that swept over us seemed to chill us to the heart; the Cossacks, who lay by our side, talked and snored, and shook our frail platform by their motion. The trouble of bringing up our baggage caused loud talking and scolding among the sürijies till almost morning, and all together produced such an effect upon my weak nerves, that to sleep was impossible, and I lay and wept like a child."

Fortunately, the next day they were able to reach a place called Shoosha, the station of some Swiss-German missionaries from Basel. They stayed at Shoosha almost three months while Smith recovered. By November he felt well enough to go on, and they set out for Tabriz, their final objective. After a few days, however, he was again in excruciating pain. Arriving at a village, they sought out the best room available. "It was about eight or ten feet square, with walls and floor of clay attaching a thick coat of dust to every thing that touched them, destitute of a fire-place, and with a door so loose, that when it was shut, the cats and hens found no difficulty in visiting us."

Another night their accommodation was, if anything, worse. Even now Smith's account of their stay in the village of Khoik makes the flesh creep: "The house, apparently the best in the village, was built of mud. . . . It had two rooms.

The one assigned to us, being the principal family apartment was, of course, filled with every species of dirt, vermin, and litter; and withal, as they were in the midst of the process of baking, the insufferable smoke of the dried cowdung which heated their tannoor, or cylindrical oven, detained us a long time before we could take possession. Persuaded at last by impatience, that the bread must be done, I entered, and found our host and chief muleteer shaking their shirts in the oven, to dislodge the 'crawling creatures' that inhabited them. . . . This use of the tannoor is common. . . . In such ovens was our bread baked, by being stuck upon their sides, and though we would fain have quieted our fastidiousness by imagining that they were purified by fire, the nature of the fuel [i.e., dung] of which that was almost invariably made, left little room upon which to found such a conception."

Throughout these trying experiences Smith and Dwight found time to observe and report on Christian activities. Once they were given shelter in an Armenian convent, where Smith inhospitably described the celebration of the mass as "more objectionable in every feature than any papal mass I ever witnessed." He watched as a confessor was preparing some women for mass: "Seated on the floor *à la turque*, he caused each one successively to kneel by his side, with her head in his lap; and then, putting his hand upon her head, listened to her confession. In another instance, we have seen a confessor, in the presence of company, reclining upon his arm, with the woman he was confessing kneeling by his side, her head being upon his bosom, and his arm upon her person."

In December Smith was once again very ill. "Now my strength soon failed. Pain in my back made the motion of my horse intolerable, and I dismounted to walk. Thus I could proceed but a few rods, and that only by the aid of my companion's arm, before weakness forced me to my horse again."

At last they reached a village and found a stable. "I remember no more, for a stupor, which had been gradually increasing during the morning's ride, now completely overcame me. I sunk upon the ground, and remained unconscious of what passed for two days. . . . On awakening from stupor, I could neither walk nor stand." Dwight sent an urgent message to an English doctor in Tabriz, now only seventy miles away, who came and guided poor Smith and his worried companion into Tabriz, where they arrived on December 18, 1830, the first Americans who had ever been there.

They spent the winter in the home of a British official (the British embassy was at Tabriz at the time) while Smith was slowly nursed to recovery. Ever mindful of their calling, they again organized religious services for the English community, of whom about a score were regular attendants. In March Smith was well enough to join Dwight on a trip to Urmia (now known as Rezaiya) some seventy miles southwest of Tabriz, reported to be the main center of the Nestorians. They forwarded to the American Board an elaborate and favorable report on Urmia as a site for mission work. As for the Nestorians themselves, Smith was enthusiastic: "I felt a stronger desire to settle among them at once as a missionary than among any people I have ever seen." [6]

Eli Smith and Harrison Dwight, their exploratory work completed, left Tabriz in April, 1831, and were back in Constantinople in May. Soon afterwards the Dwights joined the Goodells at Constantinople (see Chapter 4), and Smith embarked for America to attend to the publication of their book.

JUSTIN PERKINS

The American Board lost little time in following up on the glowing reports of Smith and Dwight. The Nestorians were singled out as a promising missionary target, and in 1833 Justin Perkins and his wife were sent forth to set up a permanent station at Urmia. Justin and Charlotte Perkins were the first Americans who ever called Persia their home.

Perkins was born on a farm near Holyoke, Massachusetts, in 1805. A graduate of Amherst and Andover, he acquired a reputation for highly polished and courtly manners, an iron will, and a robust constitution. Shortly after their marriage in July, 1833, Perkins and his wife left Boston with instructions to set up a mission among the Nestorians, the ambitious objective being "to enable the Nestorian church, through the grace of God, to exert a commanding influence in the spiritual regeneration of Asia." The voyage aboard the brig *George*, two hundred seventy tons, was quite tolerable, according to Perkins: "The profaneness of the crew was the only circumstance which we had occasion to regret." In November they landed at Malta, where Perkins had two suits made for $29, "in the prospect of being beyond the reach of European tailors in Persia." After only a week they were off again on a Greek brig, whose captain was "a very superior man for a Greek," and arrived in Constantinople just before Christmas. Here they received a jolt in the form of a letter from the British ambassador in Tabriz, Sir John Campbell, advising them to postpone their trip because of political instability in northern Persia.* His Excellency also noted in passing that Urmia, which was to be the Perkinses' new home, had been

---

* Until 1883 the United States had no diplomatic relations with Persia and hence no legation there. Aside from the missionaries, no one seems to have felt the need for one until Moritz Jackson, a New York merchant, found himself stranded in Bushire (a Persian Gulf port) on his way to Teheran with his wife and daughter in August, 1841. Jackson, finding himself "in the greatest danger," was nevertheless reluctant to put himself under British protection and wrote to Commodore Porter in Constantinople for advice. Porter replied that there was nothing he could do, as no diplomatic relations existed between Persia and the United States. Porter to S/S, Nov. 27, 1841 (with enclosures), DSD.

"devastated by the plague." Scoffing at this advice, which was later rescinded anyhow, the couple set sail for Trebizond, on the Black Sea, on May 17, 1834. From there they proposed to go overland to Persia. Their ship, incidentally, was an old American slaver, captured earlier by the British. Perkins proudly noted that Charlotte was the first American woman to sail the Black Sea.

Benefiting from the experience of Smith and Dwight, they took a tent, so as to avoid the vermin and dirt of the towns and villages. They also carried a "portable kitchen" (consisting of fitted copper pans, a kettle, frying pan, gridiron, and tea pot), two six-foot crates of books, and bedding from America. Unlike Smith and Dwight, however, they went unarmed; Perkins' only "weapon" was an old pair of holsters, with a telescope in one and a rolling portfolio in the other. Charlotte was not much of a horsewoman, and besides, she was pregnant. However, they fully expected to reach Tabriz in ample time for her confinement.

All went reasonably well until they had to decide whether to take the direct caravan route from Erzurum to Tabriz (then imperiled by bandits) or to swing around to the north through Russian Georgia, by way of Erivan. They opted for the latter. After eight weeks on the road from Trebizond, they reached the Russian frontier, then as now on the Araxes (or Aras) River. Having crossed the river without incident, they were led to a quarantine area, where they spent two solid weeks: "We were situated in a hollow, on the bank of a small muddy brook. Six or eight dozen of geese thronged us on every side; flies, like the swarms of Egypt, flocked into our tent, to devour us and our provisions; sand, from the surrounding sunburnt hills, sifted upon us, on every breeze; and a stench, from animals that had died during quarantine, their bodies being left unburied, annoyed us sometimes almost to the point of suffocation. . . . During our quarantine, scarcely a day passed without bringing with it instances of flogging, within a few rods of our tent. . . . Often we were unable to procure a morsel until afternoon; and in one or two instances, we could obtain none, during the whole day. . . . If milk, it was generally sour; and if eggs, they were repeatedly far more than stale."

Eventually they were released from quarantine and directed to the Tsarist customhouse, where it now became clear that they were being deliberately harassed. After a full day's examination of their luggage, complete with a minute and ribald inspection of Charlotte's underwear, a drunken inspector announced that most of their luggage would have to go back to Turkey. All arguments and attempts at bribery proved futile; Perkins, with Charlotte's time approaching, had no choice but to submit. Next day they set wearily forth toward the Russian-Persian frontier, a journey of seven days. At the Russian border they were told that their passports would have to go back to Erivan to be endorsed. Arguments, appeals to common humanity, tears, attempts at bribery — no luck. A messenger with the passports was dispatched to Erivan, through which they had already passed five days before. "With sad hearts, we now found ourselves both virtually and really again in quarantine. . . . We were on a great plain of sand, as barren as desert. We were unable to find a single patch of grass on which to pitch our tent." There was a strong, scorching wind, "at times sifting clouds of sand through every joint and seam of our tent, upon our beds, our provisions and ourselves, like light snow in the fury of a winter storm, and frequently upsetting our frail canopy for the want of sufficient soil to retain the pins of our tent in the ground. . . . The only means by which we kept ourselves from starvation was to induce the Persian boatmen, on the opposite side of the river, to bring us food from their village. . . . By paying an exorbitant price, we thus obtained bread and melons, once in two or three days."

After seven days of deepening despair the messenger mirac-ulously appeared from Erivan with their passports, and they were finally released. They successfully crossed the river into Persia, half-expecting at each moment to be pulled back by some new excuse. Now help was near. On hearing of their plight, the British once again came to the rescue. Ambassador Sir John Campbell sent an English doctor to meet them, and on August 23 they were safely in Tabriz. Three days later Charlotte gave birth to a daughter. Complications set in: Charlotte had convulsions and vomiting for more than a week. The doctors saw no hope for her recovery; and Justin Perkins was faced with "only the cheerless prospect of being so soon left, a solitary pilgrim in that dark and distant land." Probably it would never have occurred to him to give up and bring his infant daughter home.

But Charlotte eventually recovered, and Justin's final word on her ghastly introduction to life in the Middle East was, and still is, very touching: "It were grateful to offer a passing tribute to female fortitude in the missionary enterprise, might a husband be allowed to do it." [7]

The baby, however, died five months later, after a three-day bout of "lung fever" with no doctor available. (By this time the British embassy had moved to Teheran, four hundred miles away.) Actually, the American Board had already decided to send a physician to join the Perkinses: Dr. Asahel Grant, who left Utica, New York, on a canal boat early in 1835 and reached Tabriz the following autumn, with his young wife, Judith.

ASAHEL GRANT

Grant was surely one of the most colorful and single-minded missionaries who ever lived. He was born on a farm in Marshall, New York, in 1807. The *Encyclopaedia of Missions* of 1891, ever in search of the light touch, pointed out that "the very name of Dr. Grant assures us that the foundations of his character were laid in a Christian home. Only parents who lived in the Scriptures would have called their son Asahel." (For the benefit of those not so steeped in Scripture, Asahel was a son of Zeruiah and a brother of Abishai and Joab. He was slain by Abner, who was thereupon slain by Abishai and Joab. "Asahel was as light of foot as a wild roe." [8]) He studied with a physician in Clinton, New York, but never went to college or to a regular medical school. His first wife died in 1831, leaving him with two sons. While attending a convocation of the American Board at Utica in 1834 he felt the missionary call. Perhaps it was not his métier. A story got around missionary circles that a Persian (some made it a British official in Persia) once remarked that a good soldier was spoiled when Grant became a missionary. According to the *Encyclopaedia of Missions,* he was "not tall or large, but alert and full of vigor. His complexion was dark, his eye bright, his aspect friendly, with a dash of enterprise and enthusiasm." He was also, as it turned out, a bit of a crackpot when it came to the Nestorians: he was deeply persuaded that they were the descendants of one of the Lost Tribes of Israel, a conviction not shared even by his best friends and colleagues, much less by his critics. But, as his admiring friend and biographer, Thomas Laurie, pointed out, "Though others may not share his zeal in this matter, none can deny that it imparted a tone of uncommon energy to his missionary life." [9]

The idea of sending a missionary physician was, to say the least, pragmatic; as some canny person pointed out at the American Board's annual meeting in 1834: "to relieve the sufferings of the body is the most ready access to the heart." That great missionary theorist, Dr. Rufus Anderson, put it this way: "It is in the early stage of a mission that the value of a pious physician is most apparent. With the exaggerated conceptions usually entertained of the temporal blessings he is able to confer, he is welcomed by all classes from the first." [10] In other words Grant was expected to use his medical skill to help bring in the sheaves.*

Unlike Smith, Dwight, and the Perkinses before them, Judith and Asahel Grant traveled to Tabriz in a huge caravan of some seven hundred camels and mules. At night "the bales and boxes of merchandise . . . were thrown around a hollow square, and served as a temporary fortress to protect us from the predatory Koords by whom we were surrounded." Perkins, who rode forward into Turkey to meet them, reported that "Mrs. Grant endured — I might better say, enjoyed — the journey remarkably well." [11]

MISSION AT URMIA

Soon after their arrival in October, 1835, Grant left the two ladies with Perkins in Tabriz and rode up to Urmia, the town so highly recommended by Smith and Dwight, to find a place for them all to live. In November, though their home was not quite ready, he sent word for them to join him. "After riding all day in a driving storm of rain, they were intro-

---

* Gandhi once expressed a different view: "I hold that proselytizing under the cloak of humanitarian work is, to say the least, unhealthy. . . . Why should I change my religion because a doctor who professes Christianity as his religion has cured me of some disease, or why should the doctor expect or suggest such a change whilst I am under his influence?" Quoted in *Re-Thinking Missions* (New York, 1932), p. 68.

duced into an open room, and sat down with the carpenters among the shavings. It was late in November, and very cold. Then, as Dr. Grant had not expected them in the storm, and their loads were left behind, they had neither bedding, provisions, nor a change of clothing. A large fire, however, was soon blazing; bread and kebabs (small morsels of meat roasted on skewers) were procured from the market. . . . They slept sweetly on the piles of shavings, covered with the cloaks they had dried by the fire."

Justin Perkins later had this to say about that first hard winter: "The rooms had little opportunity to dry; and while the barley, from the straw mixed with the mud, grew from the walls of our sleeping room, which communicated with the apartment in which we lived and was thus partially warmed, the frost stiffened the bedclothes of the lamented Mrs. Grant, whose sleeping room was not even thus warmed; and these exposures, during that winter, did much to undermine our systems, and render them an easy prey to disease. . . . When the first spring and summer came, sickness seized upon us like a strong man armed." But young Judith Grant wrote a fortnight after her arrival: "I am now quite well, and very, *very happy*. I feel that I have at length reached my home, and that my wanderings, for a time at least are over. O, 't is sweet to sit by one's fireside, with those we love about us." [12]

There was work to be done. Urmia had about thirty thousand inhabitants, mainly Muslim but including about six hundred Nestorians and two thousand Jews. Inclusive of the neighboring villages, there were about twenty thousand Nestorians in the area. There were no other Westerners nearer than Tabriz. In January, 1836, the missionaries opened a school. Seven boys were in the first class; they started by learning to read the Lord's Prayer, practiced writing with their fingers in a sandbox, and learned arithmetic with the aid of an abacus. The first school exercises took place in April; by that time there were thirty pupils, and the three top scholars were presented with a suit of clothes and a cap, at a cost to the mission of about $1.75 each.[13]

In the meantime Dr. Grant was making friends by healing: "The sick, the lame, and the blind gathered round by scores and hundreds [he wrote], and my fame soon spread abroad through the surrounding country. We were regarded as public benefactors." He soon was known far and wide as "Hakim Sahib," or the Noble Doctor.

Unfortunately Grant himself was not well. He suffered from chronic indigestion, and in July, 1836, he came down with cholera. Later that year he wrote his mother: "My eyes have been so inflamed as to require me to bleed and blister freely. Mrs. Perkins and the dear children have also suffered from ophthalmia." But despite his poor health he is said to have seen ten thousand patients and performed fifty cataract operations during his first year in Persia.[14]

Judith Grant, however, died in January, 1839, at the age of 25. Besides the two boys in America Dr. Grant was left with three more children, all born at Urmia. Henry was two and a half, and the twins, Judith and Mary, were five months old. The two baby girls succumbed about a year later. ("Little Mary," wrote one of the brethren, "was a delicate flower, — a breath passed over her, and she is gone!") They were buried beside their mother in the graveyard of the ancient Nestorian church.[15]

Judith Grant deserves more than this bleak word. She must have been a remarkable girl to have agreed to marry the fiery Grant and accompany him to Persia. Her own mother having died when she was three years old, she was brought up by an aunt, a woman of strong religious views. Judith was well educated for a girl of her time, with good training in mathematics, Latin, Greek, and French. She was described as "frank, artless, yet discreet, with a kindness that knew no limits; social, gentle, and full of sympathy for others in affliction, while remarkably patient under her own." She early showed a missionary bent and indeed had already been accepted for foreign duty by the Board before she met Grant. Shortly before her marriage she wrote a poignant family letter that could almost have come from an Austen or a Brontë:

You know, dear brother, how much I have thought of being a missionary, and how I have prayed to know my duty in the matter. Hitherto the way has seemed hedged up; but a door is now opened, and I am about to enter it. Yes, my dear, dear brother, I expect soon to leave these loved familiar scenes for Persia. The interesting ceremony that unites me with Dr. Grant takes place on Monday, April 6. . . . Papa feels very much about my going; still he does not oppose.

And she had great enthusiasm for her work; soon after her arrival in Urmia she wrote: "I am every day more and more convinced that this is a most *dreadfully wicked* country." [16] Her death, the first of an adult at Urmia, was a grave blow to her husband and the mission. Even now one is drawn to this lively, literate, dedicated young spirit. She deserved something better.

Sickness hit the Perkins family as well. Justin was almost carried off by fever in the summer of 1836. During their first six years in Persia their first three children died. Mrs. Perkins developed signs of epilepsy early in 1840, and Justin had to take her home to America the following year. With them they took their fourth and only remaining child, Judith, less than a year old. Later she returned to Urmia with her father but died there of cholera at the age of twelve. (Perkins later published an anonymous, two-hundred-page, unreadably sentimental biography of this little girl, who seems to have had precocious religious instincts, under the title *The Persian Flower*.) In his journal Perkins wrote glumly: "The sad experience of several English ambassadors to this country . . . has led them to the conclusion that it is impracticable for Europeans to rear families in Persia; and our own experience is a sad confirmation of the correctness of that conclusion." [17]

In spite of everything the mission thrived. The house at Urmia, once it had dried out, proved to be very suitable; there was a walled garden and a court, "where the ladies could enjoy the air, without the annoying publicity of walking through an oriental city." Two more American couples arrived in 1837, and another two men in 1840. The schools in the mission compound were full and flourishing. On November 7, 1840, Edward Breath, a printer, struggled into Urmia with a printing press. It was a red-letter day. "We took the press from the boxes in which it was brought and set it up," wrote Perkins. "It was constructed particularly for our station, being cast in smaller pieces than is usual, to render its transportation practicable on the backs of horses, over the high, steep and rugged mountains. It appears like an exotic in this dark, remote land." The first production lovingly prepared was the Lord's Prayer in ancient Syriac. The second was the Psalms.[18]

By the 1840's, then, the mission was well established, with a solid core of laborers busily and happily engaged in spreading the good word by means of the schools and the mission press. They had the support of the central Persian Government, such as it was, and they were widely respected for their pains, even by their Anglican rivals who thoroughly disagreed with their principles.[19]

Perkins himself took delight in religious debate. On one

occasion he succeeded in convincing a Nestorian bishop that the world had been created only 1656 years before the Flood and was nowhere near 7500 years old, as the Nestorians supposed.* "These cases are interesting," he reported, "as they render the errors in the old books of the Nestorians palpable, and on points which cannot be considered as *sectarian*." [20]

There were problems, of course. The American financial panic of 1837 threw the American Board into a tailspin. Contributions fell off, and the Board found itself overcommitted. In Urmia, the backwash was felt in the winter of 1837–38. "Some of our number . . . kept but one fire during the last winter, to save fuel; and were thus obliged to bring their kitchen, their study, their recitation-room, dining-room, and nursery, all into the same apartment." [21]

One evening while the Perkinses and Grants were strolling near the town with a Nestorian priest, they were set upon by a band of professional Muslim ruffians known as "lootee," who attacked the priest with a knife. Perkins, by and large a modest man, gave this account of the affair: "Seeing the defenseless priest in such peril, I instinctively sprang forward. . . . He turned for a moment from the priest upon me, and stabbed me with indescribable ferocity. . . . Being quite weak, as I sprang back to evade the weapon, I suddenly fell. It passed through all my clothing, and slightly penetrated my body. . . . We ran into a house, barred the door and found ourselves secure. . . . The ladies were of course frightened for the moment." Soon after, the attacker, on representations from Perkins, was seized and hauled before the provincial governor, by whose order he received two hundred and fifty

---

* Other Americans were beginning to question accepted doctrine about the age of the earth. A "Dr. N." of Mississippi told John Lloyd Stephens in Smyrna in 1835 that he was firmly persuaded that some of the temples of the Nile were more than 6000 years old. Stephens, *Incidents of Travel in the Russian and Turkish Empires* (London, 1839), I, 212–213.

lashes on his bare back. Perkins and Grant were guests at the punishment. "Though very athletic and with the image of Cain stamped upon his features, he soon softened down under the stripes, and raised a piteous outcry. . . . He at length appealed to me, confessing his crime and proposing to espouse *my* religion, if I would arrest his punishment. I understood of course the sincerity of such a proposition in those circumstances. The promptness of the governor, unsolicited by us as he was, in punishing this ruffian, was highly praiseworthy in a Persian magistrate." [22] After his experience, it is perhaps understandable that Perkins should have witnessed this mighty flagellation with such composure. If it ever occurred to this messenger of the New Testament to turn the other cheek, he does not mention it.

JAMES LYMAN MERRICK

And then there were personality problems. Nobody connected with the American Board had a thornier character than James Lyman Merrick. Born in Monson, Massachusetts, he was graduated from Amherst and got his theological training at Princeton and Columbia, South Carolina. He had just one aim in life: to labor among the Muslims of Persia.

As mentioned previously, the American Board had a well-settled policy about active missionary work among Muslims in the Middle East: it was not worth the risks. Under Islamic Law apostasy meant death. Anyhow there was plenty to be done among the Oriental Christians and the Jews, and some of the good work would surely rub off on their Muslim neighbors. Why then was Merrick sent as a missionary to the Muslims of Persia? Because he talked the Board into it. He had a glib tongue and a facile pen, and his arguments were fueled with intense conviction. After long wavering the Board decided to take a chance. They lived to regret it.

Merrick, a bachelor of thirty-one, arrived with the Grants in October, 1835. He soon came to realize "that the obstacles to evangelical truth in Persia were much more formidable than all my liberal allowance for difficulties had provided for." In June, 1836, he joined two German missionaries for a long trip through Persia. In Isfahan, where they took lodgings in the Armenian suburb of Julfa, they became the object of excited rumor. The governor of Isfahan, hearing that an armed mob was on its way to their house to massacre them, sent guards in the nick of time to protect them. This incident had a deterrent effect on Merrick's German colleagues, who shortly returned to Tabriz. But Merrick went on alone to Shiraz, where he spent the winter of 1836–37 studying Persian and discussing religion amiably with some friendly Sufi scholars (Muslim mystics).

It was inevitable that Merrick's reports should betray his lack of progress, and (for he was a vain man) he may have tended rather to inflate the perils and hardships. If by detailing his difficulties he aimed to enlist sympathy and support from home for his efforts, he miscalculated. Waiting for him on his return from Shiraz was a letter from Rufus Anderson, telling him gently that the Board had decided that a mission to the Muslims of Persia was hopeless, just as they had suspected all along, and that Merrick could no longer be supported. Anderson offered him the alternative of setting up a new station at Damascus. Merrick replied immediately: "My dear brother, . . . I have concluded that it is my duty to *remain in Persia.*"

While awaiting a response to his defiance, Merrick branched out. Prince Malik Kasim Mirza, an uncle of the Shah, was running a school for boys at his home on the eastern shore of Lake Urmia and wanted to engage one of the Americans as a teacher. Horatio Southgate, an American Episcopal missionary then in Tabriz, had a visit from the present teacher, a very disillusioned Armenian. This man poured out his heart: the prince's "school" was one in name only; the boys were very irregular in attendance; the attitude of Prince Mirza was "not conducive to discipline"; in fact, he intimated, the students "were all addicted to unnatural sin." (Southgate had no doubt that the Armenian's description was a fair one.[23]) Nevertheless, Merrick took the job in the bizarre household of Prince Mirza, teaching English to as many of the boys as could be rounded up at any time. He left after three months.

Rufus Anderson was not at all pleased with this activity. He wrote repeatedly to Merrick, telling him firmly to join the Nestorian mission at Urmia. The missionaries there urged him to see it Anderson's way and invited him in the most generous terms to join them. The only alternative, they warned, was to pack up and go home, since the Board was most unlikely to reverse Anderson's decision. At last he gave in and joined the Urmia mission in October, 1842.

From the outset things did not go well. Matters came to a head in the summer of 1844 with a serious dispute in the mission over whether to subsidize local Nestorian clerics, some of whom were demanding a price for their loyalty to the Americans, who depended greatly upon them to keep their flocks in line. Justin Perkins, the veteran, maintained that certain subsidies were necessary if the missions were to survive. Merrick took the high ground, holding that subsidies were indefensible as a matter of principle. Merrick insisted that Perkins refer the issue to Anderson, who gave Merrick his little victory by declaring as a matter of Board policy (how could he have done otherwise?) that payments to local clerics should be only for their services as teachers. At the same time, however, he vindicated Perkins by firing Merrick for good and all.

After ten years in Persia James Lyman Merrick left in June, 1845, and arrived in Boston in September, full of wounded pride, defensive, bitter, very poor, and brooding about litigation. But his dispute with the Board was an unequal contest. It ultimately descended to the level of arguing about how much money was due him; he finally settled his claims for $500 and the return of some Eastern mementoes he had donated to the Board in happier days.[24]

It is perhaps characteristic of the missionaries and their times that, with all the millions of words written for publication about their work, nothing about this controversy has ever come to light except in Merrick's own pamphlet, *An Appeal to the American Board*, published in 1847. A conspiracy of silence was rigidly observed. Rufus Anderson's standard history of the Board's early activities in the Middle East devotes five pages to the life and work of Harrison Dwight, six to the short-lived Pliny Fisk, three to William Goodell, four to Eli Smith, five to Levi Parsons, and so on. James Lyman Merrick, who must have given Anderson more gray hairs than all the rest, gets nine noncommittal lines. The only kind words ever published about Merrick were by good-hearted Judith Grant, who wrote home soon after she met him in Constantinople in July, 1835: "He is a lovely young man. . . . We consider it a very great favor to have his company."[25]

HORATIO SOUTHGATE

American visitors to Urmia were understandably rare. Probably the first was Horatio Southgate, who passed several days there in July, 1837. Southgate started life in Portland, Maine, in 1812 as a Congregationalist and, after attending Bowdoin and Andover, became an Episcopalian priest. In his instruction from the Episcopalian Board of Missions (which had nothing to do with the American Board), given to him at a public ceremony at the Church of the Ascension in New York in April, 1836, he was directed to consider Persia as the principal field of his mission; the choice, according to the historian of the Episcopal Church in America, having been determined by the fact that "that was where he wanted to go." [26]

Southgate's *Narrative of a Tour through Armenia, Kurdistan, Persia and Mesopotamia*, published in 1840, reveals a refreshing sense of self-examination and appraisal. In Constantinople he began to study Turkish and get acquainted with the people. "At the end of my first month's residence at Constantinople, I might have promulgated my opinions on Turkish institutions and customs with the utmost confidence. At the end of three months, I began to perceive the fallacy of most of my conclusions, and when six months had passed, I found I knew next to nothing about the object of my study. But one useful lesson I had learned. I saw that my first judgments had been inaccurate, because they had been formed from a false position. I had begun to study the East with a Western mind. . . . I resolved to throw myself among the people, and to retire as much as possible from the influence of Western associations, by departing from Western habits and society."

When Southgate left the United States he expected to be joined shortly by a physician, a Dr. Savage, but Savage decided to go to Africa instead. As no other missionary compatriot presented himself, Southgate set out from Constantinople alone at the beginning of June, 1837. As a companion and assistant he took along an Armenian named Hohannes, or John. Ordinarily Southgate dressed in native garb, but for possible use in cities he also packed a frock coat with standing collar and single breast, buttoning close to the chin, and a fez.

His route was by steamer to Trebizond, then overland to Erzurum, Lake Van, and Urmia, where he stayed with the American Board missionaries. Southgate ventured that never before had so many Americans been together in Persia at one time. After a week or so, he took the road for Tabriz. ("The reader may generally understand, when I speak of *roads,* simple footpaths, such as may be seen across pasture grounds in New England.") There he rented a house for two months. "I enjoyed tolerable comfort and quiet. The solitude only was irksome. . . . I had never as yet felt so much the burden of loneliness as now. I thought of the man who domiciliated a spider in his prison, and I did the same with a little kitten."

On September 26, 1837, Southgate and his Armenian friend John left for Teheran, Kermanshah, and Baghdad. At Kermanshah, near the Turkish (now Iraqi) border, they both fell very seriously ill. Southgate lay flat on his back for ten days in a filthy caravanserai whose owner would not even feed him. "I could not even get a little milk warmed, and during ten days tasted nothing but the half-baked bread and fresh grapes which were brought to me from the bazaars." Besides he was out of money. Just as he was beginning to despair of leaving Kermanshah alive, he found in his pocket a forgotten letter of introduction from a friend in Teheran to a merchant of Kermanshah. He was able to establish contact, got some money, and two days after Christmas left for Baghdad, becoming — it would appear — the first American ever to have traveled in what is now Iraq.

In Baghdad Southgate recuperated at the British residency for a month under the care of an English doctor. In February, 1838, he set out for Kirkuk (where he saw the so-called "eternal fire" that had burned for centuries, and still burns, in the middle of the vast oilfield discovered there in 1927),

Mosul, Mardin, Diarbekir, Samsun, and Constantinople, which he reached without further serious difficulty. By the end of 1838 he was back in the United States.[27]

Southgate traveled again to the East in 1840, having in the meantime published not only his *Narrative* but also a tract supporting the Church of England's approach to the Eastern Christian sects and criticizing the American Board, his theory being that it was better to work with local hierarchs than to undermine them. His pursuit of this policy in Constantinople with regard to the Armenians evoked an indignant reaction from Goodell, Dwight, and others of the American Board, and a tedious battle of pamphlets ensued. At home the Episcopalians backed Southgate by consecrating him a missionary bishop in 1844; but in the long run his sponsors came to the conclusion that aside from some translations they were "not aware of any other results having been accomplished, than an imperfect knowledge of the existence of the Protestant Episcopal Church, and an erroneous impression that we are on terms of communion with the 'decayed churches of the East.'" Having returned to America in 1849, Southgate declined an opportunity to become the first bishop of California and settled in as rector of a Boston church in 1852. His only other claim to fame was the publication of a novel based on his experiences in Turkey, called *The Cross above the Crescent — A Romance of Constantinople* (1878), probably the first American novel with a Middle East setting and surely one of the worst.[28]

MORE ABOUT GRANT

While the work of the mission at Urmia was progressing steadily and on the whole successfully, one of its most colorful members found life there somewhat drab. Asahel Grant, the pioneer missionary doctor, just couldn't sit still. He was happiest when he was off in the Kurdish mountains among his beloved Nestorians, surrounded by hardship and peril. The few remaining years of his turbulent life were spent in a vain effort to establish a missionary outpost in the interior. He failed partly because what he tried to do was utterly unrealistic and was viewed as folly even by his own colleagues (who on the whole were not prone to shrink from difficulty in the service of the Lord) and partly because he ran out of Nestorians, under the most cruel and sensational circumstances.

Grant felt that having a mission at Urmia was all very well, but it really did not reach the heart of the problem. He was convinced that the Kurdish mountains harbored the main body of the Nestorians, and they were ripe for plucking, in the missionary sense, if they could only be reached. He appreciated the difficulties from the outset: "The way of access to them appeared to be hedged round by the sanguinary Koords, by whom they are surrounded, and who had treacherously murdered Mr. Schultz,* the only European who had attempted to reach the Nestorian tribes." In February, 1839, Grant's enthusiasm persuaded the Board to let him try. His plan was to plunge directly westward across the Persian frontier into Kurdistan; the Board, on other advice, instructed him to take a more cautious route in a great counterclockwise semicircle through Erzurum, Diarbekir, and Mosul, on the supposition that there were Nestorians on the west side of the mountains — though, with the imperfect intelligence of the time, no one was just certain where they were to be found. Furthermore they told him he was going to have a companion,

---

* Schultz was a scientist sent out by the French Government some years before. The Kurds killed him because they thought he had struck gold. William Francis Ainsworth, *Travels and Researches in Asia Minor, Mesopotamia, Chaldea, and Armenia* (London, 1842), II, 294.

the Reverend Henry Augustus Homes, then stationed at Constantinople, who would meet him at Erzurum.

(A few words about Homes: he was almost unique among the missionaries in that he came from a wealthy Boston merchant family. His father once sent $30 to help the pious Pliny Fisk through college. Born in 1812, Homes attended Phillips Andover Academy, Amherst, Andover Theological Seminary, and Yale, where he studied medicine and divinity. A mild, bespectacled man, in Constantinople he was occupied mainly in the distribution of Bibles and tracts.[29])

Bowing to authority, Grant left for Erzurum on April 1, 1839, but while on the road he received a message that Homes was not coming after all. The brethren at Constantinople had just heard about the death of Judith Grant in January and had assumed that this tragedy would have slowed down Grant's plans to set up a permanent station in the mountains. They did not know their man; the withdrawal of Homes merely gave Grant the opportunity to suggest once more grasping the Kurdish nettle firmly — from the east. This card was promptly trumped by Constantinople, who allowed that since Grant was determined to carry on, Homes would join him after all, and would he please repair to Constantinople to talk the matter over.

Now for a man bent on Kurdistan, Constantinople was several hundred rugged miles in the wrong direction; fuming with impatience and frustration, Grant dutifully sped to Constantinople, only to find that after all Homes could not be spared for the moment. It was therefore arranged that Grant should go alone as far as Diarbekir, where he should remain until Homes could join him. This he did. Homes caught up with him in Diarbekir in July, and the pair traveled south together to Mardin, where they remained for about two months. (Homes gathered material for an article on an obscure sect, the "Yezidis of Mesopotamia," published in 1842 in the *American Biblical Repository*.) Their stay in Mardin was abruptly ended on September 6, when, wrote Grant, "the Koords of Mardin rose in insurrection, and in open day, in the court of the public palace, killed their late governor and several more of the chief men of the place, and then came with their bloody weapons to the house where Mr. Homes and myself were residing, with the avowed intention of adding us to the number of the slain! — calling out to know where we were. Most providentially, we had just left the city, and when we returned we found the gates closed to prevent the rescue or escape of any of the intended victims. . . . Seeing a great commotion within, we retired to a convent of Syrian Christians a few miles distant, where we met with a kind reception, and remained some days until the commotion subsided."

By now it had become apparent to Grant that there were no Nestorians on the western side of the mountains, just as he had maintained from the start. If the missionaries were going to find any, they would have to penetrate the mountains; and this, of course, is what Grant had been determined to do all along. At this point Homes, perhaps taking account of the fact that his head was still connected to his shoulders, opted out. He confided to Grant that he felt "called" to return to Constantinople, where he could resume his rounds as a book distributor. (He later left the mission to become American chargé d'affaires at Constantinople from 1851 to 1853. In 1854 he returned to the United States and became a librarian. He died in 1887, aged a peaceful seventy-five.)

It is hard to believe that Grant was truly sorry to see Homes go. "I yielded a cordial and cheerful acquiescence," he recalled later. "While the voice of Providence called to him to return to his station in the metropolis of Turkey" —

is there a snicker here? — "to me it seemed to cry, onward." [30]

And onward he went. Having seen Homes safely out of town, he made for Mosul and struck north for the mountains, where only two other Westerners had preceded him since the seventeenth century. His traveling companions were two Persian Nestorians, a Kurdish muleteer, and a Turkish *cavass*, or police officer, provided by the local pasha. Soon after leaving Mosul the party spent the night at a Yezidi village. "The accommodations which the village afforded were of the poorest kind; and, to avoid the vermin of the houses, we spread our carpets in the open street, and after a social chat and a mess of pottage, made of sour buttermilk and herbs boiled together, I lay down under the broad canopy of heaven."

Riding on a mule, Grant entered the country of the mountain Nestorians on October 15, 1839.* Providentially, the Kurdish chief who had murdered Schultz was ill with a fever, which Grant was able to cure; the chief gratefully presented him with a horse. Grant also stayed five weeks as a guest of the Nestorian patriarch and received on departure "a pair of scarlet *shahwars*, the wide trousers of the country, trimmed with silk, and one of the ancient manuscripts of his library." The patriarch's spinster sister Helena bestowed an even more personal gift on the dashing young widower from the New World: "a pair of warm mittens, made by her own hands from the soft goat's hair of the country." [31] Doubtless a romantic figure, Asahel Grant.

He got back to Urmia in time for Christmas, and shortly before the death of his infant, motherless daughters. "It was a great comfort to him," wrote Thomas Laurie, apparently

* The recent assertion that apparently no American visited this region before 1915 overlooks Grant. See C. J. Edmunds, *Kurds, Turks and Arabs* (London, 1957), p. 27n.

without irony, "to be with them during their sickness; and Providence kindly ordered that it should not occur during his absence in the mountains. Is not missionary experience full of such mercies?"

Whatever Grant himself may have thought of this rhetorical question, he shortly decided to take his four-year-old son, Henry, back to the United States and leave him. But even with Henry in tow he could not forbear to revisit his beloved mountains and the friendly patriarch. Henry was carried in a kind of sling lashed to one of the horses. Occasionally he would fall off into the snow, but this apparently did him no great harm, for on October 3, 1840, he and his father reached Boston, where Henry had his first chance to get acquainted with his two older half brothers. In some ways the reunion was a disappointment. Laurie hinted at the difficulty: "It is one of the sorest trials attendant on the separation of the missionary from his children, that, while his heart yearns after them, they learn to regard him as a stranger, and transfer to others the affection that, of right, is his." (Could not an unfriendly critic suggest that the missionary had in some measure forfeited such "rights" by opting for separation?) Grant found separate homes for his three boys in Utica, Clinton, and New York City "and made provision, from his own scanty funds, for their liberal education, hoping that one day God would bring them to share his missionary labors." The publication of his book, *The Nestorians*, "yielded him a small income, at a time when, but for the aid thus afforded him, he might have been compelled to return and provide otherwise for the support of his children." [32]

MISSION AT MOSUL

In America Grant found an eager audience for his theories about the mountain Nestorians as a missionary target, and indeed he was so successful that within weeks he had induced the American Board to open a new mission station at Mosul. On January 18, 1841, Abel K. Hinsdale and Colby C. Mitchell and their wives embarked for Smyrna to start operations. Grant himself left for Kurdistan in April. His plans were to join the two new couples in Aleppo for the ride across the desert to Mosul, but reports reached him that Syria was so unsettled that they were likely to be detained there for some time. He decided that his summer would be better spent in the mountains preparing the way for them. July found him again the guest of the Nestorian patriarch.

In the meantime, however, the Syrian political situation had eased, and at the end of May the Mitchells and the Hinsdales reached Aleppo, where they checked in with the American consular agent, Chevalier Durighello, and joined a caravan at Aleppo bound for Mosul.[33] A month later, not far from their destination, Mitchell died of some unnamed fever. It was reported that he went out during a sirocco and came back complaining that he could not see distinctly. An emetic relieved him somewhat, but the next morning he was evidently deranged. A helpful German traveling companion named Kotschy bled him without much success. He died at two in the morning on June 27, 1841. In the boiling Syrian desert at midsummer, it now proved impossible — because of local religious prejudice — to bury Mitchell's body. So Hinsdale lashed it across a horse and carried it for five hours to a place called Telabel, where the natives were said to be more agreeable. Anyone interested in the details of Mitchell's illness, death, and ultimate burial (complete with the dimensions of the coffin) may satisfy his curiosity by digging up Thomas Laurie's ghoulish account. Even if one makes every possible allowance, it is still curious that such minute and morbid details should have been thought suitable for exposure in the homes of pious American gentlefolk through the missionary press of the day.

A few days later the grieving Widow Mitchell fell ill, and before long the Board had another martyr to disease. The meticulous Mr. Laurie told the story:

The next morning [July 1, 1841] Mrs. Mitchell was so ill, they had to stop, after only one hour's ride, at Bowerea. There, for four days, she lay in one of its mud-hovels, among Arabs so rude they could not be kept out of the sick-room; and in it laid hands on whatever they fancied, before the very eyes of those who could not resist them. Even the women cut off the hooks-and-eyes from the dress of Mrs. Hinsdale, while busy with her suffering companion. As anything seemed preferable to such quarters, they left on the evening of the 4th, Mr. Hinsdale having had to send to a distant village, ere he could find men willing, for any price, to carry the litter he had prepared for Mrs. Mitchell; and often after, she had to be laid in the road, while he rode far and near to find four men willing to perform what they deemed the degrading service of carrying a woman. It was now so hot they were obliged to travel by night; and as, during the day, Mrs. Hinsdale was much occupied with her sick associate, she was often so drowsy on horseback that her husband had to walk by her side, to prevent her falling. Three years afterwards, she pointed out to the writer a place on the road where, wrapped in her cloak on the ground, she snatched half an hour's sleep at midnight, amid Arabs clamoring for money, and yet unwilling to earn it by carrying Mrs. Mitchell.

The party was welcomed in Mosul on July 7 by Mr. and Mrs. Rassam, the English vice-consul and his wife. "For a day or two Mrs. Mitchell seemed to improve; . . . but soon her disease took a new form, and from that time till her death, on the 12th, reason was dethroned. . . . Mr. Hinsdale, who had watched with Mrs. Mitchell till he fainted in attempting to walk from one room to another, was taken violently ill before her death, and was not able to leave his bed till August. Mrs. Hinsdale, at the same time, was too ill to render him any assistance."

About a month later, word of the death of the Mitchells reached Grant — still in the mountains — and he hastened belatedly to Mosul to attend to the ailing Hinsdales. Hinsdale was well enough to join him on a three-week trip to the mountains in November, but thereafter the three Americans spent the winter together in Mosul, organizing a school for Jacobite Christians.

By the following June Grant's foot was itching again, and off he went for Urmia, swinging around eastward through Erbil and Ruwanduz. (He wanted to go straight through the mountains, but even he had to concede they were temporarily too unsafe.) At Urmia he conferred with the brethren and finally got clearance to set up a mission station at Ashitha, an important Nestorian settlement right in the heart of the mountains, a few miles north of Amadia near the present Turkish-Iraqi border. William Stocking of the Urmia mission started out with him, but got ill and had to return to Urmia, leaving Grant to go on by himself.[34]

MISSION IN KURDISTAN

At Ashitha Grant bought a small hill for $8 and got permission from the local emir to build a house. (He was criticized later by Austen Layard, the noted British archaeologist, for his selection of this site: "These buildings had been the cause of much jealousy and suspicion among the Kurds. They stand upon the summit of an isolated hill, commanding the whole valley. A position less ostentatious and proportions more modest might certainly have been chosen.")[35] Hinsdale joined him in October to help with the construction, leaving his wife in charge of the school at Mosul. Their reception at Ashitha was favorable on the whole, but Grant ran into some unexpected problems connected with the building work: "Men of all ranks quarreled with each other for employment in the severest drudgery. If he [Grant] hired those who had brought timber gratis, all were ready to carry heavy beams for nothing one day, for the sake of ten cents daily wages the rest of the week; and at one time so serious was the uproar, he had to dismiss the whole, retire to Lezan [several miles away], and refuse to come back again till they were quiet."

In November, 1842, the Reverend Thomas Laurie and his wife, both very ill, arrived at Mosul to replace the lamented Mitchells. The following month Hinsdale, who by now had returned to Mosul, leaving Grant at Ashitha, died of typhoid. He was buried near Mrs. Mitchell in the court of the Jacobite church. Grant, the nearest doctor, arrived in Mosul too late to treat him. Impatient to finish building the mission house at Ashitha, he nevertheless spent the winter of 1842–43 at Mosul with the Lauries and the Widow Hinsdale.

Also in residence was the Reverend George Percy Badger of the Church of England, who was under explicit instructions to hinder the work of the Americans by pointing out to the local higher clergy how their own interests were being endangered by the antihierarchical tenets of the Board missionaries. Having been encouraged by the Episcopalian Bishop Southgate in Constantinople (whose Anglican blood seems to have proved thicker than his American in this case), Badger decided to snub Grant and his colleagues, and he ostentatiously declined to return their social calls. This pained him; but, as he explained, "I had a duty to perform for the Church." He did, however, condescend to let Dr. Grant treat his ailments, and the Americans forgivingly turned out for Badger's mother's funeral.[36]

Grant returned to Ashitha again in April, 1843, this time with Laurie, who vividly described their new house: "We occupied one room in common, whose walls were built of stone, laid up in mud. This last was left squeezing out between them, like plaster on the inside of laths. The earthen floor was *almost* as smooth as a muddy road after a hard frost. In the middle of this was a heap of earth, shaped like a tray, where we built our fire. Here all the cooking was done, within some five feet of our beds. These, which served also for seats by day, consisted, first, of a layer of millet-straw, to mitigate the roughness of the floor, extending a little beyond our mattresses, so as to keep us out of the dirt. These last were home-made, and stuffed with mountain wool. A quilt apiece and our Turkish cloaks made all cosey at night, and our saddlebags answered very well for pillows. We wrote with our portfolios on our knees, our ink-bottles in our hands, and various little articles deposited, for want of shelves, on the projecting stones of the wall behind us. Our wood was piled up in one corner, where it was thrown down by the men who brought it nearly a day's journey on their backs. Our bags of meal, earthen pots, and a goat-skin of honey the doctor had laid in for the winter, occupied another. Though there was no chimney, we found no inconvenience from the smoke, for, let the wind blow from whatever quarter it would, there was a place for the one to enter, and a second for the other to get out. . . . This was the only room then finished, though the plan embraced a building for the residence of three mission families, sixty feet square, besides a chapel, school-room, stables, etc."

Grant and Laurie found that their house soon became a general meeting place for idlers: "There was no being alone, even in our own house. Sometimes a visitor would take his siesta quite at his ease." These visitors, welcome as they may have been from the missionary standpoint, brought vermin: "However laboriously we rid our clothes of tormentors at night, fresh recruits were always ready for the vacant places."

About this time, the ever-ebullient Grant began to get a bit discouraged about the future of the mission. He wrote to a colleague at Urmia: "I hardly know what to say. Clouds and darkness are round about, and we can see light only by looking up. Perhaps my ill health adds gloominess to the view." Friends advised him to abandon the effort and return home, appealing mainly on behalf of his motherless boys in America. These appeals he resisted to the bitter end: "So long as I am able to labor here," he wrote in the spring of 1843, "I have no wish to return." In January, 1844, he received a letter from his eldest son, Hastings, "begging me to return, 'for the sake of his younger brothers.' I do hope yet to be allowed to stay till I see a work of grace among the dear Nestorians." [37]

But the days of the mountain Nestorians were numbered. The Kurds, with the acquiescence of the Turkish authorities, launched a two-pronged attack from east and west to annihilate them. Grant, in the middle and aware of what was happening, vainly did what he could to get the invaders to reconsider. But he himself was becoming unpopular, not only as a friend of the Nestorians, but also as a literate foreign observer who might live to tell the tale of what was about to happen. He had also neglected to clear his missionary designs with the Porte, which regarded him with great suspicion as encouraging separatism. Soon it became apparent that he could stay at Ashitha only at the risk of being massacred with the rest. With the greatest reluctance he abandoned Ashitha on July 7, 1843; he reached Mosul a week later, having traveled furtively by night through the invaders' lines.

Meanwhile, back in Constantinople, the Ottoman Foreign Minister turned down requests of two other missionaries (Edwin Bliss and Azariah Smith) to visit the Kurdish mountains. The Porte based its refusal on disapproval of Grant's activities, especially the school he proposed to build. But John P. Brown, the American chargé d'affaires, later realized that the real reason was that the extermination campaign was underway, and no witnesses were welcome. Once the slaughter had begun, the Nestorians, split among themselves and confused by the Anglican-Congregationalist rivalry fostered by Badger, offered no effective resistance. Eight hundred of them were slain in the first engagement, and these were only the first of many thousands. At the end of the bloody massacre, "the ugliest which the Nestorians of Kurdistan had experienced since the ravages of Timur Lang," the mountain Nestorians were either dead, starving, or scattered to the four winds. Grant's new house at Ashitha was occupied by a garrison of Turks, and was rudely rebuilt to serve military needs. Grant tried to look on the bright side: "Let us have the great consolation that we have been instrumental, in some measure, of awakening an interest and spirit of prayer for them." But despite these brave words his spirit was now finally broken. Much as he wanted to return to the mountains, he now realized it was out of the question. In any case, he finally admitted, "to return there is in no ways inviting to flesh and blood. All the romance of that field — if there ever were any — is now sober reality. There is no poetry in winding your weary way over rocks and cliffs, drifted snows or dashing torrents. . . . Families cannot live in the existing insecurity. . . . I frankly confess that, when in peril, the thought that, should I fall, many will only say, 'I told you so,' and hand down my dishonored memory as the only heritage of my children, and an injury to the cause of Christ, has caused me much distress. But be it so." [38]

Grant never conceded that in kindling false hopes of autonomy among the mountain Nestorians he himself undoubtedly hastened the disaster. A British missionary closely associated with Badger, William Francis Ainsworth, who had followed Grant's first trail through the mountains sowing seeds of doubt about the Americans, at least had seen what was coming several years before. Noting in 1840 that the Nestorian patriarch had been imprisoned by a Kurdish chieftain jealous of the competing favors the patriarch was receiving from the British and the American missionaries, Ainsworth wrote, rather humbly, "As far as I am concerned, I extremely regret that the mission I was engaged in should have hastened [this] catastrophe. . . . This sudden interest, so explicitly and so actively shown on the part of other Christian nations towards a tribe of people, who have almost solely prolonged their independent existence on account of their remote seclusion and comparative insignificance, has called them forth into new importance in the eyes of the Mohammedans, and will undoubtedly be the first step in their overthrow. . . . It will be the most cruel thing imaginable, to have excited so much attention from surrounding powers towards the condition of these able, courageous and pious mountaineers, only to leave them to the tender mercies of the Mohammedans." [39]

And this, of course, is exactly what happened three years after Ainsworth's prophetic words were written.

DENOUEMENT

By now the Mosul group was thoroughly demoralized, and more tragedy was in store. Young Mrs. Laurie died on

December 16, 1843. (Her husband gave the world a graphic description of her final illness, including the "rattling in her throat.") Grant himself died on April 24, 1844, of typhus brought into his house by Nestorian refugees. A child of the Hinsdales, curiously christened Abel Abdullah, was born in Mosul and was buried there early in 1844. On October 22, 1844, the Mosul survivors — the widowed and childless Mrs. Hinsdale; the widowed Mr. Laurie; and Dr. Azariah Smith, who had arrived the previous year — straggled away for good, and the mission was "suspended." (Mosul was reopened in 1849 as a mission to the Assyrians.)[40]

Of the eight Americans who had been involved in the Mosul enterprise, if one excludes the Hinsdale baby, five had died there. Of the three survivors, Azariah Smith died at Aintab, in northern Syria, seven years later, and Laurie was so broken in health at the age of twenty-three that he was "unable to resume his labors." The hardy Mrs. Hinsdale became a teacher in a school for children of American missionaries in Constantinople and stayed there until 1855.

Laurie himself did not consider the mortality rate unduly discouraging. Writing of the role of women in missionary work, he commented: "The facts, instead of discouraging woman from engaging in the work, encourage her to go forward; for, while out of five men only one survives, only two women died out of three." [41] With this exercise in statistical optimism we may well take leave of the Reverend William Laurie.

9. *East of Suez*

TODAY WE ARE APT TO THINK of the Middle East, however defined, as something of a geographical unit. During the first half of the nineteenth century, however, and in fact until the Suez Canal was opened in 1869, the Mediterranean and the Levant were physically and psychologically very remote from the Red Sea, Arabia, and the Persian Gulf. For the British, indeed, this separation was the essence of the "Eastern Question": India on one side and England on the other. With the creaky Ottomans and their unpredictable vassals astride the only two conceivable land routes (through Mesopotamia on the one hand and across the Isthmus of Suez on the other), communications with Britain's Asiatic dominions proceeded mainly by the Cape of Good Hope.

The problems of the British, of course, do not especially concern us here. What is significant for our purpose is that this separation implied a distinct split among the Americans in contact with what we know now as the Middle East. Today Dhahran, Basra, and Aden are but a few airline hours from Cairo, Beirut, or Istanbul, and a person concerned with any of them is at least aware of them all. In earlier times the Americans who knew both sides were rather rare. There were, for instance, no American missionaries in the Arabian peninsula until about 1892, though (as we have seen) the Levant and even northern Persia and Mesopotamia were "occupied" sixty or seventy years earlier. It is disappointing to find that there were no Americans among the early explorers of the Arabian peninsula.

The first contacts with the eastern part of the Arab world were actually a by-product of the China trade, in which American merchants had established a relatively strong position by the beginning of the nineteenth century. The best route to China from the eastern seaboard of the United States lay via the Cape of Good Hope, and some enterprising Yankee merchants could not overlook the profit opportunities along the way.

The fact that a Salem clergyman and poet named William Bentley was exchanging letters in Arabic with Arab scholars as early as 1805 is not without interest in itself. But the fact that his correspondents were residents of the Red Sea coffee port of Mocha is equally significant: Salem was deeply involved in the coffee trade. English naval officers used to allow that if there were a bag of coffee hanging over the middle of hell, any Yankee skipper would sell his soul to the devil to get it. Disregarding the mixture of malice and envy behind this hyperbole, it is true that American merchants would load coffee at Mocha and haul it some thirteen thousand miles around the Cape back to Smyrna, often realizing as much as three hundred percent for their pains! Among the first was a Salem trader named Elias Hasket Derby, Junior, who picked up a cargo of Mocha coffee for Smyrna as early as 1788.[1]

In 1805 the Salem brig *Essex* arrived with $60,000 in cash with which to buy Mocha coffee. Captain Orne, its master, was persuaded by one Mohammed Akil to accept the latter's services as a guide for a short run up the coast to Hodeida. Akil put thirty of his men aboard the *Essex* to help with the navigation, and tagged along in his own ship. On signal the slaughter began. Except for a ten-year-old cabin boy, John Hermann Poll, the entire crew was murdered. The *Essex* was plundered and burned. "The headless corpse of Capt. Orne and the mutilated remains of a merchant floated on shore and were decently buried." What happened to Poll, the cabin boy, is not entirely clear. According to one account he was kept as a slave until 1812, when he died. On the other hand an English traveler named Cruttendon claimed to have seen him about 1836 in Dhofar; Poll, said Cruttendon, had matured, become a Muslim, and was living peacefully in the drab village of Salalah with his wife, a local girl. Cruttendon said Poll was American, but another version of the story makes him Dutch; either way, he had a more bewildering introduction to the Middle East than he had bargained for when he signed on.[2]

American trade with Mocha persisted at least into the 1830's. A merchant from Roxbury, Massachusetts, was living there in 1834.[3] The American consul at Cairo, George Gliddon, reported in 1837: "The trade with the wild nations of the interior of Africa, and the whale fishery on the African and Arabian coasts, is carried on by American vessels to an extent but little appreciated, excepting by a few merchants of certain cities of the United States, who keep their profitable business a profound secret. To use the words of a highly scientific traveler and experienced British officer of the East India Company's marine service, . . . 'go where you will, on the wildest shores of Africa, from Madagascar to the Persian Gulf, there is hardly a petty harbor or sheltered bay large enough to admit a square-rigged craft, but you will find a Yankee boiling his oil, repairing his vessel, or in a tent planted on shore, driving a hard bargain with the natives'." [4]

As in Turkey, the flag followed trade in Eastern Arabia. In 1833 the United States became the first Western nation to enter into a commercial treaty with the formidable Sultan of Muscat, absolute ruler over the arid and forbidding eastern hook of the Arabian peninsula. But this event took place almost entirely through the energetic initiative of a frustrated Portsmouth shipowner named Edmund Roberts. His main interest was in Zanzibar, halfway down the east African coast, which was then under the Sultan's control; American cottons shipped to Zanzibar found a ready market in Persia, where they were considered superior to English fabrics. Trade with Zanzibar in this era was dominated by the Americans; over a period from September, 1832, to May, 1834, thirty-two out of the forty-one foreign ships that called there were from the United States, and of these twenty were out of Salem. The main exports were copal gum and ivory, though many observers also inferred a "blacker trade." As Gliddon noted, only a few American shippers were in on the secrets of the Zanzibar trade; one of the keys to success was getting along with the Sultan of Muscat, and it is no coincidence that the only known portrait of him now hangs in the Peabody Museum at Salem. [5]

Edmund Roberts was a supercargo on the brig *Mary Ann* when she called at Zanzibar in 1827. Suspecting that he was being diddled by the local authorities, he went over their heads and wrote a letter to the Sultan. After setting forth his complaints in detail, Roberts invited His Highness to enter into correspondence with the American Government. He suggested, in fact, that the Sultan might be interested in a treaty with the United States, which among other things would settle definitely the manner in which American merchantmen should be received and the charges to which they should be subjected.[6]

Said bin Sultan, the ruler of Muscat, was an extraordinary man. Born in 1791, he rose to power at the age of fifteen by the expedient of stabbing to death his leading rival, a Wahhabi from the Arabian interior, during an otherwise friendly conversation. The Persian Gulf was highly significant to both the British and the French during the Napoleonic Wars, when it began to look as though Bonaparte might attack India from his new foothold in Egypt. Both Powers made diplomatic approaches to him; the wily young Sultan succeeded in avoiding any commitment until he could back the winner. At last in 1817 (the French threat having receded) the British East India Company won Said's support during an attack on some troublesome pirates operating out of the island of Kishm in the straits of Hormuz, which guard the entrance to the Persian Gulf. The total victory that resulted led to the political jigsaw known as the Trucial Coast, the beginning of direct British political intervention in the Persian Gulf by means of treaties of truce (hence "Trucial") with the local chieftains. Said was rewarded the following year by British assistance in wiping out some miscellaneous rebels. Now, at the age of thirty, the Sultan found himself "the undisputed master of his country. . . . He extended over Oman a unified and undisputed power such as it had not hitherto known." His international influence grew. In 1824 he achieved great éclat by taking the pilgrimage to Mecca in his own ship of the line, the seventy-four-gun *Liverpool*, whose provenance can be inferred from its name. Two years later he mounted a naval expedition to collect an alleged debt from the Turkish pasha at Basra, returning not only with his money but also the pasha as a prisoner. In the late 1820's he also extended his sway to Zanzibar, where Arab merchants had been settled for some time. His rule, though somewhat shaky, was well enough established for Edmund Roberts to appeal to him as the final authority.[7]

Sultan Said's reply was encouraging but evasive; he asked Roberts to furnish him with ammunition and other military goods for use against the Portuguese, whom he was finding troublesome at the moment. Roberts, of course, was in no position to accommodate him, but his persistent Yankee foot was in the door. After returning to the United States Roberts approached his good friend, Levi Woodbury, a New Hampshire Senator, and broached the subject of a treaty. By the best of good fortune, in 1829 Woodbury was appointed Andrew Jackson's first Secretary of the Navy and was in an excellent position to help out his friend Roberts. Early in 1832 Roberts was made a special agent of the United States Government to negotiate a treaty with the Sultan. He was assigned as "secretary to the commander" of the U.S.S. *Peacock,* a cover for his highly secret diplomatic mission. (The commander cooperated in the subterfuge almost to excess, assigning Roberts to a very inferior sleeping space on the gun deck.) Roberts took along gifts for the Sultan: a sword, a rifle, a pair of pistols, two pairs of glass lamps, a silk flag, a map of the United States, and a complete collector's set of American coins. He had wanted to bring more: a railroad steam engine together with a miniature track that could be screwed to the floor of the Sultan's palace, but these treasures were not ready when the *Peacock* was set to sail and had to be left behind. Just how His Highness would have bolted a railroad into the stony floor of an eastern Arabian fortress was apparently not considered, but other gifts to Oriental rulers in the nineteenth century were equally incongruous: some years later good Queen Victoria, upon hearing that Sultan Said had to sleep on the ground, thoughtfully sent him out a large brass bedstead of the best English quality. (In the 1960's a British oil company gave a Trucial Coast ruler a solid-gold working model of an offshore drilling platform, which is said to have promptly disappeared into the ruler's harem.)

The *Peacock* sailed by way of the Far East, where Roberts stopped in Siam to sign another treaty in which he was interested. The mission reached Muscat in the summer of 1833, and the treaty was signed on September 21. Its main provisions dealt with most-favored-nation treatment on tariffs and extraterritorial jurisdiction for consuls in cases involving American citizens. A mishap on the party's arrival in Muscati waters accounts for one of the treaty's unusual features. The *Peacock* had suffered the indignity of running onto a shoal near the coast. Cargo and guns had to be jettisoned, and a number of American seamen found themselves cast ashore in the desert wilderness of Oman. The Sultan, learning from Roberts of the disaster, saw to the salvage. His insistence on paying for it, as well as for the expenses of repatriating the sailors, is reflected in the picturesque Article V of the treaty, which provides that "If any vessel of the United States shall suffer shipwreck on any part of the Sultan's Dominions, the persons escaping from the wreck shall be taken care of and hospitably entertain'd at the expense of the Sultan, until they shall find an opportunity to be return'd to their country — for the Sultan can never receive any remuneration for rendering succour to the distress'd. . . ." As further token of his good will, the Sultan tried to get the Americans to accept several of his fine Arabian horses as a personal gift for President Andrew Jackson. Perhaps mindful of the fate of a similar gift from the Sultan of Turkey to Charles Rhind only three years before (see Chapter 3), the Americans gracefully declined, pleading lack of space aboard the *Peacock*.

Edmund Roberts returned to the United States in May, 1834, and the Muscat treaty, as well as the one with Siam, was ratified on June 30. The following March Roberts was commissioned to exchange ratifications with Muscat and Siam. This time he went first to Muscat, successfully completed his mission, and headed across the Indian Ocean for Siam. He took sick in Bangkok and died in Macao on June 12, 1836, at the age of fifty-two.[8]

The Sultan became a devoted admirer of the United States.* As related in Chapter 1, he created a tremendous stir in New York in 1840 by sending his own ship on a goodwill mission. This was the first — and for a very long time the only — Arab vessel to cross the Atlantic.[9]

Although a certain small trade developed with Muscat proper, the merchants of Salem remained mainly interested in Zanzibar. The Roberts treaty inspired a New York firm, Scoville and Britton, to establish agencies at both Zanzibar and Muscat.[10] American consuls were stationed at Muscat from time to time, but it was not a rewarding assignment. In 1913 Consul Homer Brett wrote to the State Department: "The total result of six years of effort along trade promotion lines . . . has been the selling of two motor boats and two small pumps, none of which, owing to the mechanical ignorance of the natives, gives satisfactory service. . . . There has not been an American vessel in Muscat harbor since the year 1897, and previous to that there was not one after 1855. . . . It is respectfully submitted that two years of practically enforced idleness is not good training for one beginning a consular career." [11] The consulate was closed in 1915.

---

* An American brass twenty-four-pound gun, dated 1842, was observed guarding the Omani fortress at Buraimi in 1875. It was said to have been one of twenty procured by Sultan Said for one of his warships. S. B. Miles, *The Countries and Tribes of the Persian Gulf* (London, 1919), II, 536.

> Our whole consular system is radically wrong, disreputable, and injurious to our character and interests. . . . The American arms are blazoned on the doors, and the American flag is waving over the houses, of Greeks, Italians, Jews, and Arabs, and all the mongrel population of that inland sea.
>
> — *John Lloyd Stephens*[1]

10. The Official American Presence

IT IS NOT NECESSARY to reproduce all of Stephens' rhetoric to indicate how displeased he was with the American consuls he ran into during the course of his travels in the East. Except for David Offley at Smyrna and John Brown at Constantinople, none of them was an American citizen. But in fairness to Commodore Porter, who had made or authorized the appointments, there simply were no Americans available for these unpaid posts. For Salonica Porter named B. W. Llewellyn, a resident Welshman, "a man of observation and fond of writing." In Egypt he was fortunate to find the British father-and-son team, John and George Gliddon. (See Chapter 6.) But for the rest Porter had no choice but to turn to the locals whom Stephens so disparaged. Before long he had consuls reporting to him from such places as Beirut,

Crete, Cyprus, Aleppo, and Bursa. At Bursa, for example, there was one Nicholas Luca Perrich; even the ubiquitous British had no consul at Bursa at the time. Perrich had no commercial duties whatever to perform, but his presence was appreciated by the American missionary families there, the first of whom arrived in 1834. Porter even thought about setting up consulates at Mocha and Trebizond, but he never got around to it.[2]

The Turks, incidentally, took a while to reciprocate. The first appointment of a Turkish consul in the United States came in 1845. He was Tigbee Oglu Abraham, a merchant already settled in Boston.[3]

Beyond the consuls themselves, there were the consular agents in such places as Jaffa, Sidon, and Tyre. These, like most of the consuls who nominated them, were invariably unpaid local merchants delighted at the prestige and "protection" (mainly exemption from certain Ottoman taxes) attached to their positions. "The office," wrote Stephens indignantly, "is coveted as a means of protecting the holder against the liabilities to his own government, and of revenue by selling that protection to others." * Indeed, when the United States was thinking of setting up a consular agency at Damietta in the Nile delta in 1837, two local merchants each offered $1000 for the post; both were rejected as unsuitable. Several times Porter recommended that the State Department should at least reimburse the consuls for their expenses, which he estimated in the order of $300 a year apiece, but for many years nothing was done about paying them.**

---

* The first appointee at Jaffa was David Darmon, a Frenchman recommended by an American traveler, Colonel Mendes Cohen of Baltimore. Porter dismissed Darmon in 1835 after hearing complaints that "he sells the protection of our flag for *money*."

** When Consul David W. Offley died at Smyrna in 1846, the following inventory was made of his exiguous personal effects: 9 shirts, 11 summer

Finally in 1855 Congress provided that all consuls had to be American citizens and were to be paid regular salaries.[4]

In places where not even one of these "petty vagabonds" (Stephens' phrase) could be found to serve, Americans continued to rely for assistance on British officials, who generally had authority to accommodate them and were quite willing to do so.* This was notably true in Jerusalem, to which American travelers were flocking in increasing numbers. In 1844 Porter's successor as U.S. minister, Dabney Carr, was startled to learn of the arrival in the Holy City of Warder Cresson from Philadelphia, who claimed to have been appointed consul in Washington before his departure, though there was no record of such an appointment. Carr thought he was "deranged" and ignored him. Cresson "resigned" with a flourish in 1846. Ten years later John Warren Gorham became the first bona fide American consul in Jerusalem.[5]

Others besides Stephens were highly critical of native consuls and consular agents. Passing through the Dardanelles in 1831, James De Kay reported: "The American flag was the only one not exhibited. We were afterward informed that we have a consul here, but he was too poor to purchase a flag. He is a respectable Jew, with twenty-five children, and his consular fees amount to about six dollars per annum. It need scarcely be added that he has no salary. His official rank is, however, very great, and he enjoys the inestimable privilege of strutting the dirty streets of this village with his twenty-five children all clad in yellow slippers." Probably an ap-

trousers, 2 half-uniform tail coats, 1 black dress coat, 1 uniform and white trousers (which had belonged to his father, consul before him), a cocked hat, a sword, 38 books, a guitar, and 1 Bible.

* It has recently been asserted that American missionaries were frequently called upon by the Government to act as part-time consuls. William R. Polk, "A Decade of Discovery: America in the Middle East 1947–1958," *St. Antony's Papers No. 11, Middle Eastern Affairs, Number Two* (London, 1961), p. 50. This never occurred during the period covered herein.

pointee of the treaty negotiators the previous year, this man was soon dismissed by Porter, who replaced him with Marino Lazzaro, a surgeon employed by the Turkish Government. N. P. Willis wrote in 1833: "Our consul of the Dardanelles [Lazzaro] is an Armenian. He is absent just now, in search of a runaway female slave of the Sultan's; and his wife, a gracious Italian, full of movement and hospitality, does the honors of the house in his absence. He is a physician as well as consul and slave-catcher." (Porter himself provides corroboration for this ironic aside; he authorized Lazzaro to leave his post to pursue the slave, as a favor to the Sultan.) As usual, however, the final word on the consular situation at the Dardanelles can be left to Stephens: "The consuls in these little places are originals. They have nothing to do, but they have the government arms blazoned over their doors, and strut about in cocked hats and regimentals, and shake their heads, and look knowing, and talk about their governments." [6]

For a long time the consular agent at Jaffa, the main port for Palestine, was Murad Aroutin, a rich Armenian who spoke no English. In his house in 1844, wrote the American naval officer, Francis Schroeder, "the American eagle and shield were emblazoned on the wall, and prints of General Jackson and Mr. Van Buren, and a map of the United States decorated the salon. . . . He showed me an album in which are inscribed the names of all Americans who have been in Jaffa during his consulate." The map was a gift from Stephens, who had passed through eight years before. [7]

The weary scholar, Edward Robinson, was really quite blunt about the consular agent at Tyre, one Yakub Akkad: "We were received by him with great hospitality and kindness; and were at once quartered in the largest and best parlor, which we were to occupy by day and by night. But it is a part of oriental hospitality never to leave a guest alone; so

that we were really incommoded, by what was meant as
kindness and respect. We were hungry, and would have eaten;
weary, and would have rested; I felt myself unwell, and
would gladly have lain down for repose; but every thing of
this kind was out of the question. Our host could not think
of leaving us; his neighbors and friends came in to sit with
him and pay their respects to his visitors from a remote world;
his mother also made us a regular visit, and sat with us for
some time. . . . As dinner had been early announced, we
waited with some impatience for its appearance. But we
waited long in vain; and not until 9 o'clock at evening were
we summoned to partake of it. Here too a shabby imitation of
the Frank style was anything but welcome. As having often
to do with Franks, our host had procured a long clumsy table,
and several coarse chairs to be used with it. This was set in
an adjacent room, with plates and rusty knives and forks.
The dishes and cookery were Syrian, with a miserable red
wine, the poorest we tasted in the country. The agent and
his brother partook with us; but waiting and weariness prevented enjoyment; and we were glad to break up as speedily
as possible. We spread our own beds upon the carpet of our
parlor; and I wished myself most heartily back again upon
the ground beneath our tent." [8]

Commodore Porter himself recognized that such local types
were not as satisfactory as American citizens would have
been. "They do not always feel and act like Americans," he
wrote ruefully in 1834, "and it sometimes requires my utmost
vigilance to keep them within the bounds of prudence and
discretion and prevent them from usurping more advantages
than are permitted by treaty, and causing complaints from
the local authorities." But rather than strengthening the consular corps, in 1840 the State Department went just the other
way: orders went out to Porter to close down all the con-

sulates except those in Constantinople, Smyrna, and Alexandria, on the ground that they were "not productive of any public advantage." Porter was instructed to tell the Porte that no political motive should be attached to the action, and he later reported that the Foreign Ministry had taken the news very calmly.

At this late date it is hard to fathom why this step was taken: surely the consuls and agents were little or no drain on the revenue. Perhaps, after all, Washington took to heart the criticisms by American travelers that had been drifting home over the years and simply decided to do away with these sources of potential embarrassment. Porter, to his credit, resisted the move. "I much fear our citizens in the East will feel the want of consular protection," he wrote, "unless consular agents are permitted as formerly. They will be obliged to resort to the humiliating alternative of British consular protection, as was the case before we had a treaty with Turkey." [9]

The abolition of the consulate at Beirut created a particular stir. Beirut at the time was occupied by some 25,000 troops of Mohammed Ali — Egyptians, Turks, and Albanians — many of whom were insulting to the Franks and sometimes committed atrocities upon them. "The houses and churches round the gardens of Beyrout have been all plundered and destroyed," the missionaries wrote with alarm. "We continue still in a state of siege, the insurgents in large numbers occupy the Pines to the south of Beyrout, about 15 minutes from the city [to the modern traveler: on the way to the airport], and the river of Beyrout to the East, about 15 minutes distance, so that we can hardly find any meat, bread or vegetables of bad quality and at enormous prices." Missionary William Thomson warned: "This act of our government will involve every American citizen residing in Syria in perplexity and embarrassment. . . . Our very existence in the country has of late depended upon the efficiency of consular authority." Consul Jasper Chasseaud, his personal position at stake, backed up Thomson and added his distinctive note of bathos: "I cannot even look upon the portrait of Washington or the Declaration of Independence which decorate my parlor, without painful regret."

So, with a certain degree of unwonted constructive independence, Porter on his own initiative retained Chasseaud as consular agent (he could not be "consul" any more, as his commission had been revoked from Washington); and in due course Porter's action was endorsed by the State Department. In the meantime the missionaries took their troubles to the American Board in Boston. Pressure was put on President Van Buren to restore the Beirut consulate to its previous status. Early in 1842 Porter received instructions to this effect and also to recommend where else in Syria consulates might be useful. Chasseaud got his appointment back on August 12, 1842.[10]

Jasper Chasseaud, as a matter of fact, got along much better with the American missionaries at Beirut than he did with the ministers at Constantinople to whom he reported. As soon as the Turkish treaty was signed in 1830 he was encouraged by the missionaries to write to Washington asking for the consular appointment. Of indeterminate nationality (sometimes he seemed French, sometimes British, sometimes quite Levantine), Chasseaud explained to the Secretary of State that he had lived in the East for seven years and that his uncle was Peter Abbott, the British consul (whose widow later married William Thomson). All this sounded good to the State Department, which authorized Porter to make him a consular agent. When word of this reached Chasseaud on April 1, 1832, his first official act was to fire himself a twenty-one-gun salute, there being no vessel in the harbor at the time to which he could apply for this honor. Indeed, this was only the first of many signs that the appointment had gone to his head. So zealous was he in the protection of his missionary charges that Porter complained to Washington, "I am kept in constant alarm lest he should do something that may involve me in difficulty with the Government." (Porter conceded, however, that Chasseaud was a very respectable person and much of a gentleman in his deportment.) One specific object of Chasseaud's enthusiasm was to try to secure extraterritorial protection for servants of American citizens, a practice frowned upon by many seasoned diplomats in the Empire, including John Gliddon. When Beirut fell into Egyptian hands in 1831, Gliddon declined Chasseaud's request that he intervene with Mohammed Ali to get extraterritorial rights.[11]

Commodore Porter's successor, Dabney S. Carr, liked Chasseaud even less. On the ground that he was drinking too much and also that he was taking money on the side from consular agents whom he nominated, Carr recommended strongly in 1847 that Chasseaud be replaced, hopefully by a salaried American. If none were available, Carr suggested that a worthy British substitute could be found; however, Carr was against using any foreigners as American consuls, because such appointments led to the mistaken belief that the United States was taking part in European power politics. Finally in 1850 an American was found for the job, J. Hosford Smith of New York; he was succeeded in 1854 by Henry E. Wood of New Hampshire.[12]

THE MEDITERRANEAN SQUADRON

Partly on account of the unsatisfactory consular situation, the United States relied increasingly on its navy to show the flag. At first the navy's role was hesitant, even reluctant: it will be recalled (Chapter 2) that Commodore Bainbridge and the *George Washington* visited Constantinople in 1800 only under duress. The Barbary Wars brought our sailors and marines to "the shores of Tripoli" (which is in modern Libya), but further east on only one occasion — when General William Eaton and a detachment of marines were landed at Alexandria from the U.S.S. *Argus* on November 26, 1804, bent on a wild scheme to seek out the exiled Hamet Pasha and restore him to the Tripolitanian throne. The *Argus* was the first American warship ever seen in Egypt.[13] In 1815, after the inconclusive naval war with Britain, the Mediterranean Squadron was created. During the Greek War of Independence (1821–29) American warships patrolled the Mediterranean in an effort to halt the piracy which was disrupting the commerce of American and European traders alike. Commodore Rodgers' spirited display of ship-handling in the Aegean in 1827 (see Chapter 3) made an obvious impression on the Turks, but it was all in fun rather than out of bellicosity. In 1829, with the Turkish treaty negotiations nearing their successful climax, Secretary of State Martin Van Buren laid down a very cautious policy:

As a general instruction to all our Consuls to the Barbary States, the President wishes them carefully to avoid exciting, or being drawn into disputes with the Governments near which they reside, upon captious or trivial causes . . . and not to appear, unless with special necessity, conscious of the presence of our Squadron in the Mediterranean. . . . While the exhibition of our Naval force in the Mediterranean has the most salutary effect upon our relations with those powers, it is the President's decided opinion that our Consuls in their official intercourse with the Regencies, cannot be too sparing of their allusions to it.[14]

Strictly interpreted, of course, these instructions applied only to the consuls along the North African shore west of Egypt, but they put a restraint on an active naval presence further east as well. To Commodore Porter, the old sea dog who never quite found his land legs in his sedentary post at Constantinople, this was all wrong. Before he had been in Turkey six months he wrote home suggesting that American naval forces should be ordered to visit Turkish waters occasionally. The rendezvous of the Squadron, he said, should be shifted eastward from Port Mahon, Minorca, to one of the Greek islands, perhaps Milo. In summer ships from the Squadron could visit Egypt and Syria: they could winter comfortably at Smyrna. Porter wrote to Washington: "It was observed to me by a gentleman in connection with the Porte not long since that 'I could never expect to be protected or respected by this Government unless I had a suite of Dragomans, Secretaries, and attachés.' I told him that 'we had something better than that to cause me to be respected.' He asked me 'what'; I replied 'some twelve or fifteen line of battle ships, & a proportional number of Frigates and Corvettes.' I hope the Government will give the Turks occasionally an opportunity of seeing that this is not altogether an idle boast." He followed this up by pouring crude scorn on his former naval colleagues: "It cannot be denied that visits to the beautiful cities of Barcelona, Marseilles, Genoa, Leghorn, Florence, Naples, etc. are much more agreeable than cruises on the gloomy and pestiferous coasts I have mentioned." [15]

Although the Government in Washington never gave Porter the satisfaction of telling him so, his advice was followed. In March, 1832, Commander Matthew C. Perry (later to rise to fame in Japan) called at Alexandria in the U.S.S. *Concord*. Porter was pleased; the *Concord* was the first American warship to visit the eastern Mediterranean since the *John Adams*, which had brought Porter out to take up his post the previous year.[16]

In October, 1833, Porter obtained permission for Commodore Daniel Patterson to bring the frigate *United States* through the Dardanelles to Constantinople, a rare privilege for a foreign warship. The impact of Patterson's visit was stunning: "He has been received by all the higher authorities of this Government with the most marked attentions such as have never been manifested to the officer of any other nation, whatever his rank, since I have been here. It is a matter of much surprise among the different legations, why so much respect should be shown to an American Commodore." Patterson was received in audience by the Sultan; Porter, with his staff, was invited to come along despite his inferior rank as chargé d'affaires, which had prevented him from being received on his own.[17]

Patterson, as commander of the Mediterranean Squadron, visited Egypt and Syria the following summer, this time with the battleship *Delaware* and the schooner *Shark*. When the ships arrived at Alexandria, Mohammed Ali was off fighting the Turks, but Patterson decided to await his return, "deeming it of national importance that he, with a strong marine, should see what kind of ships we possessed to protect our rights and repel aggression." (Actually, the Egyptians were already impressed; Ibrahim Pasha had rather tactlessly observed to the British consul at Beirut earlier that year that "after the American, the English is next the best fleet at sea.") While waiting for the viceroy to come back, the Commodore, his wife, two daughters, and a large contingent of officers visited Cairo and the Pyramids. Patterson wrote: "Nothing could exceed the public honors, attentions and civilities which I received from the Government there and on my route up and down, leaving nothing to wish or ask. Horses for my whole party and a very handsome new carriage (Florence made) with four grays met us at the landing at Boulac

[Cairo] and attended us each day of our stay. The ladies were twice received in the Basha's Harem." Commodore Porter's son, Midshipman David Dixon Porter, who was in the party, wrote his father a long chatty letter from Cairo, intimating that Patterson was in a bad humor much of the time and that the trip would have been much more fun without him.[18]

From Alexandria Patterson sailed on to Jaffa, from which a party of about a hundred visited Jerusalem, and then to Tyre, Sidon, and Beirut. Chasseaud was ecstatic: it was the first American naval visit to Beirut. He reported to Porter that at least fifty thousand people came aboard to inspect the *Delaware*, including forty or fifty princes and noblemen from the mountains. One of them told Chasseaud: "When I arrived on board it appeared to me that I was dreaming, when I thought of the idea we entertained here that the Americans were savage and uncivilized people — how grateful [sic] I was surprised to find them superior in every respect to other nations that I saw, and particularly so, in politeness and kindness towards us strangers." As related in Chapter 6, the American missionaries themselves were almost equally impressed. From Beirut the party sailed back down to Sidon to honor an invitation — much prized — from Lady Hester Stanhope.[19]

While Commodore Porter was all for having the navy show the flag, he was particular about who showed it. One of his old enemies was Commodore Jesse Elliott, whom Porter had never forgiven for sitting on his court-martial back in 1825. When Elliott sent a message asking Porter to see about getting permission from the Turks to bring his ship, the *Constitution*, through the Dardanelles to Constantinople in November, 1835, Porter was singularly unhelpful. He applied only half-heartedly for the necessary *firman* and was promptly turned down; in replying to Elliott, Porter observed stiffly that there were frequent steamboats to Constantinople if Elliott wanted to come. During Porter's absence on leave in 1837 Elliott tried again and permission was granted. Among his passengers was General Lewis Cass, on vacation with his family from his post as minister to France. Porter, who by this time had returned to Constantinople, apparently stayed in bed all the time they were there, though Elliott and Cass called on him at his country retreat at San Stefano.[20]

One by-product of all this American naval activity in the eastern Mediterranean was literature. Service in the Mediterranean Squadron was much sought after by young officers with a flair for the exotic and antique, and a good number of them wrote books about what they saw during their trips ashore. The first of these was the Reverend George Jones of York County, Pennsylvania, a Yale graduate who later became the first chaplain of the Naval Academy. He visited Constantinople on a short leave from the *Constitution*, on which he served as a schoolmaster, in 1827 and later toured Egypt and Syria from the *Delaware* (1834). In each case he published his journal. Others who made similar efforts were John Israel, Franklin P. Torrey, Walter Colton, and Francis Schroeder. Details will be found in the bibliography. None of them is particularly distinguished. Schroeder's *Shores of the Mediterranean* (1846) seems to have been the first Middle Eastern travel book by an American containing the author's own pictures of what he saw.

WILLIAM FRANCIS LYNCH

Most of these American naval officers were just carrying out normal peacetime duties, patrolling the Mediterranean and showing the flag in a desultory way, and taking advantage of the opportunities for sightseeing. Lieutenant William F. Lynch, U.S.N., on the other hand, was seized with the adventurous idea of navigating the Jordan River and the Dead

Sea. In 1847 he persuaded the Secretary of the Navy to let him mount an expedition.[21]

Lynch, forty-six years old, had wanted for many years to visit the Holy Land, but had been prevented by official duties elsewhere and by some unnamed "domestic calamity." A pious and somewhat rigid man, he chose his crew of volunteers with great care: "I was very particular," he wrote, "in selecting young, muscular, native-born Americans of sober habits, from each of whom I exacted a pledge to abstain from all intoxicating drinks." Altogether they numbered fourteen, including Lieutenant John B. Dale, the only other officer.

Before leaving the United States Lynch took over the venerable store ship *Supply*. His first stop was at the Mediterranean Squadron's base at Port Mahon, where Lynch was revolted by "the facilities [for] . . . indulging in low and vicious habits, . . . the haunts of the dissipated and the vile." Quickly he steered his lumbering vessel and its worthy young crew away from these temptations to Smyrna.

It was necessary, of course, to get the Sultan's permission to explore his domains. Lynch left the *Supply* at Smyrna and took a steamer up to Constantinople. He presented himself to the American dragoman, John P. Brown, who took him along to the Imperial Palace to seek the required *firman*. In accordance with court etiquette Lynch was asked to remove his ceremonial sword in the Sultan's presence; and this, as a matter of republican principle, Lynch stubbornly refused to do. After a brisk discussion he was allowed to keep it on: "At this I truly rejoiced, for it would have been unpleasant to retire after having gone so far." Buoyed by this victory over Ottoman protocol, Lynch presented His Highness with some pictures and books about the American Indians, received his *firman*, and left immediately to return to his ship at Smyrna. The *Supply* arrived at Acre on March 28, 1848. (During a brief stop at Beirut, the expedition acquired one more member, a wandering New York physician named Henry James Anderson.)

Now the real work began. Almost everything needed for the expedition had been brought on the *Supply* and had to be offloaded through the surf at Acre and transported overland across the hills to the Sea of Galilee (or Lake Tiberias), where the Jordan begins its precipitous descent to the Dead Sea. The equipment included instruments, tents, flags (plenty of flags), sails, preserved food, rubber sleeping sheets, bedding, cooking utensils, gum-elastic bags for use as life preservers, a blunderbuss, fourteen carbines with bayonets, fourteen pistols (some fitted with bowie knives), and — above all — two boats. These were the *Fanny Mason* and the *Fanny Lynch*; both had been fabricated to order for Lynch at the Brooklyn Navy Yard, one of copper and the other of galvanized iron. For each boat there was a carriage, similar to a gun carriage, and a set of harness for horses to haul them over the hills. Lynch and his crew waded ashore, pitched their tents, and hoisted one of the flags. "For the first time, perhaps, without the consular precincts, the American flag has been raised in Palestine." After posting sentries with fixed bayonets Lynch and Dale set forth to look for horses, and received their first jolt. The only available horses were "most miserable galled jades. It was ludicrous to see how loosely the harness we had brought hung about their meagre frames." For a while it seemed there was nothing to do but take the boats apart and carry them in sections. Finally it was decided to see if camels could be made to draw the carriages. After a couple of false starts the expedition set out on April 4: three camels drawing each carriage, sixteen horses and eleven more camels as pack animals, a mule, a dozen Arab outriders supplied by the local pasha, and the American sailors and their officers. In two days they reached the ancient town of Tiberias on the western shore of Galilee. Three days later the boats were launched. "It must have been a singular sight from the shore," wrote Lynch: "our beautiful boats, the crews in man-of-war rig, with snow-white awnings spread, and their ensigns flying, the men keeping time with their oars, as we rowed along the green shores of the silent sea of Galilee." In the course of this outing Lynch found an old wooden fishing boat (the only other vessel on the lake), which was purchased, repaired, and added to the fleet to carry part of the equipment — including the blunderbuss, which was mounted in her bows. The new addition was christened *Uncle Sam*.

Lynch's plan called for splitting the group into two parties: one led by Dale, to travel overland with the pack animals, and the other under Lynch, to navigate the river. Soon after starting, Lynch and his men encountered rapids so difficult that a portage was necessary; for four hours they were up to their waists in water, and one seaman was almost swept away by the current. Another came down with dysentery. At night they pulled ashore to camp with Dale and the land party. Warned of bandits, each man slept armed, and a sentry was posted to man the blunderbuss. Two days later the *Uncle Sam*, its rotting hull battered by boulders, foundered and had to be abandoned. The other boats were inched over the rapids with ropes. "Hard work for all hands," Lynch noted in his journal. The blunderbuss was remounted in the *Fanny Mason*: "Formidable it must have looked, with its gaping mouth pointed downstream and threatening slugs and bullets to all opponents."

On April 14 the two parties rendezvoused near the spot where a Lieutenant Molyneaux, an Englishman, had been attacked and slain by Bedouins. "It was a strange sight," wrote Lynch of the camp that night; "collected near us lay all the camels, for security against sudden surprise; while in every direction, but ever in close proximity, were scattered lances and smoldering fires and bundles of garments, beneath each of which was a slumbering Arab, with his long gun by his side. The preparations for defense reminded me of Indian warfare."

Next day Lynch reported: "We have now reached a part of the river not visited by Franks, at least since the time of the Crusades, except by three English sailors [of Molyneaux's party], who were robbed and fled from it." Ultimately they reached calmer water near Jericho, startling several thousand pilgrims who had come down to the river to bathe. (Among them were two Americans, "gratified . . . at seeing the Stars and Stripes floating above the consecrated river.")

Now began the final stage of the exploration: circumnavigation of the Dead Sea, thirteen hundred feet below sea level, the lowest body of water on earth, and six times as salty as the ocean. "There is a tradition among the Arabs," wrote Lynch, "that no one can venture upon this sea and live." He called it "the dreariest waste we had ever seen." Occasionally a few wandering tribesmen were sighted, but there were no other boats on the water. The two *Fanny*'s proceeded slowly down the western shore, taking soundings and noting geographical features. About half way along, at the foot of a steep cliff, Lynch established a semipermanent base, which he promptly named Camp Washington. "Some of our party had discovered in the face of the precipice . . . several apertures, one of them arched and faced with stone. There was no perceptible access to the caverns, which were once, perhaps, the abodes of the Essenes. Our sailors could not get to them; and where they fail, none but monkeys can succeed." This may well have been the place where the Dead Sea Scrolls were discovered almost exactly a century later.

In due course Dale and the land party struggled down the escarpment to Camp Washington, bearing fresh supplies, and the voyage continued. No one, according to Lynch, had ever before ventured so far south on the waters of the Dead Sea, and it is easy to see why no one had. At one point the boats ran aground in six inches of water, three hundred yards from the shore. "Mr. Dale landed to observe for the latitude. His feet sank first through a layer of slimy mud a foot deep, then through a crust of salt, and then another foot of mud, before reaching a firm bottom. The beach was so hot as to blister the feet. From the water's edge he made his way with difficulty for more than a hundred yards over black mud, coated with salt and bitumen. . . . In returning to the boat, one of the men attempted to carry Mr. Dale to the water, but sunk down, and they were obliged separately to flounder through. When they could, they ran for it. They describe it as like running over burning ashes; the perspiration starting from every pore with the heat. It was a delightful sensation when their feet touched the water, even the salt, slimy water of the sea, then at a temperature of 88°."

Now signs of physical and moral deterioration began to appear among the men. "The figure of each one had assumed a dropsical appearance. The lean had become stout, and the stout almost corpulent; the pale faces had become florid, and those which were florid ruddy. Moreover, the slightest scratch festered, and the bodies of many of us were covered with small pustules. The men complained bitterly of the irritation of their sores, whenever the acrid water of the sea touched them." Still Lynch did not turn back. He coaxed the men, exhausted and sullen, eastward across the southern stretches of the Dead Sea to the land of Moab. He ordered the sails furled and commanded the men to row: "Action seemed better than such unnatural stupor." At the opposite shore they were met with fresh provisions, and "dined sumptuously . . . on wild boar's meat, onions, and the last of our rice." Leaving a guard on the boats, Lynch marched his reluctant crew inland to the ancient town of Kerak, previously visited by only three modern explorers.* Kerak was a dismal, run-down place of perhaps five hundred families; there was only one shop, its wares limited to "thin cakes of dried and pressed apricots, and English muslin." In his heart a child of Manifest Destiny, Lynch's spirit cried out within him: "Fifty well-armed, resolute Franks, with a large sum of money, could revolutionize the whole country."

But Lynch's own men were becoming more and more languid and demoralized, and "prudence warned us to be gone." He gave the order to return to Camp Washington, where a float was built and anchored in sixty fathoms of water. Needless to say, the American flag was left flying over this memento of the first successful exploration of the Dead Sea. By easy stages the party made its weary way back to Jerusalem, Jaffa, Damascus, Baalbeck, Zahle, and Beirut, where they were to be rejoined by the *Supply*. Nearing Damascus, Lynch asserted his patriotism once more: "Before entering the city we were advised to furl our flag, with the assurance that no foreign one had ever been tolerated within the walls; that the British Consul's had been torn down on the first attempt to raise it, and that the appearance of ours would excite commotion, and perhaps lead to serious consequences. But we had carried it to every place we had visited, and determining to take our chances with it, we kept it flying. Many angry comments were, I believe, made by the populace, but

* John Lewis Burckhardt (in disguise), Charles Leonard Irby, and James Mangles, all in the 1810's. Irby and Mangles were British naval officers.

as we did not understand what our toorgeman [guide] was too wary to interpret, we passed unmolested."

By the time the party reached the western slopes of the Lebanon Mountains, nearly all were very sick. Dale, in fact, died on July 24, 1848, at Bhamdoun in the home of Eli Smith of the Syria mission, a martyr to the single-minded exploring instinct and stubborn persistence of his commander. Dale's body was carried down to Beirut and buried in the Protestant cemetery. (His grave marker is still to be seen.) William Thomson, as he had so often done in the past, read the funeral service for a fallen compatriot. The *Supply* never showed up at Beirut as planned. After waiting around for some time Lynch chartered a brig for Malta and eventual rendezvous with the *Supply*. The party was back in the United States in December, 1848.

In a sense William Francis Lynch sums up a great deal that we have observed in other Americans in the East in those early days. His journal shows that, like the missionaries, he was a Godly man steeped in Fundamentalist doctrine and Old Testament lore. His excessive zeal for showing (literally) the flag was shared by many another American. His self-appointed mission to be the explorer of the Jordan and the Dead Sea combined pioneering spirit with religious sentiment. In traveling to the Middle East, like so many others, he was "goaded by sorrow" — to borrow once more Kinglake's memorable phrase. The scientific and practical benefits of his expedition were probably more than neutralized by the suffering of his colleagues, including the lamented Lieutenant Dale. And yet what Lynch did could hardly have been attempted or accomplished by a man of any other nationality of his time. Unlike the French, the Russians, or the English, the motives of his Government in authorizing the expedition were utterly unpolitical. Lynch simply got a bee in his bonnet, persuaded the navy to back him, did what he set out to do without fuss, wrote it all up (in a rather ponderous way), and vanished from the scene.* William Francis Lynch was pure pioneer.

* In 1861 he resigned his commission to join the Confederate navy. He died in 1865.

11. *Pioneers in Retrospect*

TEMPTING AS IT IS to try to generalize about all these way-
ward pioneers, they unfortunately fit no neat pattern. From
John Ledyard to William Lynch (alike at least in their zeal
for exploration), there is a span of some sixty years. Across
these years march what appears to be a sort of early-American awkward squad: Harriet Livermore, George English,
James Merrick, "Captain Richards," Warder Cresson, and the
fleeting figure of David Bushnell. What obscure compulsions
pulled each of them out of the orbit of convention one can
hardly begin to imagine, and in a way it seems churlish to inquire. Something drew them all eastward, just as something
drew Lady Hester Stanhope, Richard Burton, T. E. Lawrence, and many of their compatriots. The English, after all,
have a rich and honorable tradition of eccentrics in the Orient;
surely their trans-Atlantic cousins may be allowed such a tradition of their own.

But eccentricities aside, it is useful once more to return to
John Lloyd Stephens himself to ferret out some kind of unity
from all this diversity. Stephens, while lively and individual-
istic, was anything but eccentric. It may be of symbolic sig-

nificance that his later career was devoted to the Western Hemisphere, where all Americans of his age were supposed to be concentrating their energies — at least according to such diverse authorities as Monroe, Thoreau, and Horace Greeley. By nature a "doer," Stephens found his greatest material success as the head of a railroad company in Panama. Steam navigation was another of his keen interests, and in traveling around the Middle East he thought he detected great possibilities for the steamboat. Within twenty years, he predicted, "these eastern countries will be invaded by all classes of people, travelers, merchants, and mechanics, gentlemen of elegant leisure, and blacksmiths, shoemakers, tinkers and tailors, nay, even mantuamakers, milliners and bandboxes." Steamboats, he forecast, might even contribute to the transformation of Ottoman society.[1]

Stephens did not linger in the East long enough to see if his twenty-year predictions would come true (they didn't). The point, however, is this: he was characteristically American in his conviction that human energy and enterprise could bring about beneficial change. The frontier experience seemed to prove precisely this. But the Middle East was not a wilderness, and the people already there were not savages: if anything they were overcivilized. Too many American newcomers to the East saw it in frontier terms — like Lynch, who ventured that fifty well-armed men with plenty of money could turn Palestine upside down, as though the inhabitants were illiterate Indians. While Lynch's offhand comment was not meant seriously and can be quickly forgiven, even those with more experience of the area often showed misplaced confidence that the American touch could work miracles — Asahel Grant being the prime example. The East simply didn't work that way. The wisest of the Americans were those who adapted to its unfamiliar rhythm while maintaining their own identity. As long as their Government shunned all political involvement, the opportunities for effective influence by individual Americans were necessarily limited. Those who succeeded best were those who became the most acclimated: men like David Offley, Foster Rhodes, and William Thomson.

The impulsive hustlers, on the other hand, usually came off second best. Colorful as they were as individuals, they somehow failed to achieve the inner sense of proportion that alone could have brought fulfillment. Often their careers ended in frustration. If Stephens, instead of being a mere traveler in the East, had elected to stay and devote his energies to the area, he too would surely have become frustrated. This was not his fault: it was simply that the idea of progress and reform on the vigorous, roughhewn American pattern was so alien that it could never have thrived in the conservative, complex environment of the Middle East at that time. Moreover, the relative openness of American society was part of the heritage of all the Americans who ventured there; the British and others, on the other hand, raised as they were in societies far more deeply stratified, found the process of adaptation correspondingly more easy. If adaptation is a valid gauge of achievement, it is fair to conclude that on the whole the American missionaries fared the best of any of their countrymen. Despite their own rigidities, and in the face of severe setbacks, they somehow found it possible to survive, flourish, and ultimately to string out the main thread of continuity leading, however tenuously, to America's present-day position in the Middle East.*

---

* Actually, validation of this assessment must await further research on Americans in the Middle East in the second half of the nineteenth century. John A. De Novo's study, *American Interests and Policies in the Middle East, 1900–1939* (Minneapolis, 1963), picks up the story at 1900, but a gap remains between this work and his.

Nowadays, probably, more Americans visit the Middle East each month than ever saw it in all the years before 1850. American investments in the area run into many hundreds of millions. The wooden-hulled Mediterranean Squadron has given way to the sleek and powerful Sixth Fleet. Twelve ambassadors now serve the area originally covered by Commodore Porter alone. It is hard to pick up a new book about the Middle East that does not stress the area's significance in the Cold War, its cautious and sometimes resentful awareness of America's political commitments there, and, above all, its oil resources, so important to Western strategy and security. Steamboats on the Nile, discussed in theory by Stephens with Mohammed Ali in 1836, have had their day; a sturdy survivor, bedecked with neon, is tied up as a restaurant within a dragoman's shout of the Nile Hilton. Burj Bird, designed in the 1830's by missionaries as the largest structure outside Beirut's city walls, and still American owned, maintains a calm but precarious dignity in the center of the modern city. Barren Kharg Island, where the baffled Moritz Jackson of New York and his family considered seeking refuge in 1841, now boasts the largest crude-oil loading terminal in the world. Boeings, not frigates, provide the vantage point for viewing the glorious Mediterranean sunsets recorded by Nathaniel Parker Willis.

What, in the final analysis, does the modern Middle East have to do with the Ottoman Empire and the Persia of David Porter, George Rapelje, and Justin Perkins? The physical picture has changed indeed — and irrevocably. One would think that only an incurable romantic could wish to take six days floating from Alexandria to Cairo (though an American yacht did it recently, according to the *National Geographic*), much less suffer Josiah Brewer's fleas or John Lowell's shipwreck in the Red Sea. But the East is still there for those who seek it. Go to Djoun and visit the grave where William Thomson laid Lady Hester Stanhope to rest; for fifty piasters a whiskery villager in black baggy pants will lead you through the garden, hold up the loose tombstone with its weathered inscription and let you take his picture. Try a visit to Petra (a day's round trip from Jerusalem these days), where you can still find — if you look hard — John Lloyd Stephens' name below Burckhardt's deep inside a smoke-blackened rock-hewn temple. Go down to the Dead Sea and stoop to taste the brine; turn around, and you can almost see the dancing girls of Jericho who bemused Stephens on one occasion and offended Edward Robinson's stern Calvinist sensibilities on another. There are quite probably old men who can remember Cornelius Van Dyck, who arrived as a missionary in 1840 and died in Syria fifty-six years later. And Eli Smith's New Testament is treasured in many an Arab Protestant home. But above all there are the colleges and schools: Robert College near Istanbul, the American University of Beirut, and a string of secondary schools of high standard and continuing dedication. These are the most direct heritage of the early pioneers.

And perhaps today's Americans in the Middle East are not all so different from some of the early ones. Was George English a general in the Egyptian army? An American "colonel" has recently been serving with the Yemeni Royalists. Isaac Bird was taunted and molested by a rowdy platoon of Ibrahim Pasha's troops? A youngster from Brooklyn recently emerged from two years' solitary confinement in a Syrian prison. Tylden and George De Kay were offered high commands in the Ottoman navy? Executives from Pan Am manage Iranian Airways, and others from TWA do the same for the Saudis.

Tourists still fume at petty border bureaucrats; they still are laid low by "jippy tummy" or the equivalent (though they rarely die of it any more). As always, they filch little antiquities and carve their names on large ones. The archaeologists find plenty to do with their measuring tapes, just as Robinson did. Stephens found the Frankish merchants of Smyrna chattering about "stocks, exchanges, freights, and quarter percent less"; their modern counterparts in Beirut have Merrill Lynch's Telex to Wall Street. The young Foreign Service officer learning Arabic struggles with the same conjugations, plurals, and "consonants without vowels" that so bewildered Pliny Fisk.

What is new, of course, about America in the Middle East is a sense of strategic and political concern and responsibility, inevitably dominated by the subterranean treasures of the world's greatest sedimentary basin. "Oil" in the early nineteenth century meant olive oil or whale oil, and it was used in clay hand lamps of the sort to be found by the dozen in any museum of antiquities. Today's Middle East oil fuels the Free World's economy; after World War I Turkey yielded no treasure so significant as the oil benefits that now accrue to her former Arab provinces, now independent. American enterprise and technology, perhaps more than those of any other nation (even Britain), have contributed to the Middle East's material revolution.

But the need for adaptation remains. In pursuing his business affairs an American today can use the patience and tact of a David Offley, the sympathetic understanding of a William Thomson, and the old-fashioned Yankee know-how of a Henry Eckford or Foster Rhodes. So can the AID official and the diplomat, the archaeologist and the educator. Those eastward pioneers, and others like them, gave the New World its first direct exposure to what is still in many ways a remote and difficult culture and society. The lives they led, the reports they brought home, and the books they published —

even if largely forgotten now — awakened Americans of their own and succeeding generations to the romantic inscrutability of the Middle East and to its importance and challenge as well. To try to bring the pioneers to life after all these years is more than a sentimental pastime; it is an exercise in the rehabilitation of a significant aspect of our national heritage.

APPENDIX I: CHARLES RHIND'S SEPARATE AND SECRET ARTICLE

The reason of the writing of this document and the motive of the drawing up of this writ are as follows:

As there has not been concluded heretofore any kind of official treaty between the everlasting Sublime Government and the Government of the United States of America, now, as we, the undersigned functionary, occupying the elevated degree of Chief of the Secretaries of the ever-stable Sublime Government and of the exalted Sultanate, eternally enduring, have been authorized by the Most Noble Imperial Excellency, there have been negotiations between us and our friend Charles Rhind, who has been charged and commissioned with complete authority by the aforesaid Government, separately by coming to the Gate of Felicity and jointly with the functionaries named Commodore Biddle and David Offley, now being in the town of Smyrna.

The documents containing the treaty articles that have been drawn up and established as a result of these negotiations, have been exchanged and will be undersigned hereafter by the two aforesaid functionaries.

Now that in this way a new treaty and an increased friendship and amity have been established between the two Governments, in observance of the principles of mutual profit and common interest and with regard to the fact that in the state of America timber is abundant and strong and that the building expenses are there light and small, the aforesaid functionary, our friend, in confirmation of the sincere feelings of the said Government towards the glorious Imperial Sultanate, has contracted the obligation that, whenever the Sublime Government shall order the building and construction in the dominion of America of whatever quantity of war vessels, such as two-deckers, frigates, corvettes, and brigs, this shall be communicated and notified by the office of the Chief (of the Secretaries) to the functionary of the said Government who will be at that time at the Gate of Felicity; that there shall be drawn up a contractual document stating in which way it has been negotiated and agreed upon with regard to the building expenses, the time of construction, and also to the mode of sending and conveying to the Gate of Felicity, according to which contract the required ships shall be built and constructed after the design and model to be fixed and explained by the Imperial Arsenal, so as to be as strong and tight as the Government ships of the said Government, and provided that the building expenses be not higher than the expenses of the war ships of the said Government; and that, in case of an order being given, and so as to prevent the required ships from arriving empty at the Imperial Arsenal, there shall be negotiations between the functionaries of both parties, according to which there shall be laden and sent in each ship the timber necessary for the construction of another ship like that ship itself, provided that the price be in accordance with the official price of the said Government and that the material be calculated carefully and prepared in its place, after having been cut and well executed according to the measure.

This separate article, after having been signed by the two aforesaid functionaries, is destined to be a secret article and to be counted as a part of the mentioned treaty. By the exchange of the ratifications within ten months after the day of this document it shall be observed in every way.*

* (This English translation was made by J. H. Kramers in 1931 and printed in Hunter Miller, *Treaties and Other International Acts of the United States of America* [Washington, 1933] III, 580–581. It also appears in J. C. Hurewitz, *Diplomacy in the Near and Middle East* [Princeton: Van Nostrand, 1956], I, 104–105, from which it is reproduced by permission.)

APPENDIX II: AMERICANS IN EGYPT, 1832 TO 1842

Listed below are all the American travelers who registered with John and George Gliddon, the first U.S. consuls at Alexandria and Cairo, respectively, over the decade beginning with the opening of the consulates in 1832. The list is based on George Gliddon's *Appendix to "The American in Egypt"* (an intemperate review of James Cooley's book of that title), published as a pamphlet in Philadelphia in 1842. An asterisk indicates the author of published work relating to the area.

Year	Name and Home	Comments
1832	Dr. John Thornton Kirkland * Boston	Former president of Harvard. Accompanied by his wife, Elizabeth Cabot Kirkland.* Passengers on U.S.S. *Concord*, Capt. Matthew Perry. See Chap. 6 and 10.
	Col. Mendes J. Cohen Baltimore	Important collector of antiquities. See Chap. 6.
	Rev. Eli Smith* Beirut	Missionary. See Chap. 7. Also registered in 1837 and 1838.
1833	John W. Hammersley New York	
	J. L. Stackpole Boston	Traveled together.
	Ralph J. Izard South Carolina	

1834	Commodore Daniel Patterson, U.S.N.	Commander of Mediterranean Squadron. Accompanied by wife, two daughters, and about 20 naval officers. See Chap. 6 and 10.
	William B. Hodgson Virginia	State Department employee on official business. See Chap. 4.
	John A. Lowell, "Jr." Boston	See Chap. 6.
1835	None	
1836	John Lloyd Stephens* New York	See Chap. 6.
	James Augustus Dorr Boston	
	Richard K. Haight New York	Accompanied by wife, Sarah,* and a "Mr. R." See Chap. 6.
	Richard Randolph Philadelphia	Probably the "Mr. R." referred to by Sarah Haight.
	Horatio Allen New York	
	W. McHenry Boyd Baltimore	
1837	Lewis Cass Michigan	U.S. minister to France. Accompanied by wife and family. Passengers on the U.S.S. *Constitution*, Commodore Jesse Elliott. See Chap. 6 and 10.
1838	Rev. Dr. Edward Robinson* New York	Archaeologist. See Chap. 7.

Henry McVickar
New York

Mr. Bard
New York

Dr. Valentine Mott*   Prominent surgeon. See
New York   Chap. 6.

Dr. Jackson
New York

Samuel Waring   Traveled with Dr. Mott.
New York

Dudley M. Haydon
Kentucky

H. P. Marshall   Operator of cotton machin-
New York   ery at Rosetta. See Chap. 6.
                           Also registered in 1839.

Rev. George Whiting   Missionary. See Chap. 7.
Jerusalem

1839   William J. Bennett
        New York

        C. R. Swords
        New York

        A. S. Willington
        Charleston

        J. I. Tucker
        New York

        S. H. Whitlock
        New York

        F. R. Fleming
        New York

        H. A. Cram
        New York

	Col. H. A. Ireland New York	
	Rev. Simeon H. Calhoun South Carolina	Representative of American Bible Society.
	Rev. Dr. C. Lowell Boston	Accompanied by wife and daughter.
	George Sumner* Boston	
	Rev. S. R. Houston Virginia	
1840	H. B. Humphrey Boston	
	Edward Joy Morris* Philadelphia	See Chap. 6. Later U.S. minister to Turkey.
	Fairfax Catlett New York	
	Prof. Nathaniel Fish Moore New York	Later president of Columbia College
	Daniel Lowe New York	
	Mr. Paine New York	
	John S. Miller Philadelphia	
	Thomas M. Preston Charleston	
	Mr. Dehone Charleston	
	George Lewis New London	

	Rev. J. H. Hill Athens and New York	Missionary.
	Rev. ——— May Philadelphia	
1841	Charles W. King Canton and New York	Merchant in the China trade. Died in the Red Sea, 1845.
	Gen. Josiah Harlan Philadelphia	Returning to U.S. after being governor of Goozerat, India. See Chap. 6.
	F. Oliver Baltimore	
	J. O. Colt Baltimore	
	Alexander Van Rensellaer Albany	
1842	John Cooke Philadelphia	
	Rev. C. W. Andrews Virginia	
	Daniel Giraud New York	
	Jacob Giraud New York	

Americans known from other sources to have been in Egypt during this period, but not mentioned above:

Year	*Name and Home*	*Comments*
1835	"Dr. N." and son Mississippi	See Chap. 8.
c.1835	Mr. Curtis Boston	Mentioned by Sarah Haight. Died in Greece.

	Mr. Clarke	Mentioned by Sarah Haight.
	Mr. Morton	Mentioned by G. Gliddon: said to be author of *Crania Americana.*
1839	Dr. Stephen Olin*	President of Wesleyan College. Wife died in Italy en route to Egypt. See Chap. 5.
	James Ewing Cooley* New York	Accompanied by wife. Traveled with Olin. See Chap. 6.
	David Bushnell Ohio	See Chap. 6.
	Dr. June	Mentioned by Cooley.

APPENDIX III: CONTEMPORARY ACCOUNTS

This bibliography lists early publications by Americans relating to American activities in the Middle East before 1850. Many of them are hard to find, and not all of them have been seen by the present author. About half of the titles relate to missionary activities; the others are, on the whole, the more interesting. Except for some minor (and largely repetitious) missionary material, I believe the list is substantially complete. Asterisks indicate material that could be read for pleasure by the modern general reader with an interest in Middle Eastern affairs.

Adger, John B. *My Life and Times, 1810–1899*. Richmond, Va.: The Presbyterian Committee of Publication, 1899.

An American [John P. Brown?], "An Audience with Sultan Abdul Mejud," *The Knickerbocker*, XIX (June 1842), pp. 497–505.

Anderson, Rufus. *History of the Missions of the American Board of Commissioners for Foreign Missions to the Oriental Churches.* 2 vols. Boston: Congregational Publishing Society, 1872.

——— *Report to the Prudential Committee of a Visit to the Missions in the Levant.* Boston, 1844.

Anonymous. *Letters from Asia, Written by a Gentleman of Boston to His Friend in That Place.* New York: Goodrich, 1819.

Baker, John Martin. *A View of the Commerce of the Mediterranean; . . . Embellished with a View of the Harbor of Port Mahon, with the United States Squadron as It Rode at Anchor There, in November 1815.* Washington, 1819.

Bird, Isaac. *Bible Work in Bible Lands; or Events in the History of the Syria Mission.* Philadelphia: Presbyterian Board of Missions, 1872.

———— *The Martyr of Lebanon*. Boston: American Tract Society, 1864.

Brewer, Josiah. *Patmos, and the Seven Churches of Asia, . . . Compiled Principally from the Ms. Journals of Rev. Josiah Brewer . . . by John W. Barber*. Bridgeport, Conn., 1851.

———— *A Residence at Constantinople in the Year 1827. With Notes to the Present Time*. New Haven, Conn.: Durrie and Peck, 1830.

Brown, John P. A Letter, *Journal of the American Oriental Society* (New York), 1 (1851), liv–lv.

Colton, Rev. Walter. *Ship and Shore, in Madeira, Lisbon and the Mediterranean*. New York: Barnes, 1851.

———— *Visit to Constantinople and Athens*. New York: Leavitt Lord & Co., 1836.

Cooley, James Ewing. *The American in Egypt, with Rambles through Arabia Petraea, and the Holy Land, during the Years 1839 and 1840*. New York: Appleton, 1842.

Curtis, George William. *Nile Notes of a Howadji*. New York: Harper, 1851.

———— *The Howadji in Syria*. New York: Harper, 1852.

Dearborn, Henry A. S. *A Memoir on the Commerce and Navigation of the Black Sea, and the Trade and Maritime Geography of Turkey and Egypt*. Boston: Wells & Lilly, 1819.

**De Kay, James E. *Sketches of Turkey in 1831 and 1832, by an American*. New York: Harper, 1833.

Durbin, John P. *Observations in the East, Chiefly in Egypt, Palestine, Syria, and Asia-Minor*. New York: Harper, 1845.

Dwight, Harrison Gray Otis. *Christianity in Turkey: A Narrative of the Protestant Reformation in the Armenian Church*. London, 1854.

———— *Memoir of Mrs. Elizabeth B. Dwight, Including an Account of the Plague of 1837 (with a Sketch of the Life of Judith S. Grant)*. New York: Dodd, 1840.

Eddy, Daniel C. *Heroines of the Missionary Enterprise*. Boston, 1850.

**English, George Bethune. *A Narrative of the Expedition to*

Dongola and Sennaer, under the Command of Ismael Pasha. London, 1822 and Boston, 1823.

Forbes, Robert B. *Personal Reminiscences,* 3rd ed. Boston: Little, Brown, 1892.

Goodell, William. *Mr. Southgate and the Missionaries at Constantinople.* Boston, 1844.

——— The Old and the New; or Changes of Thirty Years in the East. New York, 1853.

——— *The Power of Faith: A Sermon Preached at Constantinople Aug. 6, 1837, on the Death of E. Dwight.* New York, 1838.

——— *The Rest of Heaven: A Sermon Preached at Reading, Mass., August 13, 1851, at the Funeral of the Rev. Daniel Temple.* Boston, 1851.

*Grant, Asahel. *The Nestorians.* London: Murray, 1841 (New York: Harper, 1841).

*Haight, Sarah. *Letters from the Old World, by a Lady of New York.* 2 vols. New York: Harper, 1840.

Haines, Mrs. F. E. H. *Jonas King: Missionary to Syria and Greece.* New York: American Tract Society, 1879.

Hamlin, Cyrus. *Among the Turks.* London: Carter, 1878.

——— *My Life and Times.* New York, 1893.

Hawes, Joel. *The Religion of the East, with Impressions of Foreign Travel.* Hartford, 1845.

Hawes, Louisa. *Memoir of Mrs. M. E. Van Lennep, by Her Mother.* Hartford, 1851.

Hooker, Edward W. *Memoir of Mrs. Sarah Lanman Smith,* 2nd ed. Boston, 1840.

Horner, Gustavus R. B. *Medical and Topographical Observations upon the Mediterranean.* Philadelphia, 1839.

Innes, William, ed. *Memoir of the Rev. Levi Parsons, First Missionary to Palestine from the United States, originally compiled by the Rev. Dan. O. Morton, M.A.* Edinburgh, 1832.

Israel, John and Henry N. Lundt. *Journal of a Cruise in the U.S.S. Ship Delaware 74, in the Mediterranean in the Years 1833 and 1834.* Port Mahon, Minorca, 1835.

**Jessup, Henry Harris. *Fifty-Three Years in Syria*. 2 vols. New York: Revell, 1910.

———— *The Setting of the Crescent and the Rising of the Cross, or Kamil Abdul Messiah*. Philadelphia, 1908.

Jones, George. *Excursions to Cairo, Jerusalem, Damascus, and Balbec, from the U.S.S. Delaware during Her Recent Cruise*. New York: Van Nostrand, 1836.

———— *Sketches of Naval Life*. New Haven, 1829.

King, Jonas. *Extraits d'un ouvrage écrit vers la fin de l'année 1826 et au commencement de 1827, sous le titre de coup d'oeil sur la Palestine et la Syrie*. Athens, 1859.

Kirkland, Elizabeth Cabot. "Letters" in *Proceedings of the Massachusetts Historical Society*, 2nd ser. (Boston), XIX (1906), 440–504.

Kirkland, John Thornton. "Letters on the Holy Land," *Christian Examiner*, 23 (1837), 262–9.

Lathrop, A. C. *Memoir of Asahel Grant M.D., Missionary to the Nestorians, Compiled at the Request of His Mother, Mrs. Rachel Grant*. New York, 1847.

*Laurie, Thomas. *Dr. Grant and the Mountain Nestorians*. Boston: Gould and Lincoln, 1853.

———— *Historical Sketch of the Syria Mission*. Boston: American Board of Commissioners for Foreign Missions, 1866.

———— *Woman and Her Saviour in Persia, by a Returned Missionary*. New York, 1863.

Lawrence, Margaret Oliver Woods. *Light on the Dark River; or, Memorials of Mrs. Henrietta A. L. Hamlin, Missionary in Turkey*. Boston, 1854.

*Lynch, William Francis. *Narrative of the United States' Expedition to the River Jordan and the Dead Sea*. Philadelphia and London, 1849.

———— *Official Report of the United States' Expedition to Explore the Dead Sea and the River Jordan*. Baltimore: John Murphy, 1852.

Massett, Stephen C. *Drifting About*. New York: Carlton, 1863.

Merrick, James Lyman. *An Appeal to the American Board of*

Commissioners for Foreign Missions. Springfield, Mass., 1847.

Millard, David. *A Journal of Travels in Egypt, Arabia Petraea, and the Holy Land during 1841–2.* Rochester, N.Y., 1843.

Morris, Edward Joy. *Notes of a Tour through Turkey, Greece, Egypt, Arabia Petraea to the Holy Land.* Philadelphia, 1842.

Mott, Valentine. *Travels in Europe and the East.* New York, 1842.

Olin, Stephen. *Greece and the Golden Horn.* New York: Derby, 1854.

——— *Travels in Egypt, Arabia Petraea, and the Holy Land.* 2 vols. New York: Harper. 1843.

Parish, Elijah. *Sacred Geography; or a Gazetteer of the Bible.* Boston, 1813. (Not about Americans, but worth including as the first book by an American about the area.)

Paxton, John D. *Letters from Palestine, Written during a Residence There in the Years 1836, 7, and 8.* Lexington, Ky., and London, 1839.

Perkins, Henry Martyn. *Life of Rev. Justin Perkins, D.D., Pioneer Missionary to Persia.* Chicago: Presbyterian Board of Missions, 1887.

Perkins, Justin. *A Good Missionary: A sermon Occasioned by the Death of Rev. William Redfield Stocking, Missionary to the Nestorians, Preached at Oroomiah, Persia, July 9, 1854.* Boston, 1854.

——— "Journal of a Tour from Oroomiah to Mosul, through the Koordish Mountains," *Journal of the American Oriental Society* (New York), 2 (1851), pp. 71–118.

——— *Missionary Life in Persia.* 1861.

——— *The Persian Flower: A Memoir of Judith Grant Perkins of Oroomiah, Persia.* Boston, 1853.

*——— *A Residence of Eight Years in Persia among the Nestorian Christians.* Andover, Mass., 1843.

——— and Thomas Laurie. *Historical Sketch of the Mission to the Nestorians.* New York, 1862.

Pierson, Hamilton W. *American Missionary Memorial.* New York, 1853.

Porter, David. Constantinople and Its Environs, by an American. 2 vols. New York: Harper, 1835.

Porter, David Dixon. *Memoir of Commodore David Porter of the United States Navy.* Albany, N.Y.: Munsell, 1875.

Post, Henry A. V. *A Visit to Greece and Constantinople in the Year 1827–8.* New York, 1830.

Prime, E. D. G. Forty Years in the Turkish Empire; or, Memoirs of Rev. William Goodell, D.D., Late Missionary of the A.B.C.F.M. at Constantinople. New York: Carter, 1876.

Prime, William C. *Boat Life in Egypt and Nubia.* New York: Harper, 1857.

——— *Tent Life in the Holy Land.* New York: Harper, 1857.

Rapelje, George. *A Narrative of Excursions, Voyages and Travels, Performed at Different Periods in America, Europe, Asia, and Africa.* New York, 1834.

Ricketts, Clemuel G. *Notes of Travel in Europe, Egypt, and the Holy Land, including a Visit to the City of Constantinople, in 1841 and 1842.* Philadelphia, 1844.

Roberts, Edmund. *Embassy to the Eastern Courts of Cochin-China, Siam, and Muscat; in the U.S. Sloop-of-War Peacock . . . during the Years 1832–3–4.* New York: Harper, 1837.

Robinson, Edward. *Biblical Researches in Palestine, Mount Sinai and Arabia Petraea.* 3 vols. London and Boston, 1841.

——— *Later Biblical Researches in Palestine and the Adjacent Regions.* Boston, 1856.

Ruschenberger, William S. W. *Narrative of a Voyage Round the World during the Years 1835, 36, and 37, Including a Narrative of an Embassy to the Sultan of Muscat and the King of Siam.* 2 vols. London: Bentley, 1838.

Schauffler, Adolph Frederick. *Memories of a Happy Boyhood.* New York: Revell, 1919.

Schauffler, William G. *Autobiography, Edited by his Sons.* New York, 1887.

Schneider, Mrs. E. C. A. *Letters from Broosa, Asia Minor, with an Essay on the Prospects of the Heathen and Our Duties to Them,* by Rev. B. *Schneider.* Chambersburg, Pa., 1846.

Schroeder, Francis. *Shores of the Mediterranean, with Sketches of Travel.* New York, 1846.

Smith, Eli, trans. "A Treatise on Arab Music" by Mikhael Meshakah, *Journal of the American Oriental Society* (New York), 1 (1849), pp. 173–217.

**—— and H. G. O. Dwight. *Missionary Researches in Armenia.* London, 1834.

—— *Trials of Missionaries* (A Sermon). Boston, 1832.

Smith, Henry Boynton, and R. D. Hitchcock. *The Life, Writings and Character of Edward Robinson.* New York: Randolph, 1863.

Smith, L. E. *Heroes and Martyrs of the Modern Missionary Enterprise.* Hartford, 1852.

Smith, Maria W. A Letter, reprinted in *Middle East Forum,* January 1964, p. 11.

Southgate, Horatio. *The Cross above the Crescent: A Romance of Constantinople.* Philadelphia: Lippincott, 1878.

—— *Narrative of a Tour through Armenia, Kurdistan, Persia and Mesopotamia.* 2 vols. New York: Appleton, 1840.

—— *Narrative of a Visit to the Syrian Church of Mesopotamia.* New York: Appleton, 1844.

***Stephens, John Lloyd. *Incidents of Travel in Egypt, Arabia Petraea, and the Holy Land.* 2 vols. New York: Harper, 1837 and London, 1838.

***—— *Incidents of Travel in Greece, Turkey, Russia, and Poland.* 2 vols. New York and London, 1838. (Also published under the title *Incidents of Travel in the Russian and Turkish Empires.* London: Bentley, 1839: the edition quoted herein.)

Sumner, George. Letters, in *Proceedings of the Massachusetts Historical Society,* XLVI (1913), 341–370.

Temple, Daniel H. *Life and Letters of Rev. Daniel Temple.* Boston: Congregational Board of Publication, 1855.

*Thomson, William M. *The Land and the Book.* 2 vols. New

York: Harper, 1859. (Also many other editions, at least to 1911.)

Torrey, Franklin P. *Journal of the Cruise of the United States Ship Ohio, Commodore Isaac Hull, Commander, in the Mediterranean in the Years 1839, '40, and '41.* Boston, 1841.

*Van Dyck, C. V. A. "On the Present Condition of the Medical Profession in Syria," *Journal of the American Oriental Society* (New York), I (1849), pp. 561–580.

Wells, Thomas. *Letters on Palestine.* Boston: Mussey, 1846.

*Willis, Nathaniel Parker. *Pencillings by the Way.* London and Philadelphia, 1836. (Available in a modern edition, London, 1942.)

—— *Summer Cruise in the Mediterranean on Board an American Frigate.* New York: Scribner, 1853.

Wines, Enoch Cobb. *Two Years and a Half in the Navy; or, Journal of a Cruise in the Mediterranean and Levant, on Board of the U.S. Frigate Constellation, in the Years 1829, 1830 and 1831.* 2 vols. Philadelphia: Carey & Lea, 1832.

Woodruff, Samuel. *Journal of a Tour to Malta, Greece, Asia Minor, Carthage, Algiers, Port Mahon, and Spain, in 1828.* Hartford, 1831.

SOURCES

Extensive use has been made of books, articles, pamphlets, and the like by Americans, mostly published in their own lifetimes, and relating to events before 1850. In a sense this is "primary" material, because it is all (or almost all) long out of print and forgotten. Since no list of such material appears to have been assembled before now, I have thought it worthwhile to make one (see Appendix III). There are over a hundred titles, of which about three-quarters were first published before the Civil War — an astonishing number under the circumstances.

Some of this material is heavy going; the British editor of the life of Levi Parsons remarked frankly (1832): "It has been a frequent complaint that some of the specimens we have had of American biography, however excellent in many respects, have been too long." (Innes, pp. iii–iv). Professor Parrington has suggested another difficulty: "In the formal biographies written in that golden age of myth-making [1800–60] criticism too often gave way to eulogy. Our fathers wrote like gentlemen, but unfortunately too often they believed that in preparing a biography a gentleman was under obligation to speak well of the dead. . . . The critic is reduced to patching together his account out of scanty odds and ends." To which I can only say amen and add that the problem applies equally to autobiography and biography. Nevertheless, these books have on the whole been extremely useful.

As for unpublished material, I have examined the appropriate records of the State Department from the U.S. National Archives (on microfilm). Commodore Porter's dispatches from Constantinople (1831–43), with their immoderately copious enclosures, are a goldmine of information about the activities of Americans. As far as I know, almost nothing has been published based on these records for the period after 1830. The Porter Papers and Van Buren Papers at the Library of Congress have also been useful.

For the period up to 1831, especially for commercial and diplomatic activities, there is nothing to compare with the late Walter Livingstone Wright's "American Relations with Turkey to 1831," an unpublished Princeton doctoral dissertation (1928). Through the great courtesy of Professor Wright's widow, for several years I have been privileged to have at my elbow Wright's own copy to refer to. For her kindness in this regard I am deeply grateful.

For general background and history of the area I have drawn on the available published literature in Western languages, both contemporary and modern. Detailed references appear in the notes that follow. In the introduction to their seminal work, *Islamic Society and the West* (London, 1950), Gibb and Bowen lament the lack of trustworthy monographic material. Though I can only speak with far less authority, I too have found this frustrating — for example, I have been assured by specialists that there is no systematic history of the Ottoman navy against which to place the events set forth in Chapter 3. However, I believe this kind of deficiency is gradually being remedied.

Many academic historians and other specialists have been exceedingly helpful and hospitable in their attentions to the inquiries of an amateur intruding into their midst. Among them I have particularly to thank Roderic H. Davison, J. C. Hurewitz, D. W. Lockard, Maurice Lee, Bernard Lewis, Norman Lewis, Thomas Naff, Stanford J. Shaw, Gordon H. Torrey, Bayly Winder, and Cuyler Young. None of them, of course, is in any way responsible for the result.

A word about orthography. Because most of my research was done in London, mainly in the extraordinary resources of the British Museum and the London Library, a good many of the American books I worked with were actually English editions, in which American spelling was frequently adapted to English convention. In principle it seemed appropriate to revert to American usage, in order to re-establish the flavor (not flavour) of the original. But American spelling itself was in transition, and in some cases I may have overcorrected.

Finally, early nineteenth-century writers were prone to be much more liberal with the comma and the initial capital than is now considered necessary or desirable, and to speed the flow I have sometimes taken the liberty of making modernizing amendments where the sense of the passage would not be impaired. Otherwise, I have taken pains to reproduce the style and mood, as well as the content, of the material quoted.

Certain abbreviations will appear without further explanation in the detailed notes which follow:

DAB   *Dictionary of American Biography* (New York, 1928–36).

DI   United States, National Archives, Records of the Department of State, Diplomatic Instructions, Turkey, I (1823–59). Microfilm. Mainly communications from the State Department, though some early incoming dispatches were misfiled here rather than in DSD.

DSD   United States, National Archives, Records of the Department of State, Dispatches, Turkey (1818–50). Microfilm.

Porter   Unless otherwise indicated, this always means Commodore David Porter, and not any of his many kin.

S/S   The Secretary of State of the United States, in his official capacity.

NOTES

CHAPTER 1. INTRODUCTION

1. Max Weston Thornburg, *People and Policy in the Middle East* (New York, 1964), p. 5.

2. Publishing details from Eugene Exman, *The Brothers Harper* (New York, 1965), pp. 94–95, 104, 121.

3. "Stephens's 'Arabia Petra,'" reprinted in Poe's *Complete Works* (New York, 1902), VIII, 80–119. Brooks's enthusiastic assessment appears in *The World of Washington Irving* (London, 1944), pp. 370–374.

4. John Lloyd Stephens, *Incidents of Travel in the Russian and Turkish Empires* (London, 1839), I, 232.

5. Thomas Naff, "Ottoman Diplomacy and the Great European Powers, 1789–1802," unpub. diss., University of California (Berkeley), 1960, p. 30.

6. The best treatment from the diplomatic standpoint is still Harold Temperley, *England and the Near East: The Crimea* (London, 1936).

7. Roderic H. Davison, *Reform in the Ottoman Empire, 1856–1876* (Princeton, 1936), pp. 35–36. The definitive treatment of its subject.

8. E. D. G. Prime, *Forty Years in the Turkish Empire* (New York, 1876), p. 216. Data on education, newspapers, and transport in the United States from various sources, including John Bristed, *America and Her Resources* (London, 1818) and Francis J. Grund, *The Americans in their Moral, Social, and Political Relations* (London, 1837). On Ottoman newspapers: Stanford J. Shaw, "Selected List of Turkish Newspapers Published in the Ottoman Empire in the Nineteenth and Early Twentieth Centuries," unpub. pamphlet, Harvard University, *c.*1965; Naff, pp. 119–120.

9. Stephens, I, 227.

10. For instance, William Miller, *The Ottoman Empire and Its Successors, 1801–1927* (Cambridge, 1934), a standard text, makes no mention of the United States or Americans in the nineteenth century.

11. Comparisons with Italy were suggested by Paul R. Baker, *The Fortunate Pilgrims: Americans in Italy 1800–1860* (Cambridge, Mass.,

1964), pp. 13–14, 21, 163. "Every Cape Cod sailor": Stephens, I, 180. The mummy: Lenoir C. Wright, "United States Policy toward Egypt, 1830–1914," unpub. diss., Columbia University, 1954, p. 177. Immigrants to the U.S.: Walter Livingstone Wright, Jr., "American Relations with Turkey to 1831," unpub. diss., Princeton University, 1928, p. 75, and United States, *Compendium of the Seventh Census* (Washington, 1854), p. 118. *Al-Sultanah:* Hermann Frederick Eilts, "Ahmad Bin Na'aman's Mission to the United States in 1840: The Voyage of Al-Sultanah to New York City," *Essex Institute Historical Collections,* October 1962, pp. 219–277 (an inspired piece of research by a distinguished American diplomat); John Gray, *History of Zanzibar from the Middle Ages to 1856* (London, 1962), p. 213; Adele L. Younis, "The Arabs Who Followed Columbus," *The Arab World,* XII, no. 3 (March 1966), which reproduces a splendid portrait of Ahmad Bin Na'aman by the American artist, Edward Mooney, now in the Peabody Museum of Salem.

12. Van Wyck Brooks, *The Flowering of New England* (London, 1936), pp. 69–70.

13. Stephens, I, 229.

14. Josiah Brewer, *A Residence at Constantinople in the Year 1827* (New Haven, 1830), p. 18; Henry Harris Jessup, *Fifty-Three Years in Syria* (New York 1910), I, 105.

15. Stephen A. Larrabee, *Hellas Observed: The American Experience in Greece, 1775–1865* (New York, 1957), pp. 11, 20; James Fred Rippy, *Joel R. Poinsett: Versatile American* (Durham, N.C., 1935), pp. 24–29.

16. Ralph D. Paine, *Ships and Sailors of Old Salem* (London, 1924), pp. 174–176.

17. Larrabee, pp. 40, 47; Benjamin Seebohm, ed., *Memoirs of the Life and Gospel Labours of Stephen Grellet* (London, 1860), II, 10.

18. Larrabee, pp. 123–124, 128–132; John Rodgers (from Smyrna) to S/S, Aug. 31, 1825, DI.

19. Charles MacFarlane, *Constantinople in 1828* (London, 1829), II, 338–340.

20. Larrabee, p. 173.

21. Henry A. V. Post, *A Visit to Greece and Constantinople in the Year 1827–8* (New York, 1830), pp. 282 (ambassador's lady), 283 (renegade), 293 (slaughter), 319–330 (sightseeing in Constantinople).

22. Brooks, *The World of Washington Irving*, pp. 338–339; Henry A. Beers, *Nathaniel Parker Willis* (Boston, 1899), p. 126.

23. Nathaniel Parker Willis, *Pencillings by the Way*, L. Stanley Just, ed. (London, 1942), pp. 268–304.

CHAPTER 2. SMYRNA

1. Samuel Woodruff, *Journal of a Tour to Malta, Greece, Asia Minor, Carthage, Algiers, Port Mahon, and Spain, in 1828* (Hartford, 1831), p. 165.

2. John Lloyd Stephens, *Incidents of Travel in the Russian and Turkish Empires* (London, 1839), I, 175.

3. *Ibid.*, p. 179. For the costume, see Helmuth von Moltke, *Briefe über Zustände and Begebenheiten in der Turkei . . . 1835–39*, 8th ed. (Berlin, 1917), p. 76.

4. *Letters from Asia, Written by a Gentleman of Boston to His Friend in That Place* (New York, 1819), p. 10.

5. Henry A. V. Post, *A Visit to Greece and Constantinople in the Year 1827–8* (New York, 1830), pp. 291–292.

6. *Letters from Asia*, p. 11; N. P. Willis, *Pencillings by the Way* (London, 1942), pp. 366–367.

7. Stephens, I, 200–201.

8. Sarah Haight, *Letters from the Old World, by a Lady of New York* (New York, 1840), I, 64–65; James E. De Kay, *Sketches of Turkey in 1831 and 1832, by an American* (New York, 1833), p. 478.

9. Alvan Bond, *Memoir of the Rev. Pliny Fisk, A.M.* (Edinburgh, 1828), pp. 142–144, 148, 149.

10. Stephens, I, 198–199.

11. Samuel Eliot Morison, *The Maritime History of Massachusetts, 1783–1860* (Boston, 1921), pp. 13–14, 181; also, Morison, "Forcing the Dardanelles in 1810," *New England Quarterly*, I (April 1928), 208–225; Stephen A. Larrabee, *Hellas Observed: The American Experience in Greece, 1775–1865* (New York, 1957), p. 7; Walter Livingstone Wright, Jr., "American Relations with Turkey to 1831," unpub. diss., Princeton University, 1928, p. 44; Bernard Lewis, *The Emergence of Modern Turkey* (London, 1961), p. 63.

12. Wright, pp. 47–50; Sen. Doc. 200 25th Congress, 3rd Session, (Washington, 1839), p. 82.

13. Benjamin Seebohm, ed., *Memoirs of the Life and Gospel Labours of Stephen Grellet* (London, 1860), II, 10. This unlikely source documents Offley's family background, of which Professor Wright was apparently uncertain; see Wright's sketch of Offley in *DAB*.

14. Morison, *New England Quarterly*, p. 223; De Kay, p. 196; Wright, pp. 76–78; Charles Oscar Paullin, *Diplomatic Negotiations of American Naval Officers, 1778–1883* (Baltimore, 1912), p. 125.

15. Wright, pp. 62–65.

16. Offley to Commodore John Rodgers, Nov. 30, 1825, DI.

17. Offley to S/S, Jan. 24, 1824, DSD. Also, Wright, pp. 66–67b.

18. Stephens, I, 195.

19. S/S to Porter, April 3, 1832, DI. Porter to S/S, Oct. 4, 1834, DSD.

20. Elliot Snow and H. A. Gosnell, *On the Decks of 'Old Ironsides'* (New York, 1932), p. 165.

21. Stephens, I, 195; John P. Brown to S/S, March 1, 1846, DSD.

22. Charles MacFarlane, *Constantinople in 1828* (London, 1829) I, 65; Wright, p. 69; De Kay, p. 496; William B. Hodgson to S/S, Aug. 25, 1834, DSD.

23. Robert B. Forbes, *Personal Reminiscences* (Boston, 1892), p. 124; Morison, *Maritime History*, pp. 181–194; Morison, *New England Quarterly*, p. 210.

24. Eli Smith and H. G. O. Dwight, *Missionary Researches in Armenia* (London, 1834), p. 131; Leland James Gordon, *American Relations with Turkey, 1830–1930: An Economic Interpretation* (Philadelphia, 1932), p. 43; Sen. Doc. 200, pp. 55, 73.

25. Porter to S/S, Jan. 12, 1832, DSD; Gordon, p. 42; Paullin, p. 124; Sen. Doc. 200, p. 82; William B. Hodgson to S/S, Aug. 25, 1834, DSD; Morison, *New England Quarterly;* Wright, pp. 60–64. As for the *Calumet,* see Henry A. S. Dearborn, *A Memoir on the Commerce and Navigation of the Black Sea, and the Trade and Maritime Geography of Turkey and Egypt* (Boston, 1819), I, xxiii, for a biased contemporary version which Wright sets straight.

26. David Porter, *Constantinople and Its Environs, by an American* (New York, 1835), I, 184.

27. MacFarlane, I, 131–132.

28. Forbes, p. 125; Letters of Elizabeth Cabot Kirkland, *Proceedings of the Massachusetts Historical Society,* 2nd ser., XIX (1906), p. 500. Also, Dabney S. Carr to S/S, June 6, 1847, and Porter to S/S, Aug. 11, 1841, DSD; MacFarlane I, 41–42; Larrabee, p. 158; Woodruff, p. 148.

29. Carr to S/S, Nov. 18, 1846, Aug. 3, 1848, and Oct. 14, 1848, DSD; S/S to Carr, April 27, 1847, DI.

30. Vernon Louis Parrington, *The Romantic Revolution in America, 1800–1860* (New York, 1927), p. 272.

31. Stephens, I, 199.

32. Enoch Cobb Wines, *Two Years and a Half in the Navy* (Philadelphia, 1832), II, 133.

33. Wines, p. 133; Larrabee, p. 191; De Kay, p. 500.

34. Josiah Brewer, *A Residence at Constantinople in the Year 1827* (New Haven, 1830), pp. 258–259.

35. *Ibid.,* pp. 55, 86, 120.

36. This curious story appears in F. W. Hasluck, *Christianity and Islam under the Sultans* (Oxford, 1929), II, 643–644, citing W. J. Hamilton, *Researches in Asia Minor, Pontus and Armenia* (London, 1842), II, 275. For the facts, see Brewer, pp. 214, 246.

37. Wines, p. 123.

38. Daniel H. Temple, *Life and Letters of Rev. Daniel Temple* (Boston, 1855). The quotations by William Goodell are from *The Rest of Heaven: A Sermon Preached at Reading, Mass., August 13, 1851, at the Funeral of the Rev. Daniel Temple* (Boston, 1851), p. 20; also, E. D. G. Prime, *Forty Years in the Turkish Empire* (New York, 1876), p. 273.

39. John B. Adger, *My Life and Times, 1810–1899* (Richmond, 1899).

CHAPTER 3. CONSTANTINOPLE: THE TREATY OF *1830* AND THE TURKISH NAVY

1. John Lloyd Stephens, *Incidents of Travel in the Russian and Turkish Empires* (London, 1839), I, 221–226.

2. Walter Livingstone Wright, Jr., "American Relations with Turkey to 1831," unpub. diss., Princeton University, 1928, pp. 10–30.

3. *Ibid.,* p. 34. Thomas Harris, *Life and Services of Commodore Bainbridge* (Philadelphia, 1837).

4. Wright, pp. 36–41; a very readable and readily available account appears in Glenn Tucker, *Dawn Like Thunder: The Barbary Wars and the Birth of the U.S. Navy* (Indianapolis, 1963), pp. 11–23.

5. E. D. Clarke, *Travels in Various Countries of Europe, Asia and Africa,* 4th ed. (London, 1817), III, 79. Wright, pp. 38–41. Bainbridge's own account of the visit appears unexpectedly in the British archives, which contain two of his reports from Constantinople to the Secretary of the Navy, dated December 22 and 26, 1800. Great Britain, Public Records Office, Reference F. O. 78/31. Photocopies of these documents were kindly lent to the author by Professor Thomas Naff of Harvard.

6. C. M. Woodhouse, *The Battle of Navarino* (London, 1965), pp. 140–141; William Miller, *The Ottoman Empire and Its Successors, 1801–1927* (Cambridge, England, 1934), p. 97.

7. Wright, pp. 81–91. Bradish to Adams, Dec. 20, 1820, DI.

8. Offley to Adams, Jan. 24, 1824, DSD.

9. Adams to English, April 2, 1823; English to Adams, Dec. 27, 1823, Feb. 8, May 14, July 8, Dec. 9, and Dec. 30, 1824; Adams to English, Jan. 3, 1825, DI.

10. Charles Oscar Paullin, *Commodore John Rodgers, 1773–1838* (Cleveland, 1910), pp. 329–332.

11. Adams to Rodgers, Feb. 7, 1825. United States, National Archives, Records of the Department of State, Special Missions.

12. Paullin, *Rodgers*, p. 336; Wright, p. 111.

13. Rodgers to S/S, July 19, 1826, DI. Charles Oscar Paullin, *Diplomatic Negotiations of American Naval Officers, 1778–1883* (Baltimore, 1912), pp. 138–140; Wright, pp. 119–124.

14. Rodgers to S/S, Feb. 14, 1827, DI.

15. Robert Curzon, *Visits to Monasteries in the Levant,* new ed. (London, 1955), p. 65.

16. Offley to S/S, Feb. 17, 1828, quoted in Wright, p. 133.

17. Stephen Larrabee, *Hellas Observed* (New York, 1957), p. 182.

18. A detailed account of the negotiations appears in Wright, pp. 144–159.

19. Graham H. Stuart, *The Department of State* (New York, 1949), p. 72.

20. *DAB;* Rhind to S/S, Aug. 8, 1831, DSD.

21. James A. Hamilton to Martin Van Buren, Aug. 23, 1829, Van Buren Papers, Library of Congress; Wright, p. 164; James A. Hamilton, *Reminiscences* (New York, 1869), p. 143.

22. E. D. G. Prime, *Forty Years in the Turkish Empire* (New York, 1876), p. 421. Wright, pp. 162–190, gives a detailed account of the negotiations. See also Hamilton, pp. 144–148.

23. Offley to S/S, June 7, 1830, DSD.

24. All quotations are from correspondence filed in DSD. A fully documented account of the Rhind-Offley-Biddle quarrel appears in Wright, pp. 192–206, and an abbreviated account in Hunter Miller, *Treaties and Other International Acts of the United States of America* (Washington, 1933), III, 558–569. See also J. C. Hurewitz, *Diplomacy in the Near and Middle East* (Princeton, 1956), I, 102–105.

25. Wright, p. 206.

26. For details of the ratification, see Wright, pp. 207–211 and Hunter Miller, p. 575.

27. Rhind to Van Buren, March 29, 1831, DSD.

28. Phyllis De Kay Wheelock, "Henry Eckford (1775–1832), An American Shipbuilder," *The American Neptune,* VII (1947), 177–195.

29. Van Buren to Porter, March 21, 1831. Curiously, this letter is missing from the State Department archives, but it is quoted at length in Van Buren to Porter, April 15, 1831, DI.

30. Rhind to Van Buren, April 13 and April 16, 1831, DSD.

31. Van Buren to Porter, April 15, 1831, DI.

32. Hunter Miller, p. 586. Miller confesses ignorance of the date of

Porter's note; clearly, it is the one referred to in Porter's letter to the reis effendi following Eckford's death and was dated Sept. 27, 1831. See note 55.

33. Van Buren to Porter, April 22, 1831, DI.

34. Porter to Van Buren, June 13, 1831, DSD.

35. G. W. Sheldon, "The Old Shipbuilders of New York," *Harper's Magazine*, July 1882, p. 228.

36. This hypothesis has apparently never been advanced before. Oddly, Professor Wright hardly mentions Eckford in his otherwise minute coverage of the events of 1830 and 1831.

37. James E. De Kay, *Sketches of Turkey in 1831 and 1832* (New York, 1833), p. 27; Wheelock; Larrabee, p. 217; *DAB*.

38. Van Wyck Brooks, *The World of Washington Irving* (London, 1944), p. 183; Prime, p. 120.

39. De Kay, p. 293.

40. Porter to S/S, Aug. 11, 1831, DSD.

41. Porter to S/S, Aug. 25, 1831, Feb. 16, April 4, and April 12, 1832, DSD.

42. Porter to S/S, Sept. 19, 1832; Porter to S/S, April 24, 1834 (enclosing Rhind to Porter, Dec. 7, 1832, and Porter to Rhind, Dec. 15, 1832), DSD.

43. Porter to S/S, April 4, 1832, and October ? (undated, filed between Oct. 12 and Oct. 26) 1832, DSD; De Kay, p. 311.

44. David Porter, *Constantinople and Its Environs* (New York, 1835), II, 7–8.

45. Porter to S/S, Dec. 16, 1832, DSD.

46. Stephens, I, 216.

47. Stanley Lane-Poole, *The Life of Stratford Canning* (London, 1888), II, 77.

48. De Kay, p. 120.

49. Thomas Naff, "Ottoman Diplomacy and the Great European Powers, 1789–1802," unpub. diss., University of California (Berkeley), 1960, pp. 25, 36–40, 120; Woodhouse, p. 20.

50. Curzon, p. 49.

51. Bernard Lewis, *The Emergence of Modern Turkey* (London, 1961), p. 102.

52. John Gliddon to Porter, March 14, 1832, enclosed with Porter to S/S, April 9, 1832; William B. Hodgson to S/S, Aug. 25, 1834, DSD. For the situation before Navarino, see Woodhouse, p. 38.

53. Wheelock; Robert G. Albion, *The Rise of the New York Port, 1815–1860* (Hamden, Conn., 1961), p. 289. *Diary of William Dunlap, 1766–1839* (New-York Historical Society, 1930), III, 654.

54. Porter to S/S, Nov. 18 and Dec. 16, 1832, DSD.

55. Porter to reis effendi, Dec. 26, 1832, copy enclosed with William B. Hodgson to S/S, May 8, 1833, DSD. For identification of the "agreement of the 27th day of Sept. 1831," see Note 32 above. For some reason Porter himself did not send a copy of this letter to Washington, though he was in the habit of forwarding much less significant correspondence than this, as a matter of routine. Hodgson, who remedied the omission without Porter's knowledge, was the Commodore's disaffected dragoman and wished him nothing but trouble. (See Chapter 4.) Hodgson was seeking to sow the suspicion that Porter was out to make money from the naval arrangements, as Eckford had. Perhaps Porter was.

56. Porter to S/S, Oct. 25, 1834, enclosing Rhodes to Porter, Oct. 11, 1834, DSD.

57. Stephens, I, 234–236.

58. Stephen Olin, *Travels in Egypt, Arabia Petraea, and the Holy Land* (New York, 1843), I, 20; Edward Joy Morris, *Notes of a Tour through Turkey, Greece, Egypt and Arabia Petraea to the Holy Land* (London, 1843), pp. 15, 63; Sarah Haight, *Letters from the Old World, by a Lady of New York* (New York, 1840), I, 42; Valentine Mott, *Travels in Europe and the East* (New York, 1842), p. 408; Cyrus Hamlin, *Among the Turks* (London, 1878), p. 29; H. G. O. Dwight, *Memoir of Mrs. Elizabeth B. Dwight . . . (with a Sketch of the Life of Judith S. Grant)* (New York, 1840), p. 263; Horatio Southgate, *Narrative of a Tour through Armenia, Kurdistan, Persia and Mesopotamia* (New York, 1840), II, 92.

59. *A Handbook for Travellers in Turkey,* 3rd ed. (London: John Murray, 1854), p. 94; Adolphus Slade, *Turkey, Greece, and Malta* (London, 1837), II, 17–18.

60. Porter to S/S, April 22, May 13, May 19, and June 6, 1835, DSD.

61. Stephens, I, 237–241.

62. Porter to S/S, April 22 and June 6, 1835, May 23, 1836, Aug. 3, Aug. 22, and Sept. 9, 1837, and May 1, 1838, DSD.

63. David Porter to S/S, Jan. 11, 1837 (enclosing George A. Porter to David Porter, Nov. 26, 1836, and David Porter to George A. Porter, Jan. 11, 1837); Porter to S/S, Aug. 3 and Aug. 9, 1837, March 12 and Nov. 1, 1838, DSD. S/S to Porter, May 16, 1837, DI. John P. Brown to S/S, April 5, 1839, and Feb. 7, 1846. DSD.

64. Porter to S/S, Feb. 10, 1840, DSD. Morris, p. 14n. David Dixon Porter, *Memoir of Commodore David Porter of the United States Navy* (Albany, N.Y., 1875), p. 413.

65. J. A. R. Marriott, *The Eastern Question,* 2nd ed. (Oxford, 1918), pp. 238, 243; William Miller, *The Ottoman Empire and Its Successors, 1801–1927* (Cambridge, England, 1934), p. 149; Harold

Temperley, *England and the Near East: The Crimea* (London, 1936), pp. 105, 135.

CHAPTER 4. DAVID PORTER'S CONSTANTINOPLE

1. John Lloyd Stephens, *Incidents of Travel in the Russian and Turkish Empires* (London, 1839), I, 231, 232.

2. David Porter to Evelina Porter, March 19 and May 20, 1831. Porter Papers, Library of Congress.

3. Porter to S/S, Sept. 30, 1831; Rhind to S/S, Oct. 18, 1831, DSD.

4. James E. De Kay, *Sketches of Turkey in 1831 and 1832* (New York, 1833), pp. 289–290.

5. David Porter, *Constantinople and Its Environs* (New York, 1835), I, 49–51. The reference to Porter as "minister" is an exaggeration; this rank came to him only in 1839.

6. De Kay, p. 164; Porter, *Constantinople*, I, 140, 153. Porter to S/S, March 21 and Oct. 27, 1832, Jan. 4, 1833, DSD.

7. S/S to Porter, April 15, 1831, DI.

8. Porter, *Constantinople*, II, 306; David Porter to Theodoric Porter, June 14, 1835, Porter Papers.

9. David Dixon Porter, *Memoir of Commodore David Porter of the United States Navy* (Albany, 1875), pp. 405–410.

10. Archibald Douglas Turnbull, *Commodore David Porter, 1780–1843* (New York, 1929), p. 308.

11. Letters of Elizabeth Cabot Kirkland, *Proceedings of the Massachusetts Historical Society*, 2nd ser., XIX (1906), 502; Turnbull, pp. 304–305.

12. Thomas H. Benton, *Abridgement of the Debates of Congress from 1789 to 1856* (New York, 1859), XI, 195, 255.

13. Quoted (with indignation) in Porter to S/S, April 24, 1834. Presents: Porter to S/S, May 30, 1832, DSD.

14. S/S to Hodgson, Jan. 14, 1826; S/S to William Shaler (consul-general at Algiers), Dec. 29, 1825; S/S to Samuel D. Heap (consul at Tunis), April 20, 1826; S/S to Henry Lee (consul-general designate, Algiers), July 17, 1829; S/S to Hodgson, July 24, 1829. All in United States, National Archives, Records of the Department of State, Consular Instructions.

15. Hodgson to S/S, Sept. 12, 1831, DSD.

16. Porter to S/S, Aug. 15, 1832, DSD.

17. Hodgson to S/S, Dec. 1 and 7, 1832; May 7, 8, 9, 11, and 24, 1833; Porter to S/S, March 27 and June 19, 1833, DSD. Hunter Miller, *Treaties and Other International Acts of the United States of America* (Washington, 1933), III, 591.

18. Hodgson to S/S, June 25, 1835, DSD.

19. Porter to S/S, Nov. 6, 1833, enclosing much correspondence, DSD.

20. Hodgson to Patterson, Nov. 19, 1833; Porter to S/S, Feb. 13, 1834, DSD.

21. S/S to Hodgson, Oct. 10, 1833; S/S to Porter, Oct. 10, 1833, DI. Porter to S/S, July 10 and Sept. 1, 1834, DSD.

22. Hodgson, Report on Commerce of Egypt, March 2, 1835, DSD.

23. David Porter to Evelina Porter, March 20, 1835. Porter Papers. Porter to S/S, Nov. 11, 1834, and Nov. 2, 1835, DSD. Biographical data on Hodgson from *DAB*.

24. Porter to S/S, June 23, 1835, DSD.

25. Porter to S/S, March 21, 1834, July 31 and Oct. 15, 1835 (enclosing Porter to Jasper Chasseaud, Oct. 13, 1835), DSD.

26. Porter to S/S, July 18, 1833, June 25, 1834, Jan. 17, Feb. 3, and Oct. 21, 1835, DSD. D. D. Porter, *Memoir*, p. 412; Turnbull, p. 309.

27. Porter to S/S, Dec. 22, 1833, March 31, 1834, April 22, 1835, DSD.

28. S/S to Dabney S. Carr, July 6, 1844, DI.

29. S/S to Porter, July 2, 1832, March 31, 1834, Sept. 10, 1835, DI. Porter to S/S, June 31 [sic], 1835, DSD.

30. Porter to S/S, Oct. 17, 1840, DSD.

31. An American [John P. Brown?], "An Audience with Sultan Abdul Mejud," *The Knickerbocker*, XIX (1842), 497–505. Porter to S/S, May 24 and June 1, 1840, DSD.

32. Stephen C. Massett, *Drifting About* (New York, 1863), pp. 81–82. (For "Eni Dunia" read "Yeni Dunia" and see p. 111.) Also, Brown to S/S, March 6, Aug. 17, and Oct. 18, 1843, DSD.

33. S/S to Frederick E. Bunker, Jan. 13, 1832 and July 27, 1833; S/S to Churchill, Dec. 18, 1833, Consular Instructions. Porter to S/S, Sept. 17 and 26, 1831, Sept. 17, 1833, June 3, 1834; Brown to S/S, Jan. 4, 1842, DSD. S/S to Porter, April 1, 1833, and March 31, 1834, DI. (For more on Churchill see Chapter 2.)

34. Porter to S/S, May 1, 1835 (enclosing letter to Porter from Brown) and June 21, 1835, DSD. S/S to Brown, April 21 and 23, 1836; S/S to Porter, May 14, 1936, DI.

35. Allan Cunningham, "'Dragomania': The Dragomans of the British Embassy in Turkey," *St. Antony's Papers Number 11, Middle Eastern Affairs, Number Two* (London, 1961), pp. 81–100. The French and Austrian missions had *jeunes de langues* as early as the 18th century: see Thomas Naff, "Ottoman Diplomacy and the Great European Powers, 1789–1802," unpub. diss., University of California (Berkeley), 1960, p. 54. On dragomans generally, see H. A. R. Gibb

and Harold Bowen, *Islamic Society and the West*, I, pt. I (London, 1950), p. 123 and references cited therein. Porter to S/S, Dec. 29, 1831, Jan. 20, 1839, Dec. 16, 1840, May 27, July 25, and Oct. 4, 1842; Brown to S/S, Sept. 1, 1840, and Nov. 14, 1842; Asker to S/S, July 27, 1836, DSD. S/S to Porter, Sept. 22, 1841, and Aug. 26, 1842; S/S to Brown, Sept. 22, 1841, and Sept. 9, 1842, DI.

36. Brown to S/S, Aug. 16, 1843; Carr to S/S, Feb. 16, 1844, and July 25, 1845, DSD.

37. Brown to S/S June 4, 1846, DSD.

38. J. P. Brown, *The Dervishes; or Oriental Spiritualism* (London, 1868); new edition, H. A. Ross, ed. (London, 1927).

39. *DAB*.

40. William Goodell, *The Old and the New* (New York, 1883), pp. xiii–xiv; E. D. G. Prime, *Forty Years in the Turkish Empire* (New York, 1876), pp. 2–3, 18–19.

41. De Kay, p. 144.

42. Prime, pp. 114–121.

43. De Kay, p. 93.

44. Kirkland Letters, p. 503 (Porter considered Abigail "all but an angel"); Prime, pp. 116–123, 135.

45. Porter to S/S, April 22 and July 25, 1835, DSD.

46. H. G. O. Dwight, *Memoir of Mrs. Elizabeth B. Dwight . . . (with a Sketch of the Life of Judith S. Grant)* (New York, 1840), pp. 186–187.

47. *Ibid.*, p. 26; William Goodell, *The Power of Faith: A Sermon . . . on the Death of Mrs. E. Dwight* (New York, 1838), p. 50.

48. Porter to S/S, July 25, 1835, DSD.

49. Stephens, I, 228.

50. Horatio Southgate, *Narrative of a Tour through Armenia, Kurdistan, Persia and Mesopotamia* (New York, 1840), I, 89.

51. Josiah Brewer, *A Residence at Constantinople in the Year 1827* (New Haven, 1830), pp. 110–111; De Kay, pp. 176, 190.

52. Stephens, I, 228; Cyrus Hamlin, *Among the Turks* (London, 1878), p. 303; *Handbook for Travellers in Turkey*, 3rd ed. (London: John Murray, 1854), p. 95.

53. Dwight, *Memoir.*

54. Adolph Frederick Schauffler, *Memories of a Happy Boyhood* (New York, 1919), pp. 33–41; William G. Schauffler, *Autobiography, edited by His Sons* (New York, 1887), pp. 77–85.

55. Henry Otis Dwight, *Constantinople and Its Problems* (London, 1901), pp. 249–250; H. G. O. Dwight, *Christianity in Turkey* (London, 1854), pp. 93–97, 105, 291, 308. Porter to S/S, Nov. 3, 1839 (enclosing report by Brown), DSD.

56. Brown to S/S, March 1, 1846, DSD.

57. The quotation is from Henry Otis Dwight, *et al.*, *The Encyclopedia of Missions* (New York, 1904), I, 286. Cyrus Hamlin, *Among the Turks* (London, 1878); Cyrus Hamlin, *My Life and Times* (New York, 1893).

58. Porter to S/S, March 9, 11, and 12, 1835, April 5, June 6, Aug. 29, and Oct. 2, 1835; Brown to S/S, Sept. 25, 1838, DSD.

59. Brown to S/S, Dec. 19, 1849, DSD.

60. Hamlin, *Among the Turks*, pp. 185–194; Carleton Mabel, *The American Leonardo: A Life of Samuel B. Morse* (New York, 1942), p. 221; *Journal of the American Oriental Society*, I (1851), liv–lv; Carr to S/S, Oct. 24, 1848, DSD.

61. S/S to Carr, June 15, 1844, DI. Porter to S/S, Jan. 12, 1843 (with enclosures); Brown to S/S, May 24, 1843, Feb. 7, 1846; Carr to S/S, Aug. 24, 1847, DSD.

62. William F. Lynch, *Narrative of the United States' Expedition to the River Jordan and the Dead Sea* (London, 1849), pp. 59, 64; Hamlin, *Among the Turks*, p. 186; S/S to Brown, March 26 and May 14, 1846; S/S to Carr, Aug. 18, 1846, DI. Brown to S/S, Jan. 5 and May 16, 1846; Carr to S/S, June 6, 1847, Oct. 24 and Dec. 14, 1848; Brown to S/S, Jan. 14, 1850, DSD.

CHAPTER 5. MISSIONS

1. H. C. Horsford, ed., *Journal of a Visit to Europe and the Levant, October 11, 1856–May 6, 1857* (Princeton, 1955).

2. Russel Blaine Nye, *The Cultural Life of the New Nation 1776–1830* (London, 1960), p. 152; Harriet Martineau, *Society in America*, 2nd ed. (London, 1839), III, 273.

3. Edward Robinson, *Biblical Researches in Palestine* (London, 1841), I, 46.

4. Rufus Anderson, *Foreign Missions: Their Relations and Claims* (New York, 1870), pp. 21–22.

5. *Re-thinking Missions: A Laymen's Inquiry after One Hundred Years*, by the Commission of Appraisal, William Ernest Hocking, chairman (New York, 1932), p. 8.

6. Eli Smith and H. G. O. Dwight, *Missionary Researches in Armenia* (London, 1834), pp. 30, 60, 104; Eliza Schneider, *Letters from Broosa* (Chambersburg, Pa., 1846), pp. 49, 148–149; Edward W. Hooker, *Memoir of Mrs. Sarah Lanman Smith*, 2nd ed. (Boston, 1840), p. 241.

7. William M. Thomson, *The Land and the Book* (New York,

1859), II, 346, 445; Stephen Olin, *Travels in Egypt, Arabia Petraea, and the Holy Land* (New York, 1843), I, 52, 133–134.

8. Anderson, *Foreign Missions*, pp. 94–95.

9. Vernon Louis Parrington, *The Romantic Revolution in America, 1800–1860* (New York, 1927), p. 273.

10. Eli Smith, *Trials of Missionaries* (Boston, 1832). The characterization of Riggs is from Julius Richter, *A History of Protestant Missions in the Near East* (Edinburgh, 1910), p. 110.

11. E. D. G. Prime, *Forty Years in the Turkish Empire* (New York, 1876), pp. 79, 106; Thomson, I, 475.

12. Anderson, *Foreign Missions*, p. 145.

13. James Lyman Merrick, *An Appeal to the American Board of Commissioners for Foreign Missions* (Springfield, Mass., 1847), p. 26.

14. Rufus Anderson, *Report to the Prudential Committee of a Visit to the Missions in the Levant* (Boston, 1844), p. 53; Kirkland Letters, p. 503; Prime, p. 213; Henry Jessup, *Fifty-Three Years in Syria* (New York, 1910), I, 52.

15. Gregory M. Wortabet, *Syria and the Syrians; or, Turkey in the Dependencies* (London, 1856), I, 60.

16. Anderson, *Foreign Missions*, pp. 100–101.

17. Edward Meade Earle, "American Missions in the Near East," *Foreign Affairs*, 7 (April 1929), 400.

18. Prime, p. 95.

19. A. L. Tibawi, *British Interests in Palestine 1800–1901* (London, 1962), p. 10.

20. Stanley Lane-Poole, *The Life of Stratford Canning* (London, 1888), I, 307.

21. *The Missionary Register for 1825* (London, 1825), p. 40; Justin Perkins, *A Residence of Eight Years in Persia among the Nestorian Christians* (Andover, Mass., 1843), p. 219.

22. Dabney S. Carr to S/S, March 5, 1845, with enclosure, DSD. It is not clear whether Stratford Canning had instructions to this effect or whether he was simply ignoring instructions similar to those given to the British embassy in Persia. He was perfectly capable of the latter.

23. Martineau, III, 23.

24. Porter to S/S, May 16, 1841 (enclosing his exchange of letters with the Turkish Foreign Minister), July 31 and Oct. 16, 1841 (with enclosures), July 16, 1842, DSD. S/S to Porter, Feb. 2, 1842, DI. The story is told briefly by Rufus Anderson in his *Foreign Missions*, pp. 195–196 and also in his *History of the Missions of the American Board of Commissioners for Foreign Missions to the Oriental Churches* (Boston, 1872), I, 254, 303–304.

25. Carr to S/S, March 5, 1845 (with enclosures), DSD. S/S to Carr, Dec. 7, 1848, DI.

26. Quoted in Zeine N. Zeine, *Arab-Turkish Relations and the Emergence of Arab Nationalism* (Beirut, 1958), p. 50. My translation from the French.

27. *Missionary Register for 1824* (London, 1824), p. 547, quoting King; John Joseph, *The Nestorians and Their Muslim Neighbors* (Princeton, 1951), p. 47, quoting Perkins; Justin Perkins, *Residence*, p. 403; Anderson, *Foreign Missions*, pp. 2–4.

28. Robinson, III, 464–466.

29. Prime, pp. 352–353; Lane-Poole, II, 451.

30. Anderson, *Foreign Missions*, p. 6.

31. F. W. Hasluck, *Christianity and Islam under the Sultans* (Oxford, 1929), II, 641; Smith and Dwight, *Missionary Researches*, pp. 49, 69; Justin Perkins, "Journal of a Tour from Oroomiah to Mosul, through the Koordish Mountains," *Journal of the American Oriental Society*, II (1851), 82.

32. H. G. O. Dwight, *Christianity in Turkey* (London, 1854), p. 87.

33. F. V. J. Arundell, *Discoveries in Asia Minor* (London, 1834), II, 287; R. Walsh, *A Residence at Constantinople* (London, 1836), II, 343.

34. A good example of the anti-Protestant material appears in T. W. M. Marshall, *Christian Missions* (London, 1862), pp. 434, 575; the other side is indicated in Ray Allen Billington, *The Protestant Crusade, 1800–1860* (New York, 1938).

35. Jessup, I, 360–361.

36. Joseph, p. 77; Anderson, *Report*, p. 75; Wortabet, I, 45; Hamlin, *Among the Turks*, p. 30; Walsh, II, p. 10.

37. Kenneth Scott Latourette, *A History of the Expansion of Christianity*, vol. VI: *The Great Century in Northern Africa and Asia, A.D. 1800–1914* (London, c. 1945), pp. 51, 62.

38. Pro: George Antonius, *The Arab Awakening* (1938); new edition (Beirut, 1955); and A. L. Tibawi, "The American Missionaries in Beirut and Butrus al-Bustani," *St. Antony's Papers, Number 16, Middle Eastern Affairs, Number Four* (London, 1963). Con: George E. Kirk, *A Short History of the Middle East* (London, 1948), pp. 103–105.

39. *Re-thinking Missions*, pp. 10, 298.

CHAPTER 6. EGYPT

1. Julian Boyd, ed., *The Papers of Thomas Jefferson*, 9 (Princeton, 1954), 261n; Jared Sparks, *Memoirs of the Life and Travels of*

John Ledyard (London, 1828); Helen Augur, *Passage to Glory: John Ledyard's America* (New York, 1946).

2. *Proceedings of the Association for Promoting the Discovery of the Interior Parts of Africa*, I (London, 1810), 14, 20, 43, 45–46.

3. *Ibid.*, I, 25–26; Sparks, pp. 398–425.

4. Thomas Legh, *Narrative of a Journey in Egypt and the Country Beyond the Cataracts* (London, 1816), pp. 33, 111–123.

5. Round One: George Bethune English's *The Grounds of Christianity Examined by Comparing the New Testament with the Old* (Boston, 1813). Round Two: Edward Everett's *A Defence of Christianity against the Work of G. B. English* (Boston, 1814). Round Three: English's *Five Pebbles from the Brook* (Philadelphia, 1824).

6. James E. De Kay, *Sketches of Turkey in 1831 and 1832* (New York, 1833), p. 488. See also *DAB*.

7. George Bethune English, *A Narrative of the Expedition to Dongola and Sennaer* (Boston, 1823), p. 5. One exotic feature of this rare and beautifully printed book is the exclusive use of the Muslim calendar; English's first journal entry, for example, is dated "Zilghadge 16, 1235," the same as September 24, 1820. English also affected the device of footnotes to footnotes, when he had something really subordinate on his mind. Despite these peculiarities, the *Narrative* is regarded by one modern scholar as the best account of the climax of Ismael's campaign. Richard Hill, *Egypt in the Sudan, 1820–1881* (London, 1959), p. 174.

8. George Waddington and Bernard Hanbury, *Journal of a Visit to Some Parts of Ethiopia* (London, 1822), pp. 114–117.

9. English, *Narrative*, pp. 68–84, 113–114, 128–149, 158, 171.

10. John Bayford, ed., *Missionary Journal and Memoir of the Rev. Joseph Wolf* [sic: Wolff] (London, 1824), pp. 141–195; Anon., *Travels and Adventures of the Rev. Joseph Wolff* (London, 1860), I, 187.

11. C. F. Adams, ed., *Memoirs of John Quincy Adams* (Philadelphia, 1874–1877), VIII, 62.

12. Alvan Bond, *Memoir of the Rev. Pliny Fisk, A. M.* (Edinburgh, 1828), p. 190; Walter Livingstone Wright, Jr., "American Relations with Turkey to 1831," unpub. diss., Princeton University, 1928, p. 96.

13. William Innes, ed., *Memoir of the Rev. Levi Parsons* (Edinburgh, 1832), pp. 27, 33, 43, 123–133, 139.

14. Bond, pp. 24, 84–88.

15. Henry Jessup, *Fifty-Three Years in Syria* (New York, 1910), I, 32.

16. *Missionary Register for 1823* (London, 1823), pp. 122–124; Jessup, I, 34; Innes, pp. 239–240.

17. *Missionary Register for 1827* (London, 1827), pp. 145–149.

18. John Lloyd Stephens, *Incidents of Travel in Egypt, Arabia Petraea, and the Holy Land*, 10th ed. (New York: Harper, 1839), I, 14.

19. John Gliddon to David Porter, April 26, 1834, enclosed with Porter to S/S, June 3, 1834, DSD; Dabney S. Carr to S/S, Aug. 7, 1844, DSD; S/S to Carr, Oct. 23, 1848, DI. George R. Gliddon, *Appendix to "The American in Egypt"* (Philadelphia, 1842); George R. Gliddon, *Hand-Book to the American Panorama of the Nile* (London, 1849), p. 21; David R. Serpell, "American Consular Activities in Egypt, 1849–63," *Journal of Modern History*, 10 (1938), 345; Lenoir C. Wright, "United States Policy Toward Egypt: 1830–1914," unpub. diss., Columbia University, 1954, p. 26.

20. Porter to S/S, May 19, 1832, DSD; George R. Gliddon, Letter to the Editor of *The American Mail* (New York), July 3, 1847; George R. Gliddon, *An Appeal to the Antiquaries of Europe on the Destruction of the Monuments of Egypt* (London, 1841), pp. 97–104; Helen Rivlin, *The Agricultural Policy of Muhammad Ali* (Cambridge, Mass., 1961), p. 140. For George Gliddon's career in America, see John A. Wilson, *Signs and Wonders upon Pharaoh* (Chicago, 1964), p. 41.

21. It is sometimes asserted that because of their inferior status the Gliddons did not have access to the viceroy and that American interests had to depend on consuls-general of other nations to represent them. (See, for example, Rivlin, p. 292.) But John Gliddon was granted an audience "in my official capacity" shortly after his appointment as consular agent (Gliddon to Porter, March 14, 1832, enclosed with Porter to S/S, April 9, 1832, DSD), and both Gliddons often took visiting Americans to call upon the viceroy — an event reported by many of them, including Sarah Haight, Edward Robinson, Alexander Mott, Edward Joy Morris, Stephen Olin, John Durbin, and Francis Schroeder. See Letter from George Gliddon to the Editor, Philadelphia *North American*, Feb. 10, 1847; also Lenoir C. Wright, p. 27.

22. Porter to S/S, Sept. 1, 1834, enclosing Patterson to Porter, Aug. 9, 1834, DSD.

23. Stephens, *Incidents, Egypt*, I, 53.

24. Quoted in Russel Blaine Nye, *The Cultural Life of the New Nation, 1776–1830* (London, 1960), p. 49.

25. English, *Narrative*, pp. 15, 114; Edward Joy Morris, *Notes of a Tour through Turkey, Greece, Egypt and Arabia Petraea to the Holy*

Land (London, 1843), pp. 102, 114; Sparks, p. 402; Africa Society, *Proceedings*, II, 27; Bond, p. 242; Sarah Haight, *Letters from the Old World, by a Lady of New York* (New York, 1840), I, 88.

26. Stephens, *Incidents, Egypt*, I, 45, 103.

27. *Ibid.*, pp. 174–176.

28. *Ibid.*, p. 115.

29. *Ibid.*, pp. 84–85.

30. Gregory M. Wortabet, *Syria and the Syrians, or, Turkey in the Dependencies* (London, 1856), I, 200; Haight, I, 107; David Millard, *A Journal of Travels in Egypt, Arabia Petraea, and the Holy Land during 1841–2* (Rochester, N.Y., 1843), pp. 105, 253; Stephen Olin, *Travels in Egypt, Arabia Petraea, and the Holy Land* (New York, 1843), I, 35, 54–55.

31. Letters of Elizabeth Cabot Kirkland, *Proceedings of the Massachusetts Historical Society*, 2nd ser., XIX (Boston, 1906), 491, 497.

32. Walter Barrett, *The Old Merchants of New York City*, 3rd ser. (New York, 1864), pp. 186, 199.

33. Haight, I, 128, 154–158, 160, 230, 298; Gliddon, *Handbook*, p. 23.

34. Gliddon, *Appendix;* Gliddon, *Appeal*, p. 143; James Ewing Cooley, *The American in Egypt* (New York, 1842), pp. 91–132; Stephen A. Larrabee, *Hellas Observed* (New York, 1957), p. 243.

35. Ferris Greenslet, *The Lowells and Their Seven Worlds* (London, 1947), pp. 82, 174–186; Edward Weeks, *The Lowells and Their Institute* (Boston, 1966), pp. 13–35; Edward Everett, *Orations and Speeches* (Boston, 1859), Vol. II, pp. 379ff, an address in honor of Lowell delivered before the Lowell Institute on December 31, 1839.

36. Cohen: John A. Wilson, *Signs and Wonders*, p. 38; Cass: A. C. McLaughlin, *Lewis Cass* (Boston, 1891) and William C. Prime, *Tent Life in the Holy Land* (New York, 1857); Patterson: Porter to S/S, Sept. 1, 1834, with enclosure from Patterson to Porter, Aug. 9, 1834, DSD. Also a letter from David Dixon Porter to Commodore Porter, July 23, 1834, Porter Papers, Library of Congress; Mott: Valentine Mott, *Travels in Europe and the East* (New York, 1842); Harlan: Joseph Wolff, *Researches and Missionary Labours among the Jews, Mohammedans and Other Sects*, 2nd ed. (London, 1835), pp. 258–260.

37. Morris, p. 107; Serpell, p. 354.

CHAPTER 7. PALESTINE AND SYRIA

1. John Lloyd Stephens, *Incidents of Travel in Egypt, Arabia Petraea, and the Holy Land*, 10th ed. (New York, 1839), II, 9.

2. John William Burgon, *Petra*, Newdigate Prize Poem, 1845.

3. Stephens, *Incidents, Egypt*, II, 56, 110.

4. *Ibid.*, pp. 224–226. S/S to Bradford, Feb. 4 and Sept. 21, 1829, June 7, 1830; S/S (Van Buren) to General Lafayette, June 7, 1830, United States, National Archives, Records of the Department of State, Consular Instructions. William C. Prime, *Tent Life in the Holy Land* (New York, 1857) p. 122; Edward Robinson, *Biblical Researches in Palestine, Mount Sinai and Arabia Petraea* (London, 1841), I, 338.

5. Stephens, *Incidents, Egypt*, II, 156, 158.

6. *Missionary Register for 1825* (London, 1825), pp. 320–324.

7. Letter from William A. Jowett, quoted in *Missionary Register for 1824* (London, 1824), p. 501.

8. William M. Thomson, *The Land and the Book* (New York, 1859), I, 106, 217; II, 227, 274, 299. Thomson to Jasper Chasseaud, May 31 and June 11, 1834, enclosed with Porter to S/S, July 23, 1834, DSD. Henry Harris Jessup, *Fifty-Three Years in Syria* (New York, 1910), I, 57–58.

9. Stephens, *Incidents, Egypt*, II, 202–203.

10. Robinson, II, 280–281.

11. Stephens, *Incidents, Egypt*, II, 137–138.

12. Robinson, I, 327, 331–332, 363, 378.

13. *Ibid.*, pp. 501–503.

14. Thomson, I, 355n.

15. Frederick J. Bliss, *The Development of Palestine Exploration* (London, 1906), p. 212.

16. *Ibid.*, pp. 194–202.

17. Robinson, II, 632; I, 289; III, 25–26.

18. W. F. Albright, *The Archaeology of Palestine* (Penguin, 1956), p. 25. See also H. V. Hilprecht, *Explorations in Bible Lands during the Nineteenth Century* (Edinburgh, 1903), pp. 585, 588.

19. Jessup, I, 52; H. B. Smith and R. D. Hitchcock, *The Life, Writings and Character of Edward Robinson* (New York, 1863).

20. Stephens, *Incidents, Egypt*, II, 280–281.

21. George Rapelje, *A Narrative of Excursions, Voyages and Travels, Performed at Different Periods in America, Europe, Asia, and Africa* (New York, 1834), pp. 5, 57, 225, 369–374.

22. Harriet Livermore, *The Harp of Israel to Meet the Loud Echo in the Wilds of America* (Philadelphia, 1835), p. 6; Harriet Livermore, *A Narration of Religious Experience* (Concord, N.H., 1826), p. 25; Rebecca Davis, *Gleanings from Merrimac Valley* (Portland, Maine, 1881), pp. 16–33; Fred Myron Colby, "Holderness and the Livermores," *Granite Monthly*, IV, no. 5 (February 1881), 175–181; Elizabeth F. Hoxie, "Harriet Livermore: 'Vixen and De-

votee,'" *New England Quarterly*, 18, no. 1 (March 1945), 39–50; S/S to Porter, April 28, 1834, DI; Ian Bruce, *The Nun of Lebanon* (London, 1951), p. 401 (the only one of many biographies of Lady Hester that mentions Harriet Livermore); Edward Everett to Harriet Livermore, Dec. 21 and Dec. 24, 1841, and Everett to Lord Aberdeen, Dec. 24, 1841, Everett Papers, Massachusetts Historical Society; John C. Currier, *History of Newburyport, Mass., 1764–1909* (Newburyport, 1909), II, 477; C. C. Chase, "Harriet Livermore," *Contributions of the Old Residents "Historical Association"* (Lowell, Mass., 1891); Samuel T. Livermore, *Harriet Livermore, The Pilgrim Stranger* (Hartford, 1884).

23. Thomson, I, 110–111.

24. James Thayer Addison, *The Christian Approach to the Moslem* (New York, 1942), p. 92.

25. Thomson, II, 88, 91.

26. *Ibid.*, pp. 162–163; Jessup, I, 57.

27. Stephens, *Incidents, Egypt*, II, 281–282.

28. Sarah Haight, *Letters from the Old World, by a Lady of New York* (New York, 1840), I, 297.

29. Edward W. Hooker, *Memoir of Mrs. Sarah Lanman Smith*, 2nd ed. (Boston, 1840), p. 181.

30. William B. Hodgson to S/S, Aug. 25, 1834; David Darmon to Porter, Feb. 5, 1835, enclosed with Porter to S/S, July 13, 1835; Jasper Chasseaud to Porter, March 20, 1832, enclosed with Porter to S/S, May 19, 1832, DSD. William R. Polk, *The Opening of South Lebanon, 1788–1840* (Cambridge, Mass., 1963), pp. 162–163.

31. E. D. G. Prime, *Forty Years in the Turkish Empire* (New York, 1876), pp. 79–80; Jessup, I, 26; *Missionary Register for 1824* (London, 1824), pp. 544–545.

32. *Missionary Register for 1827* (London, 1827), p. 37; *Missionary Register for 1828* (London, 1828), p. 580. Polk, *Opening*, pp. 113–115, has further details.

33. William Goodell, *The Old and the New; or Changes of Thirty Years in the East* (New York, 1853), pp. 51–52.

34. *Ibid.*, pp. 69–76.

35. Prime, *Forty Years*, p. 99.

36. Eli Smith to Hannah Smith; MS letter made available by courtesy of Mr. Gordon H. Torrey of Washington, D.C. and published by permission.

37. Prime, *Forty Years*, p. 105; Henry Otis Dwight *et al.*, *The Encyclopedia of Missions* (New York, 1904), p. 92.

38. Jessup, I, 45; A. L. Tibawi, *British Interests in Palestine, 1800–1901* (London, 1962), pp. 13, 16; Harold Temperley, *England and*

the Near East: The Crimea (London, 1936), p. 100. For the school as seen by an alumnus: Gregory M. Wortabet, *Syria and the Syrians; or, Turkey in the Dependencies* (London, 1856), I, 60, 70–71.

39. Quarantine conditions: William Thomson and L. W. Pease to Jasper Chasseaud, enclosed with Porter to S/S, June 31 [sic], 1835. Bird incident: Porter to S/S, Sept. 8 and Nov. 22, 1833 (enclosing Chasseaud to Porter, Oct. 19, 1833), Jan. 7 and July 23, 1834 (enclosing Chasseaud to Porter, June 26, 1834); Porter to Patterson, Jan. 15, 1834, all DSD.

40. Josiah Brewer, *A Residence at Constantinople in the Year 1827* (New Haven, 1830), p. 197; Eli Smith to Hannah Smith, June 23, 1827 (MS letter courtesy Mr. Torrey); Alvan Bond, *Memoir of the Rev. Pliny Fisk* (Edinburgh, 1828), p. 287.

41. Hooker, pp. 108, 190, 233, 288, 312; Daniel C. Eddy, *Heroines of the Missionary Enterprise* (Boston, 1850), pp. 128–129, 133.

42. Isaac Bird, *Bible Work in Bible Lands* (Philadelphia, 1872), p. 340.

43. Hooker, pp. 201–203; J. D. Paxton, *Letters from Palestine* (Lexington, Ky., 1839), p. 84.

44. Eddy, pp. 137–139.

45. *Journal of the American Oriental Society*, I (1849), 173–217.

46. Porter to S/S, July 14, Sept. 10, Sept. 17, Oct. 2, Oct. 20, Nov. 3, Nov. 19 and Dec. 1, 1840, all with enclosures from Jasper Chasseaud describing events in Beirut, DSD.

CHAPTER 8. PERSIA AND MESOPOTAMIA

1. John Joseph, *The Nestorians and Their Muslim Neighbors* (Princeton, 1961), p. 43.

2. Cyrus Hamlin, *Among the Turks* (London, 1878), p. 149.

3. Eli Smith and H. G. O. Dwight, *Missionary Researches in Armenia* (London, 1834), p. 45.

4. *Ibid.*, p. lxiv.

5. Hamlin, p. 210.

6. Smith and Dwight, pp. 22, 57, 79, 84, 103, 175, 254–255, 263, 287, 289, 315–317, 410.

7. Justin Perkins, *A Residence of Eight Years in Persia among the Nestorian Christians* (Andover, Mass., 1843), pp. 27–32, 43, 51, 79–83, 92–94, 100, 115, 123–143.

8. Edwin Munsell Bliss, ed., *The Encyclopaedia of Missions* (New York, 1891), I, 394–395. The original Asahel appears in II Sam. 2. Canal boat: Dwight W. Marsh, *The Tennesseean in Persia and Koordistan* (Philadelphia, 1869), p. 156.

9. Thomas Laurie, *Dr. Grant and the Mountain Nestorians* (Boston, 1853), p. 58; William Francis Ainsworth, *Travels and Researches in Asia Minor, Mesopotamia, Chaldea, and Armenia* (London, 1842), II, 256.

10. Asahel Grant, *The Nestorians* (London, 1841), p. 3; Rufus Anderson, *History of the Missions . . . to the Oriental Churches* (Boston, 1872), I, 176–177.

11. Grant, p. 4; Perkins, p. 217.

12. Laurie, pp. 62–63; Perkins, p. 285.

13. Laurie, pp. 60, 71; Perkins, pp. 249–251, 266.

14. Grant, p. 6; Horatio Southgate, *Narrative of a Tour through Armenia, Kurdistan, Persia and Mesopotamia* (New York, 1840), I, 317; Laurie, pp. 72–75.

15. Laurie, pp. 155–156; Grant, p. 9.

16. Laurie, pp. 33–34, 86 (Judith's emphasis).

17. Perkins, p. 342.

18. Laurie, pp. 45–46; Perkins, pp. 444, 446.

19. See, for example, Southgate, I, 302–305, 311; Ainsworth, II, 303.

20. Perkins, p. 335 (his emphasis).

21. *Ibid.*, p. 347.

22. *Ibid.*, pp. 289–292.

23. James Lyman Merrick, *An Appeal to the American Board of Commissioners for Foreign Missions* (Springfield, Mass., 1847), pp. 14–29; Southgate, II, 17–18.

24. Merrick, pp. 29–46; 90–114.

25. Anderson, I, 324; H. G. O. Dwight, *Memoir of Mrs. Elizabeth B. Dwight . . . (with a Sketch of the Life of Judith S. Grant)* (New York, 1840), p. 260.

26. James Thayer Addison, *The Episcopal Church in the United States, 1789–1936* (New York, 1951), p. 148.

27. Southgate, I, 72–73, 131–135, 231, 325; II, 3, 127–130, 164, 197, 212.

28. H. G. O. Dwight, *Christianity in Turkey* (London, 1854), p. 243; Harvey Newcomb, *A Cyclopedia of Missions* (New York, 1855), pp. 631–634; W. B. Boyce, *Statistics of Protestant Missionary Societies, 1872–1873* (London, 1874), p. 25; Kenneth Walter Cameron, "The Manuscripts of Horatio Southgate — A Discovery," *The American Church Monthly*, 42, no. 4 (October 1937), 155–173.

29. Alvan Bond, *Memoir of the Rev. Pliny Fisk* (Edinburgh, 1828), p. 28; Edward Robinson, *Biblical Researches in Palestine* (London, 1841), I, 364; Anderson, I, 130.

30. Grant, pp. 9–10, 14–15, 19, 21, 24.

31. *Ibid.*, 28–49, 87–88; Joseph, p. 50.

32. Laurie, pp. 155–167.
33. Chevalier Durighello to Porter, May 8 and 31, 1841, enclosed with Porter to S/S, July 14, 1841, DSD.
34. Laurie, pp. 167–173, 190, 195–202, 215–231, 255.
35. Austen Henry Layard, *Nineveh and Its Remains* (London, 1849), I, 178–179.
36. Laurie, pp. 269–281; George Percy Badger, *The Nestorians and Their Rituals* (London, 1852), I, 6, 9, 192, 297; Joseph, p. 60.
37. Laurie, pp. 288, 306–318, 383.
38. Laurie, pp. 342–369; Joseph, pp. 56, 64–65. Bliss and Smith: John P. Brown to S/S, Aug. 7 and 17, 1843, DSD.
39. Ainsworth, II, 253–255.
40. Laurie, pp. 379–380, 390–396, 406–412; Layard, I, 179.
41. Laurie, p. 31.

CHAPTER 9. EAST OF SUEZ

1. Walter Livingstone Wright, Jr., "American Relations with Turkey to 1831," unpub. diss., Princeton University, 1928, p. 54; Samuel Eliot Morison, "Forcing the Dardanelles in 1810," *New England Quarterly*, I (April 1928), 210; Ralph D. Paine, *Ships and Sailors of Old Salem* (London, 1924), p. 150.
2. For the two versions (there may well be others), see Paine, pp. 184–185, quoting Felt's *Annals of Salem;* and Rudolph Said-Ruete, *Said Bin Sultan (1791–1856), Ruler of Oman and Zanzibar* (London, 1929), pp. 124–125.
3. William B. Hodgson to S/S, Report on the Commerce of Egypt, March 2, 1835, p. 215, DSD.
4. Sen. Doc. 200, 25th Congress, 3rd Session (Washington, 1839), pp. 203–205.
5. W. S. W. Ruschenberger, *Narrative of a Voyage Round the World During the Years 1835, 36, and 37* (London, 1838), I, 66, 136; Said-Ruete, pp. 124–126; John Gray, *History of Zanzibar from the Middle Ages to 1856* (London, 1962), p. 196.
6. Tyler Dennett, *Americans in Eastern Asia* (New York, 1946), pp. 128–129; Ruschenberger, p. vi; Gray, pp. 124–125, 195.
7. Said-Ruete, pp. 37–54.
8. Dennett, pp. 129–134; Said-Ruete, p. 129; Gray, pp. 195–199.
9. Alexander I. Cotheal, "Treaty between U.S.A. and the Sultan of Muscat," *Journal of the American Oriental Society*, IV (1854), 346.
10. Walter Barrett, *The Old Merchants of New York*, 2nd ser. (New York, 1868), pp. 102–103.

11. Richard Sanger, *The Arabian Peninsula* (Ithaca, N.Y., 1954), p. 191.

CHAPTER 10. THE OFFICIAL AMERICAN PRESENCE

1. John Lloyd Stephens, *Incidents of Travel in the Russian and Turkish Empires* (London, 1839), I, 243.

2. S/S to Porter, June 27, 1835, enclosing ten consular commissions. Llewellyn: Porter to S/S, Jan. 2, 1832, DSD. Bursa: F. S. Rodkey, "Lord Palmerston and the Rejuvenation of Turkey, 1830–1841," *Journal of Modern History*, 2 (1930), 203; Porter to S/S, Aug. 5, 1839 and Oct. 29, 1840. DSD; E. C. A. Schneider, *Letters from Broosa* (Chambersburg, Pa., 1846). Trebizond: Porter to S/S, October ?, 1832 (n.d.); Mocha: Porter to S/S, Nov. 11, 1834, DSD.

3. Dabney S. Carr to S/S, April 17, 1845, DSD.

4. Stephens, I, 243. Darmon: Porter to S/S, April 19, 1832, April 20, Sept. 10, and Nov. 7, 1834, DSD. Damietta: David R. Serpell, "American Consular Activities in Egypt, 1849–63," *Journal of Modern History*, 10 (1938), 353. Offley's effects: Carr to S/S, Dec. 5, 1846, DSD. Salaries: Porter to S/S, Nov. 11, 1832, DSD; S/S to Carr, Feb. 17, 1849, DI; Graham H. Stuart, *The Department of State* (New York, 1949), p. 120.

5. Stanley Lane-Poole, *The Life of Stratford Canning* (London, 1888), II, 88. Cresson: Carr to S/S, Dec. 7, 1844, and March 5, 1845, DSD; Horatius Bonar, *The Land of Promise* (London, 1858), pp. 208–210. Gorham: S/S to Carroll Spence (U.S. minister to the Porte), Nov. 15, 1856, DI.

6. James E. De Kay, *Sketches of Turkey in 1831 and 1832* (New York, 1833), p. 66; N. P. Willis, *Pencillings by the Way* (London, 1942), p. 283; Stephens, I, 190; Porter to S/S, Aug. 10, 1833, DSD.

7. Francis Schroeder, *Shores of the Mediterranean* (London, 1846), I, 183–185.

8. Edward Robinson, *Biblical Researches in Palestine* (London, 1841), III, 393–394.

9. Porter to S/S, Sept. 10, 1834, DSD; S/S to Porter, April 9, 1840, DI; Porter to S/S, June 9 and 23, 1840, DSD.

10. Porter to S/S, July 14 and Aug. 12, 1840, May 6, 1841 (all with enclosures), DSD; S/S to Porter, Dec. 17, 1840, Feb. 2 and Aug. 12, 1842, DI.

11. Chasseaud to S/S, Sept. 24, 1830, DSD; S/S to Porter, April 15, 1831, DI; Porter to S/S, Jan. 12 and April 19, 1832 (enclosing Chasseaud to Porter, April 7, 1832), Nov. 10, 1834; John Gliddon to Porter, April 26, 1834, all DSD.

12. Carr to S/S, Jan. 7, 1847, DSD. S/S to U.S. Minister George P. Marsh, June 12, 1850; S/S to U.S. Minister Carroll Spence, Sept. 14, 1854, DI.

13. Glenn Tucker, *Dawn Like Thunder* (Indianapolis, 1963), p. 356.

14. S/S to Henry Lee, consul-designate at Algiers, July 17, 1829. United States, National Archives, Records of the Department of State, Consular Instructions.

15. Porter to S/S, Dec. 26, 1831, Jan. 12, 1832, DSD.

16. Porter to S/S, April 19, 1832 (enclosing John Gliddon to Porter, April 9, 1832); Porter to S/S, June 25, 1832, DSD.

17. Porter to S/S, Oct. 24 and Nov. 22, 1833, DSD.

18. Porter to S/S, May 6, Sept. 1, and Sept. 4, 1834 (the last enclosing Patterson to Porter, Aug. 9, 1834), DSD; David Dixon Porter to David Porter, July 23, 1834, Porter Papers, Library of Congress.

19. Porter to S/S, Oct. 28 and Nov. 7, 1834 (with enclosures from Patterson and Chasseaud), DSD.

20. David Porter to S/S, Nov. 25 and Dec. 31, 1835, May 22 and July 22, 1837; George A. Porter to S/S, May 1, 1837, DSD.

21. The following account is based on Lynch's *Narrative of the United States' Expedition to the River Jordan and the Dead Sea* (Philadelphia, 1849).

CHAPTER 11. PIONEERS IN RETROSPECT

1. John Lloyd Stephens, *Incidents of Travel in the Russian and Turkish Empires* (London, 1839), I, 318–320.

Index

HARVARD MIDDLE EASTERN STUDIES

* Published jointly by the Center for International Affairs and the Center for Middle Eastern Studies.

† Published jointly by the Center for Middle Eastern Studies and the Joint Center for Urban Studies.